LINCOLN OBSERVED

LINCOLN

THE JOHNS HOPKINS UNIVERSITY PRESS
BALTIMORE AND LONDON

Civil
War
Dispatches
of
Noah
Brooks

OBSERVED

EDITED BY MICHAEL BURLINGAME

© 1998 The Johns Hopkins University Press
All rights reserved. Published 1998
Printed in the United States of America on acid-free paper
9 8 7 6 5 4 3 2 1

The Johns Hopkins University Press
2715 North Charles Street
Baltimore, Maryland 21218-4363
The Johns Hopkins Press Ltd., London
www.press.jhu.edu

Library of Congress Cataloging-in-Publication Data
will be found at the end of this book.

A catalog record for this book is available from the British Library.

ISBN 0-8018-5842-9

For Jessica

CONTENTS

ACKNOWLEDGMENTS

I have received invaluable help from Noah Brooks's biographer, Dr. Wayne C. Temple, Chief Deputy Director of the Illinois State Archives. Under the direction of James G. Randall and Richard N. Current, Dr. Temple wrote a masterly dissertation on Brooks which was published serially in *The Lincoln Herald*. He has kindly shared with me his extensive file of research notes and his microfilmed copies of Brooks's personal letters, some of which are included in this volume.

I am grateful to Paul H. Verduin of Silver Spring, Maryland, for his invaluable help. At the Bancroft Library at the University of California, Berkeley, Alyson Belcher was most helpful in photocopying dispatches by Brooks.

At Connecticut College I have had the able assistance of Regina Foster and Anita Allen, who helped type the manuscript. The college's R. Francis Johnson Faculty Development Fund has provided much appreciated grants that have expedited my work.

To David Herbert Donald, my mentor at Princeton and later at Johns Hopkins, I owe a special debt of gratitude.

John Y. Simon has, over the past several years, been a constant and much-appreciated source of encouragement as I have pursued various Lincoln projects.

My sister, Sue Burlingame Coover, and her husband,

Edwin R. Coover, have generously shared their suburban Washington home; their hospitality, far above and beyond the call of familial duty, has made it possible for me to indulge in marathon research binges at the Library of Congress.

Lois McDonald has been an invaluable helpmate and soulmate.

EDITORIAL METHOD

In reproducing Brooks's letters, I have tried to remain as true as possible to the documents by retaining his spelling and punctuation without the cumbersome use of "[*sic*]." Words that cannot be deciphered with certainty have been included within brackets followed by a question mark, [like this?]. When Brooks added words above the line, with or without a caret, I have have simply inserted them into the text. Contractions have been retained. Raised letters have been reproduced as if they were not raised. When words are illegible, I have used brackets to enclose a blank space, like this: [————]. When Brooks inadvertently repeated a word, I have silently omitted the second occurrence of the word. When Brooks used a period when a comma is called for, the comma has silently replaced the period.

In reproducing the newspaper dispatches, I have silently corrected obvious misprints but have otherwise left the text undisturbed. All Washington correspondence bears a second date in parentheses, indicating the issue of the *Sacramento Daily Union* which carried the story after it arrived in California.

Persons mentioned by Brooks are identified in footnotes when their name first appears, if information on them has been found. When Brooks misspells a proper name, the correct spelling is given in brackets; thereafter the name is given its proper spelling without being enclosed within brackets. I have supplied no annotation for those about whom I could discover nothing. Sources for annotations derived from manuscript collections, newspapers, and specialized monographs and biographies are identified, but those taken from easily available published sources are not.

INTRODUCTION

During the Civil War, few people seem to have been closer to Abraham Lincoln than the young California journalist Noah Brooks, whom the president regarded as a surrogate son.[1] "I knew and loved Abraham Lincoln well," Brooks stated shortly after the president's death.[2] Brooks claimed that in the final two and a half years of the Civil War, when he served as a correspondent for the *Sacramento Daily Union*, he saw Lincoln "almost daily."[3] He wrote in 1865, "It was my good fortune to make his acquaintance years ago, during the early days of Republicanism, in Illinois, and since my sojourn in Washington that early acquaintance has ripened into intimacy near and confiding."[4] That same year Mary Todd Lincoln told Brooks that her husband had been "so earnest a friend of yours, that we will always remember you, with the kindest feelings & will always, be pleased to hear from you."[5] In 1866 she recalled "the great affection & confidence, my husband, cherished" for Brooks.[6] James A. Reed was told by a mutual friend of Brooks and Lincoln that the journalist "was so intimate with the President that he visited him socially at times when others were refused admission, took tea with the family, spending evenings with him, reading to him, and conversing with him freely."[7] John Conness, who served as a U.S. Senator from California during the Civil War, stated in 1896 that "no man living had better opportunity to know Lincoln's mind than Noah Brooks."[8] Another wartime California member of Congress, Cornelius Cole, thought that Lincoln and the young journalist got along well because "Noah Brooks was one of the few men about the President who never asked anything for himself, and Lincoln rewarded him by giving the best gift he had to offer—his friendship."[9]

Actually, Lincoln did plan to give Brooks something more tangible than friendship: the post of presidential secretary. As hostilities between North and South drew to a close, Schuyler Colfax, Speaker of the U.S. House of Representatives, tried to have Brooks named to that position.[10] In addition, Mary Todd Lincoln conspired with Lincoln's friend Anson G. Henry to substitute Brooks for John G. Nicolay as her husband's private secretary. "I have been working . . . with Mrs. Lincoln to get Nickolay out as private Secretary and Mr. Brooks in his place," Henry reported on 13 March 1865, the day after Nicolay's departure from the White House had been announced. "I am quite sure he will make Mr. Brooks his Secretary," Henry predicted.[11] Three weeks later Charles H. Philbrick, who assisted Nicolay in the White House, confided to a friend: "I don't know who will be in George's [i.e., Nicolay's] place; hope some good man for otherwise I won't stay. Mrs. L will try to put in her favorite, Mr. Brooks, a newspaper man. What the President may think has not yet transpired."[12]

It is not difficult to understand Mary Lincoln's partiality to Brooks, for in 1863 he had publicly defended her as a "distinguished and accomplished woman" and "the best and truest lady in our beloved land," who had been unjustly maligned. With indignation he protested that "the tales that are told of Mrs. Lincoln's vanity, pride, vulgarity and meanness ought to put any decent man or woman to the blush, when they remember that they do not *know* one particle of that which they repeat, and that they would resent as an insult to their wives, sisters or mothers that which they so glibly repeat concerning the first lady in the land."[13] (Brooks's view of Mary Lincoln changed in time. A year after the assassination he revealed to a friend his skepticism about the former First Lady's honesty and integrity: "The reports concerning Mrs. Lincoln's [unethical] conduct at the White House I have noticed with great pain, more especially, as I have reason to believe that they have foundation in fact. I know that Mrs. L. is disposed to absorb a good deal, to put a fine point on it; and, before I left Washington, I felt uneasy at indications which I observed. I have, also, always believed that she was disposed to give currency to understated reports concerning Mr. Lincoln's estate, for obvious reasons; and these things have pained me exceedingly when I have remembered how free, generous and childlike in his money matters Mr. Lincoln was, and, more especially, how scrupulously exact and honest he was in all his dealings with public, as well as private property.")[14]

Nicolay evidently resisted the proposal that he go abroad, but shortly after the second inauguration, he and assistant presidential secretary John Hay were assigned to diplomatic posts in Paris. Lincoln then invited Brooks to replace them. The assassination scotched those plans.[15]

Despite the testimony of Mary Todd Lincoln, James A. Reed, Congressman Cole, and Senator Conness, historians Don E. Fehrenbacher and Virginia Fehrenbacher contend that "corroborative evidence of the degree of intimacy [with Lincoln] that he [Brooks] described is rather thin." They note that Brooks is seldom mentioned in *The Collected Works of Lincoln* and does not appear at all in the diaries of Gideon Welles, Salmon P. Chase, or Orville H. Browning; moreover, Brooks made only two appearances in the diary and letters of John Hay and one in Edward Bates's diary.[16] But some contemporary evidence does suggest that Lincoln and Brooks were intimate. Letters by Charles H. Philbrick and Anson G. Henry corroborate Brooks's claim that Lincoln intended to make Brooks his personal secretary, a job the president would probably not have offered to someone to whom he was not close. Brooks's letters to Nicolay in August and September 1864 make it clear that Lincoln did ask him to report privately on the Democratic national convention. Brooks's dispatches from Falmouth, Virginia, in April 1863 demonstrate that Lincoln did invite Brooks to accompany the presidential party visiting the Army of the Potomac, a fact confirmed in Edward Bates's diary.[17] Similarly, Brooks's letter to Edward McPherson in April 1865 indicates that the president confided his travel plans to him. Brooks's story about Lincoln's "last, shortest, and best speech" is partially confirmed by the manuscript of that document in Lincoln's handwriting.

The paucity of references to Brooks in the diaries of Lincoln's cabinet members and that of his assistant personal secretary does not necessarily mean that Brooks was not close to Lincoln. John Hay, for example, is mentioned only thrice in Gideon Welles's Civil War diary, twice in both Edward Bates's and Orville H. Browning's, and not at all in Salmon P. Chase's. The president's intimacy with another journalist, Simon P. Hanscom, is virtually unrecorded in the sources cited by the Fehrenbachers. Hanscom's name appears in Lincoln's *Collected Works* only four times, in the Civil War diaries and correspondence of John Hay only three times, but once in Gideon Welles's Civil War diary and not at all in the diaries of Edward Bates, Orville H. Browning, or Salmon P. Chase. Yet Hanscom, who had at the beginning of the war been a correspondent for the *New York Herald* and in 1862 became editor of the *Washington National Republican*, was evidently the newspaperman closest to Lincoln, with the possible exception of Brooks.

Many years after the war, Ben: Perley Poore recalled that Lincoln's "favorite among the Washington correspondents was Mr. Simon B. [*sic*] Hanscom, a shrewd Bostonian, who had been identified with the earlier anti-slavery movements, and who used to keep Mr. Lincoln informed as to what was going on in Washington, carrying him what he heard, and seldom asking a favor."[18] A journalist reported in 1865 that daily "the irrepressible Hanscom, of the *Republican*, comes after news, and brings the gossip of the day. The *Republican* is the President's favorite paper, and he gives it what news he has."[19] Brooks himself reported in October 1863 that "during the last few months the Washington *Republican* has contrived to secure for itself the reputation of being the organ of the President, and accordingly a great deal of misplaced importance is sometimes attached to some of its few editorials. The solution of the puzzle is that Hanscomb [*sic*], the editor, who is a pushing and persevering man, has managed to so ingratiate himself with the President that he has almost exclusive access to the office of the Executive, and there obtains from our good-natured Chief Magistrate such scanty items of news as he is willing to give out for publication, and so the enterprising editor gets up his daily column of 'official intelligence,' much to the annoyance and jealousy of the New York and other Washington correspondents."[20]

It is not hard to understand why Brooks and Lincoln may have been close, for they shared much in common, though they were two decades apart in age. Each had a knack for friendship, an amiable disposition, a deep-seated hostility toward slavery, a weakness for puns, and a fondness for literature; both had survived youthful hardships to become self-made men.

Brooks, born in Castine, Maine, in 1830, was orphaned at the age of seven. He was raised by his older sisters and, at the age of seventeen, moved to Boston to study art. During his seven years in the Massachusetts capital, he also wrote freelance articles for periodicals, thus laying the foundation for his future career.

In 1854 Brooks migrated to Dixon, Illinois, where he worked as a journalist and a businessman. Five years later he pushed further west, settling in Marysville, California. There he established a paint shop, gave art lessons, and wrote for a local newspaper, the *Appeal*. On November 4, 1860, the *Appeal* ran an article by Brooks, "Some Reminiscences of Abraham Lincoln," which described a speech Lincoln had given on July 17, 1856, in Dixon:

"There was an irresistible force of logic, a clinching power of argument, and a manly disregard of everything like sophistry or clap-trap, which could not fail to arrest the attention and favorably impress the most prejudiced mind. A prominent democrat riding by the Court House square, where the speaking was going on, stopped his horse for a moment to hear the man who he had met before at Springfield, and so completely did he become drawn into the train of his argument that he staid silently listening to the end of the speech. Hard headed old Democrats who had withstood the arguments and truths of scores of able men were forced to confess that their reason was held captive while they listened to the plain, straight-forward and sledge-hammer logic of the speaker. When he first rose on the stand, his pleasant, but by no means handsome face, irradiated by a genial smile—almost every one was disappointed at the personal appearance of Lincoln. Tall, spare, sallow in complexion, square-shouldered, with long arms hanging awkwardly by his side, his small head covered with short dark hair brushed carelessly back from his high square forehead, the new speaker, who had been preceded by long John Wentworth, of Chicago, was not one who was calculated to make at once a favorable impression upon the audience. But when, after briefly sketching the history of the much agitated question of slavery in the United States and Territories, he began to argue therefrom the reasonableness of what was asked by the North, and the madness and folly of the demand of the South that all governmental power and legislative action should be sub-servient to the interests of her own peculiar institutions, his manner and appearance were entirely lost and forgotten in the magic of his eloquence and in the fund of irresistible argument which he poured forth. His manner, never tedious or harsh, became instinct with life, energy and electric vivacity. Every motion was graceful, every inflection of his voice melodious, and, when dropping for the moment, argument, he good-naturedly appealed to his fellow-republicans to admit certain alleged charges, and then went on to show how, notwithstand-ing all this, the platform and principles of the party were untouched and uninjured, his consummate shrewdness and long-headed, astute perceptions of the truth never failed to touch the audience with a sudden shock of pleasure and sur-prise, which brought forth spontaneous bursts of applause from friends and opponents.

"The chief characteristic of this, as of all other speeches to which [I] have ever listened from him, was the simplicity of statement, the honest admission of all truthful objections, and the utter absence of everything like sophistry and cunning advantage of verbal trickery. There was no wire-drawn argu-ment to prove that the speaker was right in his conclusions, and that all others were wrong—but every hearer could not fail to be impressed with the fact that the great principles of right and justice had sunk deep into the mind of the speaker, and from these flowed the perspicuous statements which overwhelmed all who heard him.

"He was always good-humored, witty and ready with a repartee for all those foolish fellows who will persist in making asses of themselves by interrupting a public speaker. Said he to one 'irrepressible' muggins who had been unusually impertinent and persistent: 'Look here, my friend, you are only making a fool of yourself by exposing yourself to the ridicule which I have thus far succeeded in bringing upon you every time you have interrupted me. You ought to know that men whose business it is to speak in public, make it a part of their business to have something always ready for just such fellows as you are. You see you stand no show against a man who has met, a hundred times, just such flings as you seem to fancy are original with yourself; so you may as well, to use a popular expression, "dry up" at once.' The individual was obliged to see the force of the remark and at once subsided."

Brooks had spoken with Lincoln earlier that day: "[I] had previously been introduced to Lincoln [at Dixon], and while wandering about the grove, during the preliminary business of the meeting, [I] met him, and sat talking with him for an hour or more, on the probable result of the campaign, the future of the Republican party, and of the national interests therein involved. He had no hope that Fremont would be elected, and deduced conclusions from premises which after events completely justified—He was disappointed at the nomination of Fremont, and charged it upon the wicked doctrine of availability, which would ruin any party. He believed that the progress of Republican sentiment would be such that in 1860 every free State would go for the Republican nominee, provided he were an exponent of the principles of the party, and not committed to any extreme or radical measures. The candidate for 1860, he

said, should be a national, conservative man, unhackneyed by
political tergiversations, and untrammeled by party obligations. A man fresh from the people, who should be able to
embody in himself the expression of the popular will, and to
thoroughly sympathize with the popular sentiment. Against
the violent doctrines of some Republicans who were prominent in Illinois politics, he expressed himself in decided terms,
saying that such men and the false impressions they made
would lose the State to Fremont."[21]

In 1857, Brooks dined with the Lincolns in Springfield. He
told Ida Tarbell that during the Civil War, when he was a
dinner guest at the White House, the president had recalled
that meal of corned beef and cabbage and how ashamed Mrs.
Lincoln had been of it. The First Lady demurred.[22]

In November 1862, a few months after his wife had died in
childbirth, Brooks left California and returned east as the
Washington correspondent for the *Sacramento Daily Union*.
During the war he wrote 258 dispatches, which were unusually
candid about the White House, not only because the president was so close to Brooks but also because of the long delay
between the time Lincoln disclosed something to Brooks and
the time the issue of the *Sacramento Daily Union* containing
that information reached Washington. The president once
told Brooks, apropos of troop strength figures, "You can send
that by letter to California, by and by, if you want. It can't get
back here in time to do any harm."[23] Brooks's letters took
about a month to reach Sacramento; another month would
pass before the paper carrying the published version would get
back to Washington. In 1896 Brooks recalled that "sending
correspondence from Washington during the war was
attended with many difficulties. Telegraph tolls for that distance overland were very high and it was only brief dispatches
on the most important events that I sent by wire. . . . I used

carbon duplicate copies and one copy of each letter was sent overland by 'pony express,' and another copy would be placed in a tri-monthly budget and sent by steamer by the Panama route. It not infrequently happened that the 'pony express' would suffer such delay by being mudbound or snowbound that the copies sent by steamer would get to Sacramento first."[24]

Brooks's dispatches not only describe Lincoln's doings but may also reflect the president's thinking. Like most American journalists of the mid–nineteenth century, Brooks drew no firm distinction between reporting and editorializing. It is impossible to say which of the opinions sprinkled throughout his dispatches were his own and which were Lincoln's, but clearly some were the president's. A conspicuous example is Brooks's Washington dispatch of 21 January 1865, commenting on the death of Edward Everett: "Everett's reputation was world-wide, but he has left no monument of his genius or his public worth."[25] Nothing in that dispatch indicates that the president himself took so dim a view of Everett's legacy, but in 1878 Brooks recalled Lincoln's commentary on that subject: "Now, do you know, I think Edward Everett was very much overrated. He hasn't left any enduring monument."[26]

After the war, Brooks continued his career as a journalist in California, editing the *San Francisco Daily Times* (where he fostered the literary aspirations of a promising young type-setter named Henry George), the *San Francisco Alta California* (where he edited dispatches by Mark Twain), and the *Overland Monthly* (where he befriended Bret Harte). In 1871 he returned east to work for the *New York Tribune* and later the *New York Times*. As a freelance writer he specialized in stories for teenagers, contributing articles to children's periodicals and publishing books like *The Boy Emigrants* (1877). For students of Lincoln, Brooks's most important pieces of young

.adult literature were a sketch of Tad Lincoln in *St. Nicholas: An Illustrated Magazine for Young Folks* and *Abraham Lincoln: A Biography for Young People.*[27] After a decade editing the Newark (New Jersey) *Daily Advertiser* (1884–94), Brooks retired to his hometown in Maine. When his health declined, he moved to California, where he died, in 1903.

Earlier than many of his contemporaries, Brooks appreciated the greatness of Lincoln. In December 1864 he told a boyhood chum: "I have never felt the lack of confidence in Mr. Lincoln that some of our own friends have expressed, but have believed and still do believe that he is *the man* for these times; I know him well—very well, and I do not hesitate to say that he is a far greater and better man than our own people think. The time will come when people generally will concede his true merit and worth."[28]

Brooks's 1895 memoir, *Washington in Lincoln's Time*, based on the dispatches to California, omits much of the detailed information in the original pieces.[29] In 1967, some of these dispatches appeared in a volume rather casually edited by Philip Staudenraus, who left out much material dealing with Lincoln, rewrote Brooks's prose, and provided neither annotations nor index.[30] While scholars often use Brooks's reminiscences of the Civil War, the original dispatches have been comparatively neglected.[31]

This volume reproduces only those portions of the dispatches that treat of Lincoln; interspersed among these are a few of the handful of Brooks's surviving private letters that shed light on the president. (Alas, there is no collection of Brooks's manuscripts.) To supplement these wartime documents, I have added one of Brooks's published recollections of Lincoln. These reminiscences did not impress Lincoln's assistant personal secretary, John Hay, who told John G. Nicolay in

1888 that a magazine editor "wants a lot of the Noah Brooks rubbish, which of course, we could invent by the ream just as Noah does. It is very readable, I suppose. . . . But I feel no call to that field."[32] In fact, much of what Brooks wrote in his reminiscences was based on his wartime dispatches and was not the figment of Brooks's imagination that the assistant secretary took it to be.

Hay's skepticism about Brooks is justified in one respect. When he wrote about Lincoln's religion, Brooks dubiously ascribed his own Christian piety to the sixteenth president. Shortly after the assassination, Brooks told a clergyman: "I am glad now that I never hesitated, when proper occasion offered, to talk with him upon religious matters, for I think that the best evidences of his belief in Christ are those which I derived in free and easy conversations with him. You know I had an intimate acquaintance with him, which was not hampered or embarrassed by any official or business relations, nor did he have the same undefined reluctance which a man in his position would have had in talking upon religious matters, if I had been a clergyman."[33] Brooks's able biographer, however, thinks it "extremely doubtful" that Lincoln "talked openly to anybody about Christ's atonement for man's sins."[34]

But with that exception, Brooks's writings on Lincoln— especially the dispatches and letters written during the war— are trustworthy sources that shed a bright light on Lincoln's personality and his presidency.

1 DISPATCHES & LETTERS
1862–1863

4 DECEMBER 1862 (30 DECEMBER)

How the President Looks.

Last Sunday [November 30] I saw the President and his wife
at church at Dr. Gurley's (Presbyterian), where they habitually
attend.[1] The building was crowded, as usual, with dignitaries
of various grades, besides sinners of lesser note and rank.
Conspicuous among them all, as the crowd poured out of the
aisles, was the tall form of the Father of the Faithful, who is
instantly recognized by his likeness to the variety of his published likenesses. The President and his wife are both in deep
mourning for their son, who died last Spring,[2] and his Excel-
lency has grievously altered from the happy-faced Springfield
lawyer of 1856, whom I then met on the stump in Illinois for
Fremont. His hair is grizzled, his gait more stooping, his
countenance sallow, and there is a sunken, deathly look about
the large, cavernous eyes, which is saddening to those who see
there the marks of care and anxiety, such as no President of
the United States has ever before known. It is a lesson for
human ambition to look upon that anxious and careworn face,
prematurely aged by public labors and private griefs, and to
remember that with the fleeting glory of his term of office
have come responsibilities which make his life one long series
of harassing care, and, while compelling him to save himself

and his country from disgrace and reprobation, mark him
with the daily scars of mental anxiety and struggle. Whatever
may be said of Abraham Lincoln by friend or foe, no one can
ever question the pure patriotism and the unblenching honesty of the man. He inspires that feeling by his personal
presence as much as by his acts, and as he moves down the
church aisle, recognizing, with a cheerful nod, his friends on
either side, his homely face lighted with a smile, there is an
involuntary expression of respect on every face, and men, who
would scorn to "toady" to any President, look with commiser-
ating admiration on that tall, mourning figure which embod-
ies Abraham Lincoln, whom may God bless.[3]

9 DECEMBER 1862 (5 JANUARY 1863)

Did the People Vote Anti-Emancipation?

. . . In a former letter your correspondent has stated what is
commonly admitted and believed—that the slow conduct of
the war had more to do with the result of the elections than
anything else. This is the view which the President took of it,
and it must be admitted that adopting, as he did, that hypoth-
esis, he was more deeply chagrined than if he had supposed
that his emancipation policy had received a signal rebuke. . . .[4]

3 JANUARY 1863 (29 JANUARY)

How We Went a-Calling on New Year's Day.

It was a small party of us, chiefly Californians, who went the
rounds of the dignitaries who "received" on New Year's Day.
The good old custom is still kept up here—the Cabinet Ministers and other public functionaries being obliged to follow the
custom or be thought exclusive, which would be bad for the
Cabinet Ministers and such, you know, and people who bore
the President with a perpetual flood of audiences, because he

was made President for the people's use, would think it very hard in Seward, Chase & Co.[5] if they should retire from their workday world to a closed house on the day for universal calling; so they keep open house, and anybody who behaves himself can go and see them at home.

Secretary Welles and Postmaster General Blair did not receive their friends, on account of recent deaths in their families;[6] Secretary Smith had handed in his resignation of the portfolio of the Department of the Interior, and had departed for the interior to assume his new duties as United States Judge for the district of Indiana;[7] so he was also exempt. But the "Pres.," as he is familiarly termed by the unwashed, had no excuse, and at eleven he commenced his labors by receiving the Foreign Diplomats and their attaches. These dignitaries made a truly gorgeous appearance, arrayed in gold lace, feathers and other trappings, not to mention very good clothes. After they had paid their respects to the President and his wife, and had departed, the naval and military officers in town went in a shining body to wish the Commander-in-Chief of the Army and Navy of the United States, "A happy New Year," which, we must suppose, was gratefully received by "Old Abe," with a sincere hope that it might be happier than his last two years have been. Precisely at 12 o'clock the great gates of the Executive Mansion were thrown open, and the crowd rushed in; our delegation from California, being vehicularly equipped, were obliged to fall into a line of coaches, and march up the drive at a truly funeral pace. The press was tremendous, and the jam most excessive; all persons, high or low, civil, uncivil, or otherwise, were obliged to fall into an immense line of surging, crowding sovereigns, who were all forcing their way along the stately portico of the White House to the main entrance. There was a detachment of police and a small detail of a Pennsylvania regiment on hand to preserve order; but, bless your soul! there was but precious little order in that crowd. Here was a Member of Congress (Kellogg of Illinois)[8] with his coat-tail half torn off, there a young lady in tears at the wreck of a "love of a bonnet" with which she must enter the presence, as there is no retreat when one has once committed oneself to the resistless torrent of that mighty sea which surged against the doors of the White House and around the noble columns thereof. Anon, a shoulder-strapped Brigadier, too late for the military *entree*, would enter the crowd with a manifest intention of going in directly; but he found his match in the sovereign crowd, which revenged its civil subordination by very uncivil hustling of the unfortunate officer. "If I could get my hand up, I would make you remember me," was the angry remark of a burly Michigander to a small Bostonian who had punched him in the victual basket. Bostonian knew that such a thing was impossible in that jam, and smiled his contempt. But the doors, closed for a few moments, open for a fresh dose of the "peops," and all, combatants and non-combatants, changed their base about five feet, with the same brilliant results which McClellan announced of his Peninsular fight.[9] The valves of the entrance close until the monster within has digested his new mouthful, and we fetch up this time against a fresh faced soldier, created in "this hour of our country's peril," to mount guard at the White House, with a piece of deer skin, meant to typify a buck-tail, on his cap. Says this military Cerberus: "My gosh! gentlemen, *will* you stan' back? You can't get in no faster by crowdin'. Oh, I say, *will* you stan' back?" To which adjuration the gay and festive crowd responded by flattening him against a pilaster, never letting him loose until his fresh country face was dark with an alarming symptom of suffocation, he the while holding his useless musket helplessly in air by his folded arms.

Inside, at last, we pour along the hall and enter a suite of

rooms, straightening bonnets, coats and other gear, with a sigh
of relief, for within the crowd are not. A single line, such as we
see at the Post Office sometimes, reaches to the President, who
is flanked on the left by Marshal Leman [Lamon],[10] who
receives the name of each and gives it to the President as each
advances to shake hands. Thus Lamon: "Mr. Snifkins of California." To whom the President, his heavy eyes brightening,
says: "I am glad to see you, Mr. Snifkins—you come from a
noble State—God bless her." Snifkins murmurs his thanks, is
as warmly pressed by the hand as though the President had just
begun his day's work on the pump handle, and he is replaced
by Mr. Biffkins, of New York, who is reminded by the Father
of the Faithful that the Empire State has some noble men in
the Army of the Union; and so we go on, leaving behind us the
poor besieged and weary President, with his blessed old pump
handle working steadily as we disappear into the famous East
Room, a magnificent and richly furnished apartment, of which
more some other time.[11] A long window in an adjacent passage
has been removed and a wooden bridge temporarily thrown
across the sunken passage around the basement of the house,
and by this egress the fortunate ones depart, smiling in com-
miseration at the struggling unfortunates who are yet among
the "outs." A primly dressed corps of cavalry officers, glorious
in lace and jingling spurs, dash up to the portico and are disgusted to find that they must be swallowed up in the omnivo-
rous crowd; but they must, for this is pre-eminently the
People's Levee, and there is no distinction of persons or dress
shown here.[12]

6 JANUARY 1863 (3 FEBRUARY)

The Germans Visiting President Lincoln.
A large delegation of Germans from Pennsylvania, New York,
New Jersey, Ohio and Illinois, waited upon the President

yesterday with a memorial setting forth the features and advantages of Eli Thayer's Florida colonization scheme,[13] and asking that it might receive his favorable attention. The President briefly replied, cordially welcoming the delegation to the White House, and heartily acknowledging the indebtedness of the country to the stable loyalty of the German element of our population. He assured the delegation that Thayer's proposed scheme met with his approval, and that its complete indorsement was only temporarily postponed on account of recent military events. . . .[14]

9 JANUARY 1863 (4 FEBRUARY)

The Sandwich Island Commissionership.
The removal of Thomas J. Dryer, United States Commissioner to the Sandwich Islands,[15] having been resolved upon, there has resulted a considerable pressure upon the President for the position.[16] The chief applicants from the Pacific coast are J. W. Foard and Frank Soule of San Francisco, and Dr. McBride of Oregon.[17] While one of the California delegation was urging upon the President, the other day, the propriety of sending a citizen of one of the Pacific States to the Sandwich Islands, the President replied that Senator Sumner had said that the city of Boston was the only place in the United States which had any considerable interest in the commerce of those islands.[18] One Mitchell is urged upon the bothered President as a candidate for the Commissionership, by the Massachusetts Senator.[19] A successor to Dryer would have been appointed long ago, as the President is convinced of his incapacity and immoral conduct, but has been tried severely by the conflicting claims urged by the friends of the different applicants for the place.[20] In reply to the statements of some of the friends of a California applicant, the President said, the other

day: "Tell me, now, are you most in favor of getting out this
man, or of getting in the other man? Which have you most at
heart?" The delegation acknowledged themselves in a tight
place.[21]

21 JANUARY 1863 (17 FEBRUARY)

President Lincoln Upsets a Beehive.

Monday morning, bright and early, Congress was greeted
with a message, informing that honorable body that he [Lin-
coln] had signed the joint resolution authorizing the issuance
of $100,000,000 of legal tender notes for the payment of the
army and navy, and at the same time giving his views on the
financial question at some length.[22] It must be confessed that
the message partook somewhat of the character of a lecture,
but the turmoil, buzzing and fretting of Congress was unnec-
essary and undignified. To the astonishment of these Congressmen, who have been wrangling and spouting for weeks
over the Revenue Bill, the President is actually found to have
an opinion and a mind of his own. Remarkable impudence
and unparalleled boldness! The President has dared to disturb
the windy lucubrations of Congress, and tell them what he
thinks is right and fit in such a deplorable fix as the present.
Instantly the House was up in arms, and a motion to refer to a
Special Committee was lost, the House adjourning without
making any disposition of it. Representatives grumbled and
swore, and Senators were indignant, and being so lectured
would not even print the message. Senator Wilson[23] fumed
and said that the President took occasion to ring in a speech
every time he sent the most trivial message to the Senate, etc.,
etc. But the people are pleased, for they are in the main
(except the bank interest) in favor of the views of Secretary
Chase, which the President indorses, and public confidence is

accordingly reassured, and the popular mind pleased with the
independence of the President, who has brought up Congress
with a round turn to a sense of its duty. It is now seven weeks
since Congress has been in session, and nothing yet has been
done to determine the financial policy of the country for the
next two years. Each individual member of the Ways and
Means Committee has had his own peculiar views and hobby
to advance, and Congress has frittered away its limited time in
long speeches, and in the consideration of impracticable
schemes, leaving, meanwhile, the credit of the country to go
steadily down to ruin, the soldiers unpaid, the war debt accu-
mulating, and the financial world unable to predicate any
action whatever upon the action of Congress and the Treasury
Department. The President's message, notwithstanding the
turmoil which it has created, will be likely to bring about a
compromise of financial views, and thus insure the speedy
action of Congress upon some sound measure. . . .

26 JANUARY 1863 (21 FEBRUARY)

The Latest Military Emeute.

Early this morning the public was astonished to learn that
Burnside had at last tendered his resignation as Commander of
the Army of the Potomac.[24] I say they were astonished, for that
expresses the sensation made by the sudden divulging of an
item of news which had been daily expected by those who are
on the inside. Last week, while some of the plans of Burnside
were being developed to the cognizance of his subordinates, a
feeling of dissatisfaction and lack of confidence in the plans of
the Commander took tangible shape by the strenuous opposition, which was made to the War Department and the President, against the plans of Burnside by some of the Generals
under his command. Brigadier General John Cochrane acted

as spokesman for these malcontents,[25] and came to Washington with the extraordinary statement that if Burnside's plan of
a movement then under contemplation was carried out, that, in
the judgment of said subordinates, the issue would be fatal, and
that they could not go into the movement with confidence.
The President did not order General Cochrane under arrest,
but listened to his arguments, and the result was that the whole
scheme of Burnside was withdrawn and he at once tendered
his resignation of a command which had been thrust upon him
and of which he had long been very sick. Burnside and Hooker
were sent for,[26] and this morning we learned that the resignation of the Commander-in-Chief of the Army of the Potomac
had been accepted, and that "Fighting Joe Hooker" was in the
place successively occupied by McClellan and Burnside. Co-
instantly with this change came the applications of Franklin
and Sumner for a relief from their commands in the Army of
the Potomac.[27] This was expected, as the dignity of these Division Generals was not supposed equal to the pressure which
would be brought upon them if they were to serve under a
commander who had been their equal and coadjutor. What
will be the result of this general pulling up and weeding out of
the Army of the Potomac it is now difficult to say. . . . The promotion of Hooker is a matter of congratulation to those who
believe that fighting qualities are of the foremost importance
just now. But it is a pity that any change[s] were necessary, and
still more a pity that the change reveals such a deplorable state
of things in the army. We can only wait and hope for better
things. The Potomac Army is so demoralized that not much
can be hoped for it now, and it is no longer so important a
matter as to who is in command as it once was. In the meantime, Hooker is a popular officer, and can carry the enthusiasm
of his own corps with him, and should he succeed in infusing
the same spirit into all of the corps under him he will achieve a

great victory and redeem the waning reputation of the Army of the Potomac.

4 FEBRUARY 1863 (3 MARCH)

The Political Situation.

. . . I have hinted heretofore at the want of harmony which exists between the Executive and the Republican party, but have not spoken so plainly as is now necessary; and it may as well be understood first as last that the President does not have the cordial and uniform support of his political friends. It is true that upon all great questions, such as emancipation, confiscation, suspension of the habeas corpus Act, and other kindred measures, the Administration party, *per se*, is a solid column; but beneath all of this there is an undercurrent of dissatisfaction and an open manifestation of the spirit of captious criticism which is painful, and is calculated to shake the confidence of every true patriot. It is a common thing to hear Republicans abuse the President and the Cabinet, as they would not allow a political opponent to do, and to see Republicans, who would vote for sustaining the President in any of his more important acts, deliberately squelch out a message from the White House, or treat it with undisguised contempt. The heads of the Departments, the Congress and the President are not in harmony with each other, and the common danger is all that appears to force them to act in common unity of purpose. This comes, say the party, of choosing a fourth-rate man for President. When Lincoln took the Executive chair, it was thought that as he did not know much of statesmanship he would be ready to be managed by those of his own party who did know a great deal. Consequently, many a prominent Republican came to Washington with the idea that he was to have the management of the President; they found their error, and were chagrined that Honest Old Abe would have none of their counsel or reproof. There was the first breach made. Next, he thought that the border States must be conciliated and kept in the Union by pleasant promises. The hyena was fed with sugar plums, and it snapped at the hand which caressed it. Buchanan's appointees from States in rebellion were retained in office, and while treason still rioted upon the fat pickings of Government patronage it served its base ends better by secret espionage and correspondence than though it were in the rebel army. What wonder that loyal friends of the President, who in vain remonstrated against such a state of things, were embittered against an Executive which through a mistaken sense of duty to the country tolerated in office those whom he confidently believed to be Union men, but who were sympathizers with rebellion and despisers of himself? The President found that he must hunt up his own friends. His political associates supported him only as the man who had been placed in power by their success, and only for the sake of the country to which they look for future support. The Border State Conservatives, which includes the Vallandigham Democracy,[28] looked upon the President's policy of conciliation as an evidence of weakness, and treated his concessions, not as grateful acts of mercy and condescension, but as surrenders to their just demands, and, consequently, deputations of borderers, impudent in their exactions, have visited the White House, presuming upon the conciliatory policy of the President, to secure their growing demands. The "Border State policy" has proved a failure, and those States which it was designed to conserve to the Union are, possibly, more dangerous and more difficultly dealt with for the reason that they are out of the Union while they profess to be in it. Were the "actual cautery" applied to Kentucky, Tennessee, Maryland, Delaware and Missouri in the beginning we should not have had the perils with them which have already overtaken us by their sending disguised secessionists to engineer for them in Congress and spy for them in the departments. Between these half-confessed traitors and the loyal Republicans the President has failed to ride easily, and it is no wonder if our honest, patriotic, and single-hearted Chief Magistrate to-day looks over the heads of mere politicians to find his best friends most distant in the mass of the people, who love and reverence Abraham Lincoln for his noble and manly qualities of mind and heart. . . .

5 MARCH 1863 (4 APRIL)

The Last Days of the Thirty-Seventh Congress.

. . . The President is in his private room in the rear of the Senate Chamber, where he has been all night, signing bills as they are sent to him from the House or Senate. Nicolay and Hay,[29] his private Secretaries, are kept busy with running to each Chamber with the rolls of parchment Acts of Congress, which the signature of Abraham Lincoln has made law, and announcing to the houses that such bills have been so signed. . . .

The Last Hours.

About four o'clock in the morning (March 4th) the House took a recess until ten o'clock A.M., the Senate having done the same a few hours before. At the appointed hour there were but few of the members present, but the galleries were crowded to suffocation. The report of a Conference Committee upon certain disagreements between the House [and Senate] upon an Appropriation Bill was agreed to, and then sprang up a lively and somewhat acrimonious debate between Washburne of Illinois, Dawes of Massachusetts and Van Wyck of New York upon a minority report made by the latter upon the investigations of a Committee to which they had severally

belonged,[30] and which report was upon the result of an examination into the New York Custom House frauds. Van Wyck
made a severe report, while the majority were disposed to
whitewash, and asked that his report should not be printed.
The matter occupied an hour, but Van Wyck was triumphant,
and his report will be given to the world.[31] This over, an
immense shower of "little local bills" poured in, each member
being half-convulsed with his own anxiety to get his bill or
resolution passed at this late hour; and at half-past eleven the
noise and confusion were great in this Hall; in the midst of
which the President's Secretary appeared at the bar of the
House, ever and anon, with new lots of bills, the hard-working
President being still hard at work in his private room. At ten
minutes to twelve, noon, the last batch came in, and the President returned word by the House Committee that he had no
further communications to make to the body. . . .

18 MARCH 1863 (14 APRIL)

The Federal Official Abuses on the Pacific Coast.
Up to the present writing no definitive action has been had
upon the proposition to remove certain officers of the Government who now hold position upon the Pacific coast. The circumstances of the case and the evidence therein have been laid
before the President, who will give it a careful examination, as
is his wont. It will not be at all unlikely if the whole of the
"slate," as it has been sketched out by Secretary Chase, should
be set aside and the California delegation be given a voice
in the selection of the new officers. The President is more
thoughtful of the interests and wishes of the people than are
some of his subordinates. The charges brought against Victor
Smith, Collector at Port Angeles, Washington Territory, are
very explicit, and his removal is asked for by all the Federal

officers in that Territory, with but a single exception, and by a
great number of loyal and influential citizens.[32] It is charged
that Smith removed the Collectorship from Townsend to
Angeles for a private speculation; that he has misused the
public moneys confided to his care, depositing a portion
thereof for security for his private debts, and diverting cash to
his own uses; that he has made false entries upon his books and
has kept his business in a loose and disreputable manner.[33] He
has said that he was "so linked into the fibers of the National
Government that he could not be removed;" but the appearances are that Father Abraham will try the experiment.[34]

21 MARCH 1863 (17 APRIL)

The San Francisco Mint and Custom House.
When I last alluded to the unpleasant state of things which
is likely to result in some radical changes in official positions
in the above named institutions, the papers in the case and
the new slate of Secretary Chase had been submitted to the
President for his review. Since that [time] a very unexpected
change of programme has occurred. . . . The California delegation, seeing that nothing more could be done than to
submit to the somewhat arbitrary ruling of Chase in the
premises, left Washington and were stopping in New York for
a few days before leaving for California, when the President
discovered what had occurred. He was at once greatly exer-
cised at what he considered to be an unfair and ungenerous
treatment of the California Congressmen by the Secretary,
and he directed that they be recalled to the Capital, if possible, informing them that their preferences in the matter
should be regarded. Low and Sargent returned to Washington
a day or two since, Phelps having sailed for California in the
meantime.[35] The President expressed his regret at the hasty

and somewhat arbitrary action which had deprived them of any opportunity of having a voice in the selection of the new appointees for the Federal positions to be made vacant by dismissal, and then asked them to submit names for Executive action. This was all very well, but, in Phelps' absence, it was not so easy to agree upon such names as would secure the approval of the entire delegation and also prove acceptable to such of their constituents as were specially interested in the matter. It was an affair of considerable delicacy to fix here upon men who are not applicants for the offices which they are to fill, and it was not easy to choose men who would be unobjectionable to the irrepressibles of San Francisco, who have as many political cliques and jealousies as ever flourished in any American city. To further obscure the muddle, a telegram was received by the President from John Conness,[36] stating that in his opinion the interests of the Administration would best be subserved by making no removals. This, coming upon the damaging report of the special agent [Thomas Brown], whose evidence appeared conclusive, was a staggerer, but the President pursued the plan marked out by him and waited for the nominations of his California friends, whose greatest difficulty lay in the selection of a suitable person for the responsible office of Collector of the Port of San Francisco, over which so much sharp fighting was made two years ago. The President suggested that the delegation should return to California and there make up a slate and send [it] on; but when it was seen that such a proceeding would constitute the delegation of a sort of Special Committee to the Pacific coast to recommend candidates, the plan was abandoned. At this juncture, when the difficulty of fixing upon a successor to Rankin,[37] whose resignation it had been agreed to ask for, it was attempted to solve the difficulty by a new suggestion, as will be seen in the following letter of Secretary Chase to one of the California Congressmen:

> Treasury Department, March 21, 1862
>
> A. A. Sargent, of California—Dear Sir: I propose to tender the appointment of Collector of the Port of San Francisco to your colleague, Low. It is a very responsible position, and requires a man of unquestionable capacity for business and equally unquestionable personal integrity. Low seems to me to possess both. Will you have the goodness to say if there is any reason whatever for a different opinion?
>
> Yours truly,
>
> S. P. CHASE

To this inquiry there could, of course, be but one answer. Low's integrity, business capacity and standing are so unimpeachable that Sargent's reply must have been satisfactory to the Secretary, who had tendered the Collectorship to Low, but that gentleman refused to accept it, giving as a reason that he neither sought nor desired it; and that he was content to yield it to those who might be ambitious to secure its honors and emoluments. For the other positions to be made vacant by dismissal or otherwise, several names, not now necessary to mention, were submitted, and so the matter rests at this present writing, not much nearer an adjustment, I am sorry to say, than when I last wrote, though it is likely that something will be done before the delegation leave for California. Californians are the best judges of the probable popularity of Low's appointment, could he be induced to take it, but the impression here is that in no other way could the important office be filled so acceptably as by the appointment of the worthy gentleman alluded to, whose known integrity, firmness of character and moral uprightness will be a sure guarantee that he will not countenance the abuses which have distinguished the administration of affairs by the present incumbent. It is a

great pity that such things have occurred in the management
of affairs in the Federal offices in California, and perhaps
some tender-footed Republicans may object to a ventilation
of the abuses. But the President is bound that corruption and
venality in office shall not pass unrebuked by him, cost what it
may; and the people may rest assured that if official abuses
come to light, investigation will be set on foot by the Administration, and punishment and disgrace will follow conviction.
It is better to expose and correct official derelictions than to
gloss over and conceal them for purposes of mere expediency.[38]

24 MARCH 1863 (20 APRIL)

Returned Prisoners from Richmond.

At the meeting of the Union League in this city last night
there was present a band of returned Federal prisoners from
Richmond, whose accounts of matters and things at the
Confederate Capital, and of their own experience, were very
interesting. The party is four in number, and is the remnant
of a small detachment of picked men, sent from Shelbyville,
Tennessee, on the 7th of April, 1862, into the rebel lines, for
the purpose of seizing an engine on the Nashville and Chattanooga railroad, to run down into Georgia, and cut off an
important rebel line of communication. The expedition failed,
for the reason that telegraphic communication south was not
cut off soon enough to prevent a knowledge of the expedition
being sent to the rebels. The party was seized, and a portion
of their number were hanged summarily, without a moment's
warning, to terrify their comrades into betrayal of their plans
and purposes. After the most terrible sufferings in prison,
repeated and dreadful floggings, incarceration in loathsome
underground prisons and in Castle Thunder, also in Parson
Brownlow's former iron cage,[39] they were exchanged at last

and are alive to tell the story of their perils and sufferings.
These soldiers say that the want and famine at Richmond is
very severe, and that the rations of the soldiers is about one-
half what it was when the war began. One of them, [Jacob]
Parrott, bears on his back the scars of one hundred lashes,
inflicted by these scions of chivalry, and his denunciations of
those in the North who are apologists and friends of a system
and a cause which has such a savage and brutal spirit as he
saw in Secessia were truly forcible and eloquent. He has good
reason to have a *feeling* recollection of the hospitalities of the
amiable rebels.

26 MARCH 1863 (22 APRIL)

The Returned Prisoners from Rebeldom.

Yesterday the six Ohio soldiers, mentioned in a former letter,
who have been brought up from Richmond on a flag-of-truce
boat, had an informal interview with the Secretary of War,
who thanked them, for the country, for their courageous
demeanor under great suffering, by which they had extorted
even the praise of their enemies. He conversed with the party,
who gave him much useful information, and at the close of
the interview he gave them each one of the medals of honor
voted by the last Congress, and also made each a present of
$100, and told them that he had requested the Governor of
Ohio to promote them from the ranks to a Lieutenancy. After
the interview at the War Office they were taken to the White
House, where they waited upon the President, who had
desired to see them. He asked them many questions and
treated them with great cordiality. The names of these returned
prisoners are E. H. Mason, Jacob Parrott, William Pettinger
[Pittenger], Robert Buffum, William Reddick and William
Benninger [Bensinger]. The expedition to which these men

belonged originally consisted of twenty-two men, and was
sent into Georgia by General D. M. Mitchell [O. M. Mitchel]
on the 7th of April, 1862,[40] the men being picked from the
Second, Twenty-first and Thirty-third Ohio regiments—one
man only being taken from any one company, and each being
chosen for his superior courage and address. They dressed in
citizens' clothing, and avoided all rebel camps, and made their
way to the vicinity of Marietta, Georgia, a short distance
above Allentown, on the Western Railroad, connecting the
latter city with Chattanooga. At an eating house a few miles
above Marietta, while passengers were getting a meal, one of
the party acting as engineer, they seized the train and made
lightning speed toward Chattanooga. In passing stations they
only slackened up a little—telling those congregated there
that they had munitions of war for the army in Virginia, and
were in consequence compelled to make the utmost speed.
Unfortunately, the telegraph wires were not cut in time, and
when the wood and water gave out they were necessitated to
abandon the train. They took to the bushes, but were subsequently captured and taken to Atlanta.

Seven of the party were tried by the rebel authoritie[s],
convicted, and sentenced to be hung. It was shown in their
examination that they were not spies, had been near no rebel
camp, and had done no more than they had known hundreds
of rebel soldiers to do in Tennessee, who when captured were
dealt with as prisoners of war. The survivors brought with
them a copy of the Atlanta *Confederacy*, in which the particulars of the trial and execution are set forth, and the facts are
now in possession of Colonel Joseph Holt, Judge Advocate
General. The death warrant of the brave men was signed by
General Ledbetter, who was in command at Chattanooga at
the time, and indorsed by General E. Kirby Smith.[41] They
were given no notice as to the time of their execution. They

were executed with the expedition that people would shoot a
dog with the hydrophobia. Two of the men, weighing over
two hundred pounds, broke the rope and fell to the ground.
They earnestly demanded only one hour, to be wholly devoted
to prayer, but the inhuman agents of this infernal order were
inexorable, and the men were again mounted on the scaffold
as soon as the rope could be adjusted. When the rebel Secretary of War was notified that seven of the prisoners were
executed, he telegraphed back inquiring why they had not all
been executed? Afterwards this same Secretary denied to our
Government that any of these men had been hung.

The cruel lashing of Parrott, who refused to tell who was the
driver of their engine and to what regiments they belonged, are
among the sworn statements of these hardly-treated prisoners,
and are new instances of the boasted chivalry of our rebel foes.
The Government will authorize the publication of the testimony of these brave and patriotic soldiers, in which they detail
the cruelties which characterized the rebel treatment of not
only themselves and comrades, but other loyal citizens and soldiers. It also intends to inaugurate a system of retaliation which
shall prevent their repetition in the future.[42]

31 MARCH 1863 (27 APRIL)

Why Burnside Went West.

In a former letter I said that Burnside would go to the
Department of the South, and, taking his old corps from the
Potomac, would operate against Charleston. That was true
when it was stated, and as you have by this time learned that a
change of plan has sent Burnside and his men westward
instead of southward, it is well enough to give the reason why.
When Hunter was ordered to the Department of the South
there ensued an irrepressible conflict between Hunter and

Foster,[43] both of whom cherished very different and incompatible plans concerning the management of military affairs in the South; and there immediately began a long and vexatious correspondence with the War Office on the part of the two Generals, who fired paper bullets at each other, instead of at the enemy. This moved the Administration, which was contemplating an attack upon Charleston, to consider that safety and dignity required a supersedure of both the officers, and the presence in the Department of the South of an abler and more popular commander than either Foster or Hunter had proven himself to be. Accordingly the difficult and responsible post was assigned to Burnside and his corps. Some 32,000 men had actually begun to arrive at Fortress Monroe, *in transitu* for the South, when the breach between Foster and Hunter was healed, and simultaneously with that announcement came the doleful and somewhat sensational tidings that the rebels contemplated an invasion of Kentucky. Rosecrans was menaced,[44] and a general alarm at the prospects of another raid upon Ohio by the rebels was felt throughout the West, and has not yet subsided. The orders which were to send Burnside South were at once countermanded, and he was ordered to the West, not to supersede or reinforce Rosecrans, but to co-operate with him, and to protect and defend Southern Ohio, Northern Kentucky, and—if need be—the left wing of Rosecrans. The Burnside corps, then at Fortress Monroe, and arriving from the Rappahannock, was transported to Baltimore in small sections very quietly, and, before any general knowledge of the fact got abroad, the redoubtable General and an advance of his army was at Cincinnati, and the rear of that force is passing through Baltimore to-day.

You will see, then, that there is a strong probability that the attack on Charleston has been indefinitely postponed, and, for one, I should be surprised if any attack upon that city should

occur before this letter shall reach you. Certainly, it will not
take place until the plan which was interrupted and changed by
the transfer of Burnside to the West shall have been succeeded
by some other programme. This is not altogether speculation
on the part of your correspondent, and the value of these statements will be tested by the fast-flying telegraph. But, in any
event, the public anticipation has been disappointed again, and
will be likely to be again obliged to submit to a postponement
of its favorite action—the siege of Charleston. This, together
with the hanging-fire of the Vicksburg expedition, serves to
dampen somewhat the ardor of our mercurial people, just now
in a fever heat at the last outburst of public confidence in the
financial credit of our Government. We have our ups and
downs, and may have such another season of depression as that
of January last, but the signs all remain favorable for a speedy
return of peace and an end of an armed rebellion. Let us take
heart and wait.

2 APRIL 1863 (30 APRIL)

The San Francisco Federal Officials.
At the last moment before leaving for California F. F. Low
consented to take the Collectorship for San Francisco, and so
that matter may be considered settled. The removal of Rankin
will not be immediate, but will probably take place at the
commencement of the new fiscal year in June next. It is due to
that officer to say that the report of Special Agent Brown does
not implicate him in any positively dishonest practices, but
rather places his offenses in the milder light of an amiable
weakness which had enabled designing men to influence him
unduly for their own corrupt ends. The appointment of Low
gives great satisfaction here, and is cordially made by the
Administration, the President remarking that he considered it

a happy solution of the difficult problem [of] who to appoint
to the place. It now appears that R[obert] B. Swain, formerly
mentioned for the Sub-Treasury (*vice* [David W.] Cheese-
man, promoted), will be Superintendent of the Mint, and
H. M. Miller, now in the Custom House, and S[amuel] J.
Bridge will be appointed Appraisers. Should there be any
change from this programme it will not be likely to be
material—except to the parties already nominated. The wishes
of the delegation from California have been consulted in this
matter, and the appointments appear to have been selected
with considerable care. It is to be hoped that this is an end to
this unhappy business, and it will be seen that the Administration never spares its seeming friends when it is found that
the public interest demands their removal.

Removal of Collector Victor Smith.

In a former letter I alluded to the fact that application had
been made to the Administration for the removal of Victor
Smith, Collector of Customs for the Puget Sound district. It
now appears that he will be removed, not so much for any
proof of dishonesty as for general bad management, and for
making himself obnoxious to the people with whom he has
been brought in contact. The Administration claims to have
consulted the wishes of the people of Washington Territory in
this matter, the petitions for removal being signed by many
influential citizens and public men.

12 APRIL 1863 (8 MAY)

A Presidential Visit to the Army.

As it is not every day that one can get an invitation to accompany the Commander-in-Chief of the Army and Navy of the
United States on an excursion to the vastest army now on the
face of the earth, you may be sure that your correspondent

promptly availed himself of a request to make one of the small suite of the President on a late visit to the Army of the Potomac. The thoughtful wife of the President, an able and a noble woman, ought to have the credit of originating the plan of a tour through the Army by the President, as she saw what an excellent effect would be given to the troops, now in good condition and ready to march, by coming in contact with their Commander-in-Chief and his family. The party was small, consisting only of the President, Mrs. Lincoln, "Tommy" Lincoln—the President's ten-year-old boy—Attorney General Bates, Dr. A. G. Henry, Surveyor General of Washington Territory, Captain Crawford of the Overland service,[45] and your humble servant. Though the trip had been postponed for several days on account of unfavorable weather, it was snowing furiously soon after the special steamer left Washington Navy Yard, and before night the wind blew a gale, so that we were obliged to come to anchor in a little cove on the Potomac, opposite Indian Head, where we remained quietly until the morning of the 5th instant.[46]

It was a rare chance for a daring rebel raid upon our little steamer had the enemy only known that the President of the United States, unattended by any escort and unarmed, was on board the "Carrie Martin," which rode peacefully at anchor all night in the lonely roadstead. And it was a scene which was peculiarly characteristic of American simplicity in the somewhat dingy but comfortable cabin of the steamer on that stormy night, where the Chief Magistrate of this mighty nation was seated familiarly chatting with his undistinguished party, telling stories, or discussing matters military and political, in just such a free and easy way as might be expected of a President who was out on a trip of relaxation from care and toil. There was no insignia of royalty or pomp, not even a liveried servant at the door, but just such plain republican

manners and style as becomes a President of a republic, were
to be seen. And though the rebels might have gobbled up the
entire party without firing a shot, nobody seemed to think
that it was worth while to mount guard to prevent so dire a
calamity; and nothing of the kind occurring, we arrived safely
at Aquia creek next morning, the snow still falling.

"The Creek" is now a point of considerable importance, as a
vast amount of supplies pass through the little *entrepôt* daily,
for the use of the army. Huge warehouses have sprung up since
the construction of the railroad to Falmouth—a large fleet of
transports and Government steamers lie at the wharf or in the
stream, and enormous freight trains are constantly moving
toward the Grand Army which is encamped among the rolling
hills of Virginia lying between the Rappahannock and the
Potomac. You can form some idea of the amount of freight
transported, when it is stated that *one million pounds* of forage
is daily transported from Aquia creek to feed 60,000 horses
and mules now in the Army of the Potomac. The railroad is a
temporary affair, but is well built and in good running order.
When our party started for the special train in waiting, there
was a tremendous cheer from the assembled crowd, who gave
another parting peal as the rude freight car, decorated with
flags, moved off with the President and suite. The day was
disagreeable and chilly, though the snowing had ceased, and
the face of the country, denuded of trees, hilly, and white with
snow, was uninviting and cheerless. All along the line of the
road are camps more or less distant from the track, and the
inmates appeared to be comfortably housed from the weather
by embankments about their log huts, covered with canvass
shelter-tents. We stopped at Falmouth Station, which is the
terminus of the railroad, and is five miles below or east of the
old town of Falmouth. The station is an important one, and, of
course, is now doing a big business in the way of receiving and

distributing supplies for the Grand Army. Several carriages
and an escort of lancers awaited the President and his party, the
honors being done by General Hooker's Chief of Staff—Major
General Butterfield.[47] We reached headquarters after a long
drive over a fearfully muddy road, the "sacred soil" red and
clayey, being almost fathomless in depth, and made more moist
by the newly fallen snow.

Headquarters Army of the Potomac.

General Hooker's headquarters are quite as simple and unpre-
tending as those of any of his men, as he abhors houses and
prefers tent-life, being unwilling, he says, to live in better
quarters than his humblest soldier. The headquarters are about
three miles from the Rappahannock in a direct line, situated
upon a high, rolling ridge, and are not very extensive, as the
staff is not large nor extravagant. The various staff officers and
aides have their tents on either side of what forms a street, at
the head of which is the wall tent of General Hooker, which
at the time of our visit was flanked by a couple of similar tents
put up for the President and his party, who were provided
with the luxury of a rough board floor, stoves and camp-made
bedsteads, and real sheets. The quarters were comfortable, and
the President and Mrs. Lincoln enjoyed the sharp contrast
with the White House hugely, while "Tod," [Tad] the juvenile
Lincoln, had made the acquaintance of nearly every tent
before the first day was done. The headquarters has every convenience for army use, as there are here a printing office, telegraph office, topographer, stenographer, artists, bakery, not to
mention various mechanical shops and their appurtenances.
The printing establishment is in a wall tent, and has as much
work as it can do printing blanks, army orders, etc. There were
nine hands employed in the establishment, detached from
various regiments, and representing New York, Pennsylvania,

Massachusetts and Minnesota. They had two small army presses, each taking a "form" of half-sheet letter paper size, and being very simple in construction; the ink being rolled upon the form by a small hand roller. The work done was very neat. . . . The printers have brevier, burgeoise, long primer and nonpareil for body type, and several varieties of fancy and "display" type besides, all of which is securely packed in cabinets and packed up when the army is on the march. The whole establishment can be packed up in a compass of an ordinary dray load, and can be set up in working order within one hour from the time of a halt. The printers shoulder "shooting-sticks" in a general engagement, and though they have no "fat takes" in their office, they manage to give the enemy a fair share of "leaded matter" whenever they get at him with a good "leader."

A Cavalry Review.

The 5th was so unpleasant that nothing was done further than to receive the officers of Hooker's staff by the President, who shook hands and had a pleasant word with each one. But on the 6th there was a grand cavalry review by the President and General Hooker. The entire cavalry corps of the Army of the Potomac is now massed as a whole, instead of being distributed among each of the corps as formerly, and is commanded by Major General Stoneman, the best cavalry officer in the service, Brigadier General Averill [Averell], the hero of Kelley's Ford, being the second in command.[48] The cavalry force is probably the largest ever known to warfare, being now about 17,000, larger than the famous force of Murat, who is esteemed the pattern of all cavalry officers.[49] This arm of our service has been of little account heretofore, owing to the mismanagement and imbecility of McClellan, but now, educated by experience, and allowed a latitude of operations by

the present commander of the Army of the Potomac, it
promises to make a brilliant record for itself when the time
comes, and already the gallant Averell, one of the most modest and quiet officers in the army, has inspirited the whole
cavalry corps with a feeling of emulation which will tell when
they are called into action.

The day for the review was not very propitious, the sky
being overcast and the air very raw and cold. The roads were
in a dreadful state, and on our way to the spot selected for the
review we had a taste of the quality of the country over which
some of the operations of Burnside, in January last, were
conducted during what is known in the army as "the Mud
Campaign."[50] The cavalcade was a brilliant one, the President
and General Hooker heading it, with several Major Generals,
while a host of Brigadiers, staff officers, Colonels and smaller
fry followed, the rear of this long tail being tipped out with
the showy accouterments of the Philadelphia Lancers, who
act as an escort of honor, and are an effective and brilliant
corps. Arrived on the ground, the President was greeted with
the usual salute of twenty-one guns, which was the first intimation, by the way, that most of the army had of his presence
among them. The troops were drawn up in squadrons on the
long swells of the rough country where we were, and the
cavalcade rode through all of the splendid lines at race horse
speed, colors dipping, drums rolling and trumpets blaring
wherever the President appeared. It was very muddy and also
windy, and the sacred soil flew in all directions, making the
gala clothes of the military big-wigs and their train appear as
though they had been bombarded with mud shells; occasionally a luckless wight got thrown and ran a narrow chance of
life among the rushing feet of the cavalcade. In the midst of
all rode little "Tad," the President's boy, clinging to the saddle
of his pony as tenaciously as the best man among them, his

gray cloak flying at the head like the famous plume of him of
Navarre. The President had the glorious privilege of riding
bareheaded, while common folks could cover their nobs from
the raw and gusty weather. It is a nice thing to be distinguished.

The tour of the cavalry in line being finished, the party
took position and the columns were set in motion, marching
past the post of the President and party. It was a grand sight
to look upon this immense mass of cavalry in motion with
banners waving, music crashing, and horses prancing, as the
vast columns came on and on, winding like a huge serpent
over hills and dales, stretching far away out of sight. Never
before upon this continent was there such a sight witnessed,
and probably never again will there be in our country so
great a number—seventeen thousand—assembled together,
men and horses, and all looking in excellent condition and
admirably fit for service. . . .

The President to-day used a saddle which had lately been
received by General Hooker from Main & Winchester, sad-
dlers in San Francisco, as a present from that firm. It is a very
handsome affair, and, as Hooker well said, could only have
been made in California, as its style and thoroughness of
workmanship is just what a military Californian can best
appreciate. The donors will, perhaps, be gratified to learn that
so excellent a horseman as the President was the first man to
sit astride their magnificent gift. . . .

The President in the Hospitals.

During the day the President and several of the commanders
reviewed the Fifth Corps, General Meade's,[51] and afterwards
went through several military hospitals. . . .

The President, with his usual kindliness of heart, insisted
upon going through all of the hospital tents of General Meade's

corps, and shaking hands with every one, asking a question or two of many of them, and leaving a kind word here and there. It was a touching scene, and one to be long remembered, as the large-hearted and noble President moved softly between the beds, his face shining with sympathy and his voice often low with emotion. No wonder that these long lines of weary sufferers, far from home and friends, often shed a tear of sad pleasure as they returned the kind salutation of the President and gazed after him with a new glow upon their faces. And no wonder that when he left the camp, after his long tour through it all, that a thundering cheer burst from the long lines of men as he rode away to the chief headquarters.[52]

A Great Infantry Review.

The 8th was a great gala day in the camp of the army, as on that day there was a grand review of the infantry and artillery of four corps of the Army of the Potomac, namely: The Fifth, under Major General Meade; the Second, under Major General Couch; the Third, under Major General Sedgwick; and the Sixth, under Major General Sickles.[53] . . . The day was brightening, and the weather a bit more emollient than heretofore, and the ground was dryer. After the usual Presidential salute and cavalcade through the lines, the troops were set in motion, and commenced passing by the usual headquarters in solid columns, by regiments and brigades. It was a splendid sight to witness these sixty thousand men all in martial array, with colors flying, drums beating and bayonets gleaming in the struggling sunlight, as they wound over hills and rolling ground, coming from miles away, their arms shining in the distance and their bayonets bristling like a forest on the horizon as they disappeared far away. . . .

The review lasted five hours and a half, during which time there was not the slightest interruption, but all moved on like

clock work, the solid and soldierly columns moving by in
perfect order, and retiring from the field in double quick time.
The general appearance of the men was first-rate, being admirable for drill, discipline and neatness, and each man bearing a
cheerful and confident look which was encouraging to note. If
these brave fellows do not fight well under their beloved commander, General Hooker, it will be for occult reasons, beyond
the ken of man. The President was highly gratified at the
appearance of the men, and many a serried rank turned eyes
involuntarily as it passed by their Chief Commander and Magistrate, who sat bareheaded in the wind in reverence in the
presence of the tattered flags of the army and the gallant men
who bore them. I noticed that the President touched his hat in
a return salute to the officers, but uncovered to the men in the
ranks. . . .

More Review of Troops.

The original intention of the President had been to stop with
the army only one day, but he found that the visit was pleasant
to the men and an agreeable respite from labor to him, and
he prolonged his stay until he should be able to see all of the
different corps of the army. When we first went down we
began to receive the first intelligence of our operations before
Charleston by the Richmond papers, brought from the rebel
pickets across the Rappahannock, and the President appeared
anxious and, if possible, more careworn than ever, though he
has never had any faith in an attack upon Charleston by sea
forces alone;[54] but after a few days the weather grew bright
and warm, and the news appeared no worse, and he rallied his
spirits somewhat, and the jaunting about appeared to rest him
physically, though he said quaintly that nothing could touch
the tired spot within, which was all tired.[55] He always speaks,
by the way, of this war as "this great trouble," just as a father

might speak of a great domestic calamity, and he never says "the Confederates," or "the Confederate States," but always "the rebels," and "the rebel States."

The 9th of April was the day after the grand review of four corps, . . . and on that day the Fifth Corps, Major General Reynolds, was reviewed by the President.[56] This corps numbers about 17,000 men, and is encamped upon a beautiful plain at the mouth of Potomac creek, where it puts into the Potomac river. The day was beautiful and bright, and the scene one of the finest which we met in our brief campaign. . . .[57]

[The last review] was held on the 10th, when the Eleventh Corps, Major General Howard, and the Twelfth, Major Gen. Slocum,[58] were inspected in due form. The first of these bodies of troops was formerly commanded by Franz Sigel,[59] who, like most of his Teutonic brethren, is a gallant man, but cannot be persuaded to live in harmony with his brother Commanders who are not Germans. The President expressed the gist of the Sigel difficulty when he said that Sigel would never forget that he and his Germans are step-sons. . . . Slocum's corps was the last reviewed, and then the cavalcade took up a line of march for the Brookes station, where we were to take the cars for Aquia. The march was a triumphal one, the troops of several corps being drawn up, without arms, along the line of travel, and for miles there was an intolerable yell of cheers for "the President," "Josey Hooker," "Mrs. Lincoln," "the boy"—meaning "Tad"—and occasionally there was a jocose cheer for "a fight, shure," or "the bully boy of Williamsburg,"[60] and once a good humored call of "and send along the greenbacks." . . .

Amid shouts and cheers, a novel salute of multitudinous steam whistles and dipping of flags, the Presidential party, accompanied by Major Generals Sickles and Schurz,[61] with several staff officers, left Aquia at sunset and arrived safely at

Washington at night, well satisfied with the ever memorable visit to the Army of the Potomac.[62]

20 APRIL 1863 (18 MAY)

A New Portrait of the President.

Some of the public spirited gentlemen of Philadelphia have commissioned E. D. Marchant, an artist of that city, to paint a portrait of President Lincoln for Independence Hall.[63] The picture is about finished and is quite successful as a likeness, though nothing wonderful as a work of art. The figure is life size, a half length, the subject being in a sitting posture, pen in hand, and with a warmly tinted background. The President says he had no idea that a painter could make so good a picture out of such excessively poor materials.

28 APRIL 1863 (22 MAY)

The Military Aspect

just now is hopeful and promising, despite the untoward rain and the backward season. From Vicksburg we hear that some of the complicated strategy of the past six months has been abandoned for the more sensible and common sense plan of running the batteries from above and practically flanking the town.[64] This has long been a pet project of the President, and he is in good spirits over what he considers a fair prospect of success. . . .

Personal Items.

. . . Mrs. Lincoln proposes a visit to the White Mountains this Summer, her eldest son Robert being her escort. The President will take no excursion of any sort unless his health should give way under the terrible pressure of his duties.

Waiting for the News.

. . . From the President down to the newsboys all watch the signs of the sky with as much anxiety as that which possesses a Wall Street broker during the rise and fall of the gold barometer. Last night, with a cloudless and moonlit sky, the President prophesied rain, and the falling flood of to-day proclaimed Abraham a veritable prophet.

2 MAY 1863 (27 MAY)

The Cabinet Sketched.

. . . Seward is small in stature, big as to nose, light as to hair and eyes, averse to all attempts upon his portrait, and very republican in dress and manner of living. He is affable and pleasant, accessible—from a newspaper point of view—smoking cigars always, ruffled or excited never, astute, keen to perceive a joke, appreciative of a good thing, and fond of "good victuals," if not of luxurious furniture. He has a desire for the Presidency, and all of the protests to the contrary cannot shake my humble belief in that fact, and Seward's consummate tact and ability. He is an advocate of conservatism and McClellan, not generally popular here, and sits on the small of his back, twirling his watch guard and telling pleasant stories of the past and present. He is unpopular with Mrs. Lincoln, who would like to see Sumner in his place.[65]

Stanton is what is popularly known as a "bull-head;"[66] that is to say, he is opinionated, implacable, intent, and not easily turned from any purpose. He is stout, spectacled, black as to hair and eyes, and Hebraic as to nose and complexion. He has a little, aristocratic wife, lives in handsome style, consuming much of his large fortune, probably, in his ample and somewhat gorgeous way of living. Stanton is exceedingly industrious, mindful of the interests of his Bureau, never off from his

post, works like a trooper and spends day and night at his
office when under a strong pressure. He does not appear to
have the maggot of the next Presidency in his brain, but plugs
right on, unmindful of what anybody says or thinks concerning him. In Cabinet Councils he is always for fight, and he
hopes to have a lick at England before he vacates his place.
He is very arbitrary, and shuts and no man openeth, or opens
and no man shutteth, with much vim and decision. The newspaper men, with the exception of the [Washington] *Chronicle,*
hate him as they do Original Sin, for he is as inexorable as
death, and as reticent as the grave. He wears good clothes,
goes to an Episcopal church—if at all—and would be much
more popular if he were not so domineering and so in love
with the beauties of military law.

Secretary Chase . . . is dignified, able, and ambitious, likewise he is the special antipathy of the New York *Herald,* and
the mirror of perfection for the [New York] *Times,* whose
Washington staff of correspondents are the favorites of Mr.
Chase and his first assistant flunkey, Mr. Harrington,[67] whose
humble origin makes him no better but much worse in his
present influential position. Mr. Chase is large, fine looking,
and his well flattered picture may be found on the left hand
end of any one dollar greenback, looking ten years handsomer
than the light haired Secretary. He is reserved, unappreciative
as to jokes, and has a low opinion of Presidential humor and
fun generally. He gained a transient reputation for fairness by
refusing to give positions to Ohio people when he first took
his seat in the Cabinet, but afterward revenged himself and
his fellow-citizens by filling his immediate office and many
subordinate ones with Ohioans. He has a long head. He lives
in a moderate style, is a widower, has a beautiful and somewhat airy daughter as the head of his household, and is a
regular church-goer. If he should be the next President of

these United States, the Executive chair would be filled with more dignity than it has known since the days of Washington. As to his ability, it is only a trifle below the dignity, or the Secretary is greatly deceived.

Father Welles, as the populace term our venerable Secretary of the Navy, is not so old as he is painted, although his white beard and snowy hair—wig, I mean—give him an apostolic mien which, in these degenerate days, is novel and unusual. He is a kind-hearted, affable and accessible man. Unlike his compeer of the Treasury, he does not hedge his dignity about him as a king, but is very simple and unaffected in his manners. He is tall, shapely, precise, sensitive to ridicule, and accommodating to the members of the press, from which stand-point I am making all of these sketches. That he is slightly fossiliferous is undeniable, but it is a slander that he pleaded, when asked to personate the grandmother of a dying sailor, that he was busy examining a model of Noah's ark; albeit, the President himself tells the story with great unction. Welles is a genial gentleman, and has, in the management of his Department, all of the industry of Stanton with all of the pride of Chase, which is saying a great deal. He will not lose his place in a hurry.

The rest of the members of the Cabinet can be "run in" in a single paragraph: Usher, of the Interior, is fair, fat, fifty and florid, well fed, unctuous, a good worker, as good a liver, an able lawyer, an accidental member of the Cabinet by the law of succession, and is socially dignified and reservedly get-at-able.[68] Bates is a nice old gentleman, short as to stature, gray headed, modest, quiet, conservative, and painfully reserved; he is somewhat of a patriarch—having a large family—is a profound student of human nature, and is one of those close, quiet observers of people who see through a man at first glance. Montgomery Blair is the best scholar in the Cabinet, but beyond that he is of but little account; awkward, shy, homely and repellent, he makes but few friends. . . .

A Pair of Lincoln Anecdotes.

No colored persons are employed about the Executive Mansion,[69] but the President has succeeded in getting about him a corps of attaches of Hibernian descent, whose manners and style are about as disagreeable as can be, barring one "Charlie," a valet, whose services during our late visit to the Army of the Potomac I hold in grateful remembrance. One morning the President happened to meet his Irish coachman at the door, and asked him to go out and get the morning paper. The Jehu departed, but, like the unfilial party of whom we read in Scripture, he said, "I go," but went not, and the anxious President went out himself and invested five cents in a *Morning Chronicle*.[70] It afterwards transpired that the coachman did not consider it his business to run errands, which coming to the President's ears he ordered up the carriage the next morning at six o'clock and sent a member of his household in the equipage to the Avenue, where he bought a paper and rode back, with the mortified coachee on the box.

That plan of punishing the hauteur of an exclusive servant was not original with the President, but this is: A gentleman who has been waiting around Washington for three months past, in vain pursuit of a pass to Richmond, applied last week, as a *dernier resort*, to the President for aid. "My dear sir," said the President, "I would be most happy to oblige you if my passes were respected; but the fact is I have within the last two years given passes to more that two hundred and fifty thousand men to go to Richmond, and not one of them has got there yet in any legitimate way."[71] The applicant withdrew with a rush of blood to the head.

Odds and Ends.

. . . Congress at its last session passed a law to authorize
Courts of Inquiry in the cases of such naval officers as were
overslaughed by the Naval Advisory Board. It has just transpired that the President "pocketed," or neglected to sign the
bill. He says that it would be constituting one Court to undo
the acts of another. The Commandant at Mare Island is among
those whom the bill was designed to give a rehearing to. . . .

8 MAY 1863 (5 JUNE)

The Effect.

. . . The first intimation of the fact [of the defeat at Chancel-
lorsville] was known here at three o'clock on Wednesday
afternoon, the 6th, when the War Department received a dispatch from General Butterfield, Hooker's Chief of Staff,
informing that Bureau that for prudential reasons the army
had been withdrawn from the south side of the Rappahannock and was safely encamped in its former position. Had a
thunderbolt fallen upon the President he could not have been
more overwhelmed. One newly risen from the dead could not
have looked more ghostlike.[72] It actually seemed that we had
been overwhelmed and forced to abandon the campaign, and
had been driven back, torn and bleeding, to our starting point,
where the heart-sickening delay, the long and tedious work of
reorganizing a decimated and demoralized army would again
commence. Despair seemed to dwell in every word of that
curt and fatal dispatch, which was the first to pass over the
wires after an interruption of a whole day, in consequence of
breakages made by the swollen streams.

Before an hour had passed the President, accompanied by
General Halleck,[73] was on his way, in a pouring rain, to the

army, having taken a special steamer at the Navy Yard for that purpose, at four o'clock in the afternoon. . . .

Sensation Newspaper Reports.

. . . From the President, who returned last night, I gained such information that I do not hesitate to say that . . . statements [in the New York *Tribune* about the catastrophic nature of the defeat] are in the main unqualifiedly false and wild. There was no "inglorious retreat" . . . no demoralization, and no "failure of the campaign," and no discussion of the "safety of the Army of the Potomac." But, on the contrary, the President— one of the most impressionable, while one of the most res- olutely practical of men—comes back satisfied that we have suffered no defeat or loss of *esprit du corps*, but have made a change in the programme (a forced one, to be sure) which promises just as well as did the opening of the campaign. . . .

Our Losses in Battle.

Of course it is now impossible to accurately state our loss in the late battle, but the highest authority—that which the President obtained at headquarters—puts it at 10,000 in killed, wounded and unaccounted for, and 1,700 made prisoners. . . .[74]

12 MAY 1863 (6 JUNE)

Hooker Criticised.

Those who are "nothing if not critical" have in the present con- dition of military affairs an opportunity for an exercise of their peculiar talents, which, of course, they are not slow to embrace. It is so easy, you know, for a knot of critics to demolish the pro- gramme of a General, while seated around a Washington breakfast table or in an editorial sanctum, that it is not strange that Hooker has had to "catch it" right and left. He who survived the thunder-burst of Stonewall Jackson and the terrific rains of May is likely to be demolished by the critics of New York and Philadelphia, of which last set, one Emile Schalk has proven himself the most unreliable, as he has either lied or misrepresented the facts in a most alarming manner in a communication in the Philadelphia *Press*. Already some of the leading newspapers are beginning to talk of Hooker's successor in command of the Army of the Potomac, as though his removal were a foregone conclusion. The New York *Herald* nominates Sickles for that position, and modestly demands that the President shall put this able Democratic politician in command, forgetful of the fact that it has never ceased to denounce Butler, Banks and Schurz for having been politicians before they were Generals.[75] But it is true, nevertheless, that the Administration has not lost its confidence in Hooker, and though it is conceded that his return to this side of the Rappahannock was a mistake, it is not true that the President considers that a fatal error, or is disposed to look for Hooker's successor anywhere at present. And allow me to say that if there should arise any necessity for a change in the command of the Army of the Potomac, either Rosecrans or Couch will be the successor of the present commander. But Hooker will, let us hope, as we believe, prove to his detractors that he can lead the patient and noble army to victory, and that he will show that he is the skillful and great General which we have been forced to believe him to be. The Army of the Potomac has been a slaughter pen for other than the rank and file. McDowell,[76] McClellan and Burnside have perished there, and now Hooker is very sick. We hope that his reputation and character as a soldier may not also be a wandering ghost behind the decimated ranks of our favorite but unfortunate army.

16 MAY 1863 (9 JUNE)

Loyal resolutions, passed by the California Legislature, are copied from the Sacramento Union into the [Washington] *Chronicle*, and are highly commended here for their spirit and conciseness. The President pronounced them as the best he had seen.

20 MAY 1863 (12 JUNE)

The Cabinet.

. . . The "radicals" have made another drive at Seward. . . .[77]

The President is exceeding loth to give up his wise and conservative counsels, and retains him against the wishes of a respectably large fraction of his own party friends, merely because he believes that to his far-seeing and astute judgment the Administration has owed more than one deliverance from a very tight place. Moreover, Seward's policy has always been of a character to avoid all things which might result in a divided North, and though it may have been too emollient at times, it has resulted in retaining to the Administration its cohesive strength, when it would have driven off its friends by following the more arbitrary and rash measures of Stanton. . . .

28 MAY 1863 (22 JUNE)

Who shall be the next President? Probably no people but ours would, while convulsed with a civil strife which our sister nations consider fatal, be so stoical as to agitate such a question as the above. But with a Roman calmness worthy of Caesar's cohorts, we have already commenced parceling out the spoils while the sword is yet in our hand. And at this moment the American people presents the extraordinary spectacle of a nation at war with rebel enemies, but not too much engrossed by war or alarmed at its results to be any less prompt than in days of peace to enter upon the excitement of a Presidential contest. While a war, alleged to spring from the result of the last election, is yet waging, we are ready to initiate another political campaign, though the life of our country may yet be at stake. The New York *Herald*, with its usual aptitude for mischief, has opened the ball by deploying a few skirmishers in front, whose salutes for Lincoln have drawn the fire of several editorial batteries, the most prominent of which have been the New York *Express* and the Woodite *News*, which Copperhead organs, of course, are exceedingly bitter upon any proposition to renominate President Lincoln. One cannot well determine if the *Herald* is in earnest or not in its explicit nomination of Lincoln for the next Presidency. It may be that the wily *Herald* takes this course as the most effectual one to weaken Lincoln; or it may be that the paper has spoken its honest convictions in saying that it believes that he will be the choice of the people. Certain it is the *Herald* is usually a most excellent weather-cock of public opinion, and its course upon any subject is a pretty correct index of what is the leading thought and wish of the people. And from a somewhat intimate and extensive acquaintance in Washington with the comers and goers of different sections of the country, I must say that I do not believe that any prominent public man appears to be so likely to receive the nomination for the next Presidency as Abraham Lincoln. His honesty, faithfulness and patriotism are unques-tioned, while his sagacity, ability and statesmanship have served to save the country from ruin, despite treason in all of the departments of the Government, imbecility and conspiracy in the army, and ill-disguised sympathy with rebellion in the North. It has been fashionable to speak of the President as weak and faltering, and to contrast his conduct with that of Andrew Jackson, but few recollect the vast and conflicting

interests which he has to direct and control, the wide scope of
thoughtful observation necessary for him to practice, and the
enormous daily and hourly pressure of duties upon him. It
would be wonderful, indeed, were he not to make some mistakes in the administration of so onerous a trust; but reviewing
the past it can be safely said that we have been blessed by
Providence in having such a man as Abraham Lincoln to hold
in his hands greater powers than were ever before given to any
President of the United States. Nevertheless, although popular
feeling is greatly with the present incumbent of the Presidential
chair, and though it would seem probable that the Seward
conservatives and Chase radicals can best be fused on Lincoln,
much does depend upon the conduct of the war for the coming
Summer. Should we be unfortunately unsuccessful, it is very
likely that popular feeling will look to a change in the Presidency, as a hopeful means of a change in the conduct of the
war; and though many—perhaps most of the masses—might
dread so radical a change while in the midst of an active war, it
is not to be supposed that continuous defeats would fail to
shake the public confidence in the present Chief Magistrate,
who stands just now so firm in the esteem and affections of the
people. The past misfortunes are not attributable to his mismanagement; the future may, with some show of justice, be
chargeable to his failure to profit by experience. At any rate,
however, he will do nothing himself to secure his renomination. I believe that he would accept it, but know that he believes
that no President has a right to allow his public or private acts
to be colored or directed by any determination to secure any
future aggrandizement for himself. He will continue to discharge his duty to his country as faithfully as he always has,
and as unmindful of his own future as he would if his tenure
of office were to expire only with his life, and were not dependent upon the will of the people. In public life this has always

been his course, and it is gratifying to know that such a policy, if policy it may be called, is generally more successful than an opposite one.

4 JULY 1863 (28 JULY)

The Removal of Hooker.

. . . Public and official confidence was shaken in him [Hooker] when he made the Chancellorsville failure; but . . . the President felt that the ineffectual end of that campaign was capable of being attributed to the inexperience of General Hooker in handling so large an army as that of the Army of the Potomac, and he felt that justice to Hooker and to the country demanded that he should have one more trial at least before he was removed. That trial was had when appearances indicated a rebel raid across the Potomac, and Hooker failed to prevent it, as it is now apparent. Allow me to put in here a bit of personal gossip: On the night of June 2d, just before leaving for South Carolina, your correspondent had a conversation with the President, in which I expressed some natural anxiety that a rebel raid might occur soon, and that activity in this vicinity might come up in my absence. The President said that all indications were that there would be nothing of the sort, and that an advance by the rebels could not possibly take place so as to put them on this side of the Rappahannock, *unless Hooker was very much mistaken, and was to be again out-generaled.* Hooker was mistaken, and was out-generaled. In the course of his somewhat blundering programme, after the army of Lee was across the Potomac, he ordered the evacuation of Harper's Ferry, as that point was of no special importance to us so long as the rebels had other channels of retreat and communication, and French's force was needed in the field.[78] Halleck protested against this action and notified French that he was not subject to Hooker's orders, at which Hooker asked to be relieved. As one of Meade's first orders was the evacuation of Harper's Ferry, and no interference was made with him, it is a fair supposition that the objection of Halleck was only a subterfuge to get rid of Hooker. General Hooker has the popular sympathy in his misfortunes, for he is unquestionably brave, high-spirited and gallant, but the public also believe that he was not the man for the emergency, and Meade assumes his difficult *role* in the face of the enemy with a great sigh of relief from the people.[79]

"The Soldiers' Home."

. . . The institution bearing the above name is a large, fine building, built of stone, in castelated style, about two miles and a half from Washington, due north.[80] The grounds are extensive and beautiful, and belong to the Government, which erected the large central building for disabled, homeless soldiers of the regular service, of whom a large number here rest from the services in the field. Near the central building are several two-story cottages, built of stone, in the Gothic style, and occupied by the Surgeon in charge, the Adjutant General and other functionaries, and one is occupied during the Summer by the President and family. Mr. Lincoln comes in early in the morning and returns about sunset, unless he has a press of business—which is often—when he sleeps at the White House and has "prog" sent up from Willard's.[81] He goes and comes attended by an escort of a cavalry company, which was raised in this city for the purpose, and the escort also stands on guard at the premises during the night; but to my unsophisticated judgment nothing seems easier than a sudden cavalry raid from the Maryland side of the fortifications, past the few small forts, to seize the President of the United States, lug him from his "chased couch," and carry him off as a hostage worth having.

8 JULY 1863 (1 AUGUST)

The National Capital Jubilant.

The official dispatch of Admiral Porter, announcing the surrender of Vicksburg,[82] was received at the Navy Department at five minutes before one o'clock yesterday [after]noon. Secretary Welles immediately went over to the Executive Mansion with the joyful news, nearly upsetting Father Abraham in his excess of enthusiasm. . . .[83]

Notables in Washington.

. . . Major General Sickles was brought here last Sunday, and is stopping with a friend on F Street. He bears his wound with great fortitude, having experienced no reaction since the amputation of his leg.[84] He was worse to-day than he has been since his wound was received, but will undoubtedly recover. The President visited him on Sunday, and General Hooker called upon him yesterday. . . .

BOONSBORO, MARYLAND, 14 JULY 1863 (10 AUGUST)

Parting Compliments.

. . . Why didn't we bag them? Of course the country will ask the question, and with the present light on the subject we can only say that if General Meade had followed his own judgment the rebel army would have been attacked upon Monday, just in the nick of time, when a portion of their force was across and the main part of the army was congregating around the scow-crossing at Williamsport and the bridge at Falling Waters. On Sunday night he called a council of corps commanders, and out of eight there were only three who favored the General's proposition to attack the next day. Those three were General Pleasanton [Pleasonton] of the cavalry corps, General Wadsworth, acting Commander of the First Corps,[85]

and General Howard of the Eleventh. General Meade, being
overruled by his officers, deferred the attack, and the rebels
escaped into Virginia. General Hooker, we cannot help thinking, would have asked the advice of his commanders and then
have done just as he thought best—attacked the rebels.

The effect of this failure to defeat the rebel army will be
unfortunate upon our army, which has accomplished wonders
during its late hard month of service, marching from Virginia
to Pennsylvania, then fighting a three days battle, and then following the rebels to Maryland, and being all the time exposed
to such privations as marching troops in rainy weather, without
full rations or shelter, can only suffer. They see that their term
of service "for the war" is lengthened a year at least by this
escape of their old foe, and they have speedily lost the high
spirits which they had but yesterday. But we must wait still,
and hope yet for a better end to all of these campaigns, and
believe that they will not all be so fruitless as the July campaign
in Maryland.[86]

22 JULY 1863 (13 AUGUST)

Too Many Generals.

Allusion has been made to the fact that the Army of the West
has not demanded so many Generals as that of the Potomac,
and that may be accounted for by observing that the latter
army is too near Washington; and the fact that it is too near
Washington is often adduced as a reason why the Army of the
Potomac does not win more victories, compared with the
Western Army. Possibly that is true, but not in the way that
the grumblers aver. The Army of the Potomac is near enough
to Washington, it is true, to be continually interfered with by
the authorities here, and it is also near enough to permit its
Colonels, brigadiers and Major Generals to be rushing in at

every frequent breathing spell in pursuit of promotion, changes, and various other favors for themselves, friends and favorites; therefore, it is no slander to say that the army is one vast hot-bed of bickerings, heart-burnings and jealousies; that is a hard thing to say, but it is true as the Book. The President says that the changes and promotions in the Army of the Potomac cost him more anxiety than the campaigns. He also says—and he ought to know—that the ratio of men to Generals in that army, is now just 800 men to each General. This is partly owing to the fact that many of the regiments are such only in name—their ranks having been decimated, and the remnants are being consolidated or recruited. These skeleton regiments make skeleton brigades, and a skeleton brigadier too often commands what is not equivalent to one full regiment. The famous Excelsior Brigade went into the Gettysburg fight with 1,000 men.[87] The First Corps had in the fight when its commander, General Reynolds, was killed, only *four thousand* men, all told, and yet that corps had all its paraphernalia of Major Generals of divisions and Brigadier Generals of brigades. This is not so in the West, where they have been too far off to ask much for promotions, and where Colonels command brigades and divisions also. This vice of promotion is of recent growth, for at the first battle of Bull Run Hunter was a Colonel, but commanded a corps, and Miles, of Harper's Ferry notoriety,[88] occupied the same position with the same rank. But a couple of years in the vicinity of Washington, and frequent visits here, and familiar acquaintance with Congressmen, have all conspired to make a change in our favorite, much abused Army of the Potomac. The Western army has more time for fighting, and when you hear that the other army is too near Washington to be successful greatly, it will be well also to recollect that its usefulness can be impaired

in other ways than the official meddling which it is popular to
believe is the rule here.

Wounded Officers in Town.

There are many wounded officers in Washington just now,
among whom is Major General Sickles, who has bravely
recovered himself after the severe illness consequent upon the
amputation of his right leg. He rides out in his carriage daily.
His corps idolize him, but he will be hardly likely to resume
the command of the Third again. As the President, to adopt
his own homely language, will have a hole for which he has no
peg in Meade's reported resignation, it may be possible that
Sickles, with his one leg, may yet be put in there. Another
wounded hero is Ulric Dahlgren, a son of the Admiral, as
brave and gallant a soldier as ever lived.[89] He was a member
of Hooker's personal staff, with the rank of Captain, and distinguished himself by various exploits of arms, one of which—
a cavalry dash into Fairfax, early in the war—furnished a
spirited theme for the gifted pencil of F. O. C. Darley.[90] Dahlgren went upon Pleasonton's staff when Hooker was relieved,
and in a brilliant dash upon Williamsport, where he captured
an invaluable rebel mail, he was wounded in the foot, and is
now very low in health in consequence of the wound, and will
lose his foot, if not worse. These are some of war's harvests.
Colonel Cradlebaugh,[91] formerly of Nevada Territory, who
was wounded in the attack upon Vicksburg, May 23d, has
been lying at a hospital in Memphis for several weeks past,
but has recovered sufficiently to come to Washington. While
calling to his men, as he led them on, a ball entered his open
mouth, cut off the tip of his tongue and passed out through
the right jaw. He was reported as killed, but yet lives to make
more anti-Mormon speeches, I hope, albeit his speaking faculty is greatly impaired by the loss of the piece of his tongue.

23 SEPTEMBER 1863 (17 OCTOBER)

The Situation.

. . . Last night the town was full of dark rumors of a great defeat of the Union army, and the President was fain to declare that he believed that Rosecrans had been badly whipped. . . .[92]

Dahlgren has not yet proved himself the brilliant officer which he was supposed to be, and his unfortunate sally by night upon the well-defended ruins of Sumter has not served to exalt his reputation much. . . . [93] The President believes in Dahlgren, and has every reason to believe that he will succeed when his occasion is fully come. . . .

Maine and California.

. . . Honest Abraham spoke affectionately and warmly of our State in a private conversation the other day, saying that he had always liked California for her large liberality and generous profusion, but now he loved her for her unswerving fidelity to the Union, under circumstances which might have shaken the patriotism of less noble States. . . .[94]

26 SEPTEMBER 1863 (21 OCTOBER)

Superintendent of Indian Affairs in Northern California.

Early last August . . . George M. Hanson was removed from the position of Superintendent of Indian Affairs for the Northern District of California,[95] and Elijah Steele, of Eureka, Humboldt county, was appointed. This removal was made in consequence of certain charges of mismanagement in office being brought against Hanson by citizens of the localities within his jurisdiction.[96] I am sorry to say that the financial transactions of the late Superintendent do not have a good look; but it is not true, as has been intimated here, that certain domestic irregularities of the Superintendent, though notorious here, had any special weight in determining his removal. The facts in the case were brought to the knowledge of the President, who wisely decided that, though both parties in the unfortunate affair may have been far from spotless, the question could not enter into the merits of the officer of the Government. Steele, as well as the new Collector of San Francisco, was appointed at the instance of Senator Conness.[97]

The President in a Fix.

Almost everybody would like to be President, and there are but few persons who realize any of the difficulties which surround a just administration of the duties of the Executive office. The other day a delegation from Baltimore called upon the President by appointment to consider the case of a certain citizen of Baltimore whom it was proposed to appoint to a responsible office in that city. The delegation filed proudly in, formed a semi-circle in front of the President, and the spokesman stepped out and read a neat address to the effect that, while they had the most implicit faith in the honesty and patriotism of the President, etc., they were ready to affirm that the person proposed to be placed in office was a consummate rascal and notoriously in sympathy, if not in correspondence, with the rebels. The speaker concluded and stepped back, and the President replied by complimenting them on their appearance and professions of loyalty, but said he was at a loss what to do with ———, as a delegation twice as large, just as respectable in appearance and no less ardent in professions of loyalty, had called upon him four days before, ready to swear, every one of them, that ——— was one of the most honest and loyal men in Baltimore. "Now," said the President, "we cannot afford to call a Court of inquiry in this case, and so, as a lawyer, I shall be obliged to decide that the weight of testi-

mony, two to one, is in favor of the client's loyalty, and as you
do not offer even any attempt to prove the truth of your suspi-
cions, I shall be compelled to ignore them for the present."
The delegation bade the President good morning and left.

2 OCTOBER 1863 (29 OCTOBER)

Pressing the President.

The Missouri-Kansas delegation, now in town for the purpose
of urging upon the President the removal of General Schofield,[98] is a large and good looking body, numbering seventy
men. You have already had a summary of their address to the
President, which, much to the disgust of the irrepressible
newspaper men, was delivered at a private interview in the
famous East Room of the White House [on September 30].
The doorkeeper, when pompously told by an applicant for
admission that he was an editor, said, "Oh yes, editors, of all
other persons, are to be denied admission during the interview." That doorkeeper knows his business. The delegation
has the sympathies of all loyal men here, apparently, but their
success is a doubtful question. They would have been more
likely to have secured Butler for a commander in their department if they had not asked it, but now I venture to predict
that General Butler will not be sent to Missouri. It is one of
the marvels of these progressive times that a Committee from
slave-holding Missouri, a fair representation of the State,
urges a more radical policy than our "sectional" Republican
President.

Publishing Contraband News.

In my letter of September 26th some items of the movement
of the Eleventh and Twelfth Corps of the Army of the Potomac were furnished,[99] and of course they were not contraband

for California, though they were here. When it was decided to
reinforce Rosecrans with the above named corps an officer
from the War Department went to every newspaper correspondent in town and requested them, at the special desire
of the President and Secretary of War, not to mention any
movement from the Army of the Potomac or in any way
allude to it, thus throwing themselves on the patriotism of the
correspondents. The request was made in a gentlemanly manner, and was so reasonable withal that all the correspondents
agreed to it, and telegraphed or wrote to their newspapers not
to allude to the event should it come to their knowledge in
any way. Thus far all was well, when everybody was astounded
on the night of the 26th by information from New York that
the *Evening Post*, an out-and-out Administration paper, had
published full particulars of the reinforcement of Rosecrans by
the Eleventh and Twelfth Army Corps, under Hooker. Some
of the Sunday morning papers copied the intelligence, and the
Philadelphia *Sunday Mercury*, a rabid secesh concern, went so
far as to republish the *Post's* news, with the addendum that it
was contraband and that if justice was done the editors of the
Post should breakfast in Fort Lafayette. The newspaper men
were in despair, Stanton raged like a lion, and the President, I
am free to say, was very mad. The Monday morning papers
discreetly held their peace, and quietly ignored the intelligence
and the whole affair, waiting for a proper opportunity to open
their batteries on the unfortunate *Post*, which made haste, in
its next edition, to explain by saying that its Washington correspondent was not responsible for the *rumors* which had
appeared in its Saturday's edition concerning army movements,
but that it had been imposed upon by irresponsible parties.
The truth of the matter was that an occasional correspondent
of the *Post*, who dabbles in stocks, was in Washington at the
time, and, to buoy up the market, which was drooping, smug-

gled the news to New York by mail, and the senior poetical editor, who has usually nothing to do with the make-up of the paper, got hold of it and put it in, greatly to the dismay of the managing editor.[100]

I have been thus particular in the account of this latest newspaper escapade for the reason that the whole report was afterward contradicted with a great deal of virtuous indignation, but it was substantially correct as it first appeared. The affair is unfortunate for the *Post*, as it not long since published President Lincoln's Springfield letter, much to his vexation and chagrin.[101] On the day before its delivery he had refused an advance copy to the Washington agent of the Associated Press, saying that, though solemn promises not to publish had repeatedly been given, he had found the practice of furnishing advance copies to newspapers to be a source of endless mischief. That night the *Post* published the letter, and it was telegraphed back to Washington before it was read at the Springfield Convention. So much for newspaper enterprise; but where they got the letter is yet a secret known to the editors only.

6 OCTOBER 1863 (31 OCTOBER)

Concerning the Next Presidential Campaign.

There is no longer any need of concealing or ignoring the fact that Lincoln is a candidate for renomination. Your correspondent has the highest authority for saying that he does not seek the nomination, but really desires it at the hands of the loyal people of the United States. In this desire, a natural ingredient, is his hope that he may receive the suffrages of the people as an approval of the policy with which he has conducted an Administration through a long and arduous struggle.[102] It is true that other Presidents may have asked the

same on the same ground, but Lincoln has been called upon
to administer the Government in strange and perilous times,
and, as it is conceded that a change in the Administration
during the present war would be, to say the least, risky, or, to
use Lincoln's own phrase, would be "swapping horses in the
middle of the stream," it would be a direct rebuke to the present incumbent of the Presidential chair to rotate him out of
office while affairs are in such a situation. It would be virtually
voting him a failure; if he is a failure he ought to go, for the
safety and welfare of the nation are of more value than any
President's personal feelings or claims. But it is also reasonable to believe that Lincoln has, so far as any man can have, a
symmetrical and coherent plan, compact in his own mind, for
the adjudication of the great questions which will arise under
the final pacification of "this great trouble," as he calls the
rebellion. If the people are satisfied that Lincoln has done
the best which could be done for the suppression of the rebellion, the protection of our varied interests, and for the whole
country, and also is willing to trust him with the pacification
of the country, he will be the next President of the United
States.

He is no seeker for a renewal of office, busies himself with
no thought of his own future, and never bestows favors with
any reference whatever to the relations of an applicant for
office toward himself. But, patient, patriotic, persevering, and
single-hearted, he goes right on with his duty, "pegging away,"
just as though, as he has said to me, his own life were to end
with his official life, content to leave his earnest labors and
conscientious discharge of duty to the disposal of God and his
country. A nobler and purer nature than his never animated
man. His chiefest errors have been that the heart overruled
the head, and a kindness, which has been mistaken for weakness, has too often prevailed when sterner counsels have been

heard. He is, also, so anxious to conserve and defend the interests of *the whole country*, that he has disappointed and alienated some portions of it, and he has thus turned away those who would have been always his friends. Here, in Washington, we have frequent occasion to hear the beratings and scoldings of politicians who have been treated just as dispassionately and coolly by the President as though they had no power at all to bring to bear upon a future Presidential canvass. Lincoln does not appear to consider for a moment that the men whom he kindly but firmly denies to-day will to-morrow be part and parcel of a Nominating Convention, but he does what he considers to be right, regardless of the consequences to himself. This is noble, but is it politic?

The Great Split.

And right here comes into prominence the widening breach between the Conservatives and the Radicals of the Union or Republican party. Radicalism and Conservatism are now the opposing forces which besiege the President, which are entering into an adjustment of all the great issues from the settlement of the rebellion, and which will divide the combatants in the contest for the next nomination, now narrowed down, as far as the Unionists are concerned, to two candidates—Lincoln, as standard bearer for the Conservatives, and Chase, so the champion of the Radicals. It is evident that Lincoln will have to fall back upon his own conservative policy, as laid down by his own Administration, and become the candidate of a People's Union party. Not that there will be more than one candidate against the Opposition or so-called Democratic party, but the fight will be in the Convention, and it promises to be almost as interesting as the old Douglas and Buchanan quarrel, without any of its bitterness. Those disloyalists who hope to see a dismemberment of the great loyal party of the

North, through a sharp feud between new and inharmonious
elements, will not be able to draw much comfort from an
apparent incoherence of the component parts. An ambition
for the chair of State is honorable, as much so in Chase as in
Lincoln, but it happens that [the] two men represent ideas
and principles which are different but not radically opposed or
irreconcilable. Chase's views and sentiments are not manufac-
tured for the occasion; his life-long record, his splendid public
services, his uncompromising hostility to every form of
oppression and slavery, his purity of character—all these are
too well known to need recapitulation, and these, added to his
statesmanlike abilities, make him an eminently fit candidate
for what is known as the radical wing of the loyal party of the
North. If our people are ready now to go into an election upon
Chase's avowed platform of "Freedom for all," he will be the
next President. Chase keeps ahead of public sentiment; Lincoln prefers to be led by it. . . .

What the Cabinet Will Do.

If any of the members of the Cabinet of President Lincoln
have had any aspirations for his uneasy chair—and it would be
surprising if they had not—all but Chase have resigned such
fond dreams. . . .

14 OCTOBER 1863 (7 NOVEMBER)

The "Republican" as an Organ.

During the last few months the Washington *Republican* has
contrived to secure for itself the reputation of being the organ
of the President, and accordingly a great deal of misplaced
importance is sometimes attached to some of its few editorials.
The solution of the puzzle is that Hanscomb [Hanscom],[103]
the editor, who is a pushing and persevering man, has managed to so ingratiate himself with the President that he has

almost exclusive access to the office of the Executive, and
there obtains from our good-natured Chief Magistrate such
scanty items of news as he is willing to give out for publication, and so the enterprising editor gets up his daily column of
"official intelligence," much to the annoyance and jealousy of
the New York and other Washington correspondents whose
dependence is upon the current news of the day, which must
be gained before a single hour has blown upon its freshness.
As for the *Republican* having any authority to reflect or indicate the views of any member of the Administration upon any
subject whatever, it is the most complete invention of those
who circulate such a foolish yarn.[104] Lincoln believes in letting
the newspapers publish all that will not benefit the enemy; he
disapproves of many of the arbitrary edicts of the press of Secretary Stanton, and he is more free to converse upon matters
pertaining to his Department than any of his Cabinet, though
the rack of torture could not extort from him what he chooses
to conceal; but he abhors the thought of an "organ."

Odds and Ends.

. . . The President was shown that telegraphic blunder which
made him say that he was "agreed" to giving up the Union,
instead of "against" it; but he thought it a very serious joke.

21 OCTOBER 1863 (20 NOVEMBER)

Three Hundred Thousand More.

Right on the heels of important State elections, in which the
mass of the people once more declare their determination to
uphold the President in a vigorous prosecution of the war,
comes a call for three hundred thousand volunteers, with a
contingent order for another draft just behind it. The call is
timely, for we have now an opportunity to test the sincerity of
those who have opposed the draft and have begged for a

chance for volunteering, as well as the sincerity of those who
have voted in such overwhelming volume for the sustenance
of the war against the rebellion. The most captious can take
no exception to this call, and on all hands we hear a general
manifestation of applause and gratification that the President
has taken the people at their word. As they have shown that
he is still trusted and upheld, so he asks them to show their
faith by their works. And it is believed that if we have the
men in the North fit for fighting they will come out at this
call. If they do come it is yet quite possible that they may not
be obliged to fire a gun. The President hopes that the moral
effect of such another rally of volunteers as we ought to
expect, *added to great victories near at hand*, will be all that we
shall need for the final crushing of the rebellion, now so weak
at home and so rapidly failing abroad. Depend upon it, there
are worse foes within the lines of the rebellion than there are
without. Ruin, bankruptcy, financial distress, loss of credit and
of military supplies—these are all the destroying worms which
are eating out the life of this modern Herod of rebellion.

Already there is some discussion as to the terms of the new
call, some persons affecting to misunderstand the relative position of the call for volunteers and the draft now in operation;
but the plain statement of the case is that the President calls for
three hundred thousand men, which shall include all those
already raised by conscription under the present draft—which
draft is to go forward in such States as it has been commenced
in, and the men so raised are to be credited on the new call.
The quota of each State under the new call, then, is just what
its deficiency under the draft is, and if we have raised one hundred thousand men from the draft, we shall have two hundred
thousand men to raise by volunteering; and if we do not raise
but one hundred thousand more by volunteering by January 5,
1864, we must expect a second draft for another hundred thou-

sand to make up the deficiency. But all States which have not yet received full credit for the men already raised by them will now have credit on the new call, and the quota of each State on the call for volunteers will be apportioned or designated by the Government. There is now on hand about nine millions of dollars, being avails of the commutation fund of the draft, which will be used for the purpose of paying the usual bounty for volunteers, as provided by the Government, veterans receiving $402 and new recruits $302. A portion of this commutation fund is to be used, however, for the reimbursement of such loyal slaveholders (is the term paradoxical?) as furnish able-bodied negro recruits—each man so furnished being forever free, and his owner, if loyal, receiving $300 for every black soldier so given to the ranks of the Federal army. The rule is to apply to all slaveholding States and parts of States excepted in the President's proclamation of freedom. Two years ago, when Governor Yates, of Illinois,[105] urged upon the President the confiscation of rebel property, emancipation and the enlistment of a million black soldiers, Old Abe telegraphed: "Hold fast, Dick, and see the salvation of the Lord." I believe that Dick begins to "see it."

24 OCTOBER 1863 (21 NOVEMBER)

Rosecrans.

It is hard to give up a popular idol, and those who have long believed that the hero of Stone River, Murfreesboro and Corinth was a consummate General will demur at his sudden fall.[106] It is sad and disheartening that such things must be, but yet they must be, and it is a sufficient answer to all cavils to be able to say that no man in the nation was more pained at the necessity of the removal of General Rosecrans than was the President himself.[107] But that honest Chief Magistrate,

whose daily labor and nightly thought is for the country
which he loves, knows that Rosecrans is not fit to command
an army where so much depends upon its success as now
depends upon the Army of the Cumberland. It is not proper
that all men should now know the reasons why Rosecrans was
removed, but they are weighty and all-sufficient, and if they
were known no right-minded man would ask that he should
be retained in command. It is enough to know that this
Administration has never dismissed a valuable public servant
or relieved any General of his command without good cause
for so doing. Some of the newspapers have tried to break
Rosecrans' fall by saying that he is outranked by Grant and
must therefore be relieved or violate military etiquette. This is
charitable, but it is not the reason, for Rosecrans, if a true soldier and a good General, should and could fight under Grant.

29 OCTOBER 1863 (26 NOVEMBER)

Chattanooga and Rosecrans.

We are waiting for the thunder which is soon to burst over the
battle fields around Chattanooga, and the popular tumult over
the summary deposition of the popular idol, Rosecrans, is
stilled before the more momentous looking for of tidings from
the dread encounter expected in the Southwest. It would be
sad indeed if the American people were so mercurial or so
unthankful that the services of so distinguished a General as
Rosecrans could be at once forgotten when a wise and honest
President relieves him from military duty. We have been
taught so long to consider Rosecrans as a demigod, inevitable
and unconquerable, that it is hard to cheerfully acquiesce in
the *dictum* of the Administration which has relieved Rosecrans from his command. Whatever "insiders" may know, and
whatever the War Department may conceal for the present,

the public generally has believed that Rosecrans was the man for the occasion, and they will not willingly give him up; but, while deferring for the present to the honest purpose of the President, they still hope that time and the future will exonerate their favorite. Still, it is instructive and encouraging to see how very generally public confidence in the President, who is solely responsible for this unexpected step, is shown by the popular deference to the superior knowledge and wisdom of the Executive. At first, people were disposed to be indignant and captious, but maturer thought, and the knowledge that honest Abraham Lincoln had himself directed the removal, without the counsel or advice of his Cabinet, seemed to convince the people that it was all right and for the best. There is no military or arbitrary despotism about Abraham Lincoln, and when such a step as the removal of Rosecrans is taken people feel that there are motives and reasons which are honest and sufficient prompting to the act, and they cheerfully acquiesce, believing that, though they know not now why such changes are made, they shall know hereafter. Of course the mischief-loving Copperheads are an exception to this general rule, and they strive to shake popular confidence in the Administration by assailing it for the removal of a General who is popular generally. They have a good opportunity now to repeat their McClellan programme, and deify a single General at the expense of the power which displaces him. But time will prove that the public confidence in the President is not misplaced; and when all men know, as they will know, that Rosecrans has shown himself to be unfit for the command of an army upon whose success so much depends, we shall see all men congratulating themselves that we have at the head of affairs a President who is not afraid to do what is right, regardless of popular clamor and popular likings.

Great preparations are going on at Chattanooga for the

defeat of the rebels who oppose our advance upon Atlanta and Northern Georgia. The artillery which was lost at Chickamauga has been replaced by large reinforcements from other departments, that of the Potomac and of Washington being pressed to spare all that can be safely taken away, so that the artillery force of Grant's grand army will be so augmented as to far exceed anything of the kind, in weight and in numbers, ever known in the history of modern warfare. The *Chronicle*— "the War Office organ"—says that we must now find our Richmond at Chattanooga, accepting Jeff. Davis' theory that a decisive battle there will practically end the war. This is believed in Washington to be one of the givings-out of Secretary Stanton, but it is unpopular, for our favorite Army of the Potomac will have been a failure, and all of the blood and treasure lavished in campaigns in Virginia will have been fruitlessly expended. Is it true that the war in the East has been of no avail, and that the campaigns against Richmond from the North are practically at an end? Such is undoubtedly the opinion of the War Office, and the Army of the Potomac, it would appear, will have no further duty than to defend the National Capital and come in, like a Greek chorus, to applaud and accompany the final "crushing" of the rebellion. General Meade has been despatched by the President "to find a fight or resign."[108] He will not find a fight, so the people say, but will give place to some new commander. He will never reach Richmond, and his days as General in command of the Army of the Potomac are numbered. Our public vituperate Halleck, as the chief bungler of all our military operations, and, baffled by the President's honest sagacity and open-hearted wisdom, they turn upon the reticent and self-possessed General-in-Chief with anger and continual reprobation. One cannot help admiring the plodding, patient, impervious character of General Halleck, who works as hard and as cheerfully as though he were not to-day the most unpopular man in Washington—always excepting Stanton.

30 OCTOBER 1863 (26 NOVEMBER)

Mass Meeting in Baltimore.

The great Union mass meeting held in Baltimore on the night of the 28th is one of the most significant evidences of the change in popular sentiment in the Border States which we have had from any quarter. But a little while ago Maryland was almost coaxed into open rebellion against the Government, in simulated defense of slavery and Southern rights; the Legislature of the State conspired to carry her out of the Union; the streets of Baltimore—that "murder-haunted town"—were sprinkled with the first blood shed by the defenders of the nation, and everywhere the spirit of secession and pro-slavery ran mad and appeared dominant for a space. But now one of the largest and most enthusiastic assemblages ever known in Baltimore congregates in Monument Square, bearing such mottoes upon banners and transparencies as these: "Union," "Emancipation," "Slavery is Dead—its Treason killed it," "Infamy the Reward of Rebels," "Emancipation and Free White Labor," "Slavery is the Mother of the Rebellion." Do we dream, or do we actually hear with our own ears loyal Marylanders making speeches in favor of immediate Emancipation, and a loyal crowd of Baltimoreans applauding to the echo the most radical utterances—the "radical" Secretary of the Treasury making the most conservative speech of them all. Is this "My Maryland" of the rebel boast, now promising 20,000 majority to the Unconditional Union Emancipation ticket? Truly, wonders will never cease; and it is not strange that President Lincoln could not find words in which to express his feelings when invited to attend a Union meeting in

Baltimore—that Baltimore through which he was secretly conveyed three years ago.

But the great outpouring at Baltimore night before last had another significance to those who watch political events and who understand the inside working of political cabals. The election of Henry Winter Davis and the triumph of the Emancipationists in Maryland is the defeat of Montgomery Blair and all of his kind.[109] It is a matter of common notoriety that he has strained every nerve to defeat Winter Davis and to give what official sanction he could to an extra-conservative policy in Maryland. Assuming to speak for the President and the majority of the Cabinet, he delivered his Rockville speech, in which he assailed Sumner and Chase, and foreshadowed a pro-slavery, States Rights theory as being that of the Administration.[110] He went to Baltimore again and again to secure, if possible, a candidate for Congress who should run against Winter Davis on some half-hearted war platform; and if he did not succeed in getting up a milk-and-water candidate for that purpose, it was not for the reason that he did not try. He *was* unsuccessful; for few dare to attempt a campaign against the noble and loyal Marylander, and Winter Davis will be triumphantly elected. The Baltimore meeting had the countenance and support of Secretary Chase, and his simple words of sympathy and cheer for the struggling sons of freedom in Maryland were received with the wildest enthusiasm. One could not but feel, as the eye took in the vast multitude which surged through the square, bearing upon the gusty waves of popular excitement banners, torches and transparencies innumerable, that a great and momentous revolution had occurred, and that a signal and grave repulse was then and there administered to that narrow-minded Cabinet officer, who had stooped so low as to try to drive popular sentiment against the policy of the Administration of which he is a member.

Postmaster General Blair and Forney.

There is but one expression, and that of reprobation, toward Postmaster General Blair for his extraordinary course, and it now remains to be seen whether Lincoln will sacrifice his chances of a renomination by tacitly indorsing Blair's ratiocinations by retaining him in the Cabinet. Although he was appointed to his place upon the urgent request of such radicals as Sumner and Wilson, against whom he now turns, we cannot expect that any sense of obligation to them would induce him to modify his own private views or restrain his public utterances. Good faith is not a characteristic trait of the Blair family. But good sense, at least, might have restrained him from loading his own wrong-headed opinions upon the Administration of which he is a member. Soon after the Pennsylvania election Judge Kelley, of Philadelphia, and John W. Forney called upon the President with their congratulations— and Forney, with his usual outspoken candor, very plainly said to the President, Blair being then present, that his conservative friend Governor Curtin desired the President to know that if the Rockville speech of Postmaster General Blair had been made thirty days earlier it would have lost the Union ticket in Pennsylvania twenty thousand votes.[111] He also expressed his astonishment to Blair that he, a Cabinet Minister, should have the hardihood to utter such sentiments in public, just on the eve of important elections in other States, as those of the Rockville speech. Blair responded that whatever Forney might think of the matter, he had only spoken at Rockville his honest sentiments. "Then," said the impetuous Forney, turning upon him, "why don't you leave the Cabinet, and not load down with your individual and peculiar sentiments the Administration to which you belong?"

The President sat by, a silent spectator of this singular and unexpected scene. I hope, however, that he was edified, for if

he does not realize the unfortunate position in which he is
being pushed by Blair, he must make up his mind to fall with
Blair, for it is morally certain that no such fossiliferous theories and narrow-minded policy as that of the Postmaster General is to be indorsed by the people of any of the loyal States.
Every State election this Fall has rejected such a notion, and
the people are too far advanced in liberal ideas to consent that
any standard bearer of theirs shall refuse to carry the banner
of "Freedom for All."

It is not pleasant or edifying to be obliged, as a faithful
chronicler, to allude to these bickerings among our public
men, but they are a part of the history of the times, and the
public must sooner or later know all about them. . . .[112]

4 NOVEMBER 1863 (1 DECEMBER)

Various Odds and Ends.
. . . The Copperhead newspapers have a great deal to say now
about the Government sending home sick soldiers to vote
down the Democratic ticket in New York. The President says
that if the soldiers are too sick to fight they are not too sick to
vote without knowing what ticket they put in. None but con-
valescents are sent home, and they are furloughed for two
weeks from November 1st. . . .

7 NOVEMBER 1863 (4 DECEMBER)

How They Live at the White House.
The edifice itself is tolerably familiar in appearance to most
people who have seen the engravings of the house, which is
usually represented with the Potomac front toward the spectator, as that really fine face of the building is higher and not
covered with the overgrown portico which so disfigures the
Avenue front that it looks like a big portico which had been

built to conceal the house behind it. The Potomac front has sloping grounds, decorated with vases, statuary and ornamental gardening, between it and the unoccupied public square on the river bank; but the main entrance to the house is on the front which faces Pennsylvania avenue, and a pair of massive gateways open from the avenue upon the semi-circular driveway which leads to the portico, and thus incloses a small park, in the center of which stands the bronze statue of Jefferson (not Davis), with the Constitution in his hand, which statue aforesaid is green and moldy with time and is in seedy contrast with the smug-looking effigy of Old Hickory, cutting off the right ear of his rampant charger, which stands in the square across the avenue, and is known as the Clark Mills statue.[113]

Let us go into the Executive mansion; there is nobody to bar our passage, and the multitude, washed or unwashed, always has free egress and ingress beneath the awful shadow of this immense portico, whose tall columns stand thickly around us. A small vestibule opens into a wide hall, handsomely carpeted, which has a bronze and ground glass screen separating the state and family apartments from the more public part of the house. At the right is an ante-room for the servants in waiting, and beyond that is the dining room—not a very sumptuous room—only accommodating thirty-five at table. Beyond this are family rooms and a large conservatory, and in the basement are servants' rooms, kitchen, etc. We have no "kitchen Cabinet" during this Administration, but the present presiding lady of the White House has caused a terrible scattering of ancient abuses which once accumulated below stairs. The suckers who grew rich on the pickings and stealings from the kitchen, garden and conservatory, and who had spies in every room in the house, have been dispersed, and when they went they circulated innumerable revengeful yarns

concerning domestic weaknesses at the White House, and
there were some credulous people who believed them.[114] The
right or west wing of the house is occupied by the President's
family, the center by the state parlors, and the east wing has
below stairs the famous East Room, and up stairs the offices
of the President and his Secretaries. The parlors which are
used for ordinary receptions are entered from a corridor
behind the screen which forms one side of the main hall of
entrance, and are three in number, being called severally the
blue, green and crimson drawing rooms, from the color of the
upholstery and fittings. The last named of these is the favorite
sitting room of Mrs. Lincoln, where she receives private calls
every evening in the week when in town, and where the President usually meets his friends socially after dinner. The furniture is very rich—of crimson satin and gold damask, with
heavy gilded cornices to the windows and a profusion of
ormolu work, vases, etc., some of which stuff is very ancient,
being bought or presented during Monroe's and Madison's
administrations. There is a grand piano in this room and a full
length portrait of Washington; but generally, the walls of the
White House are destitute of paintings, the want being
remedied by gilded and richly colored hangings. It would be
a sensible notion if some Congress, more thoughtful and
public-spirited than any which we have yet had, would make a
small appropriation for the purpose of hanging in the house of
the Chief Magistrate of the nation a few pictures by the best
American artists, which might form a nucleus for a gallery of
art in the home of the President and his family. The walls of
the house would be relieved of their unfurnished bareness, and
a portion of the severe simplicity of the White House would
be graced thereby. The blue drawing-room is much admired
by most people, as its fittings are quite sumptuous in style and
finish. The room is formed in the graceful curves of a perfect

ellipse, and the windows command a lovely view of the grounds
in the rear of the house and of the Potomac. The furniture is
of blue and silver satin damask; the woodwork of the chairs,
sofas, etc., being solidly gilt, as also are the heavy cornices of
the doors and windows; broad mirrors, with massive frames,
surmount the marble chimney-pieces, and a blue and white
velvet carpet covers the floor. The ceiling is painted in fresco,
in which blue is the prevailing tint, and the walls are covered
with blue and gold hangings; in short, it is all so "deeply,
darkly, beautifully blue," that one feels quite cerulean therein.
In this room are many of the Japanese presents to President
Buchanan, which constitute a part of the furniture of the
house, under the law which confiscates all presents to Government officials to the use of the Government. These drawing
rooms all communicate with each other and with the great
East Room, and upon some occasions they are all thrown
open. The East Room occupies the entire principal floor of
the east wing of the house, and is well known to most people
by the common engravings of it. The ceiling is frescoed in a
very ordinary style, cupids, flowers and such sprawling about
overhead in a very loose manner, the unbreeched urchins
looking as though a suit of Uncle Sam's uniform would not
come amiss this cold weather. The lace curtains, heavy cords
and tassels and damask drapery, have suffered considerably
this season from the hands of relic-hunting vandals, who actually clip off small bits of the precious stuff to carry home as
mementoes, I suppose. I wonder how they have the "cheek" to
exhibit their trophies to admiring friends at home and com-
placently relate how they stole them. Some of these aesthetic
pilferers have even cut out small bits of the gorgeous carpet,
leaving scars on the floor as large as a man's hand. Others, on
larger game intent, have actually cut off a yard or two from the
lower end of some of the heavy crimson satin window hang-

ings. It is easy enough to do this here, for though there are always one or two watchmen about the house, a thief can have an accomplice to engage the attention of the watchmen elsewhere, while he commits his petty larceny within. I suppose such fellows take it that the White House property belongs to the people, and they will take their individual share now. In this East Room the Presidents usually hold their levees or public receptions, but Mrs. Lincoln does not always receive publicly here. When large delegations or deputations wait upon the President he receives them in this room, but he usually prefers that they shall wait upon him in his private office up stairs.

If we go up stairs at any hour after Washington people are stirring we shall find the corridors and waiting-rooms full of people who have business or curiosity urging them into the presence of the President. The grim Cerberus of Teutonic descent [John G. Nicolay] who guards the last door which opens into the awful presence has a very unhappy time of it answering the impatient demands of the gathering, growing crowd of applicants which obstructs passage, hall and ante-room. It would not be a bad idea if an inside guardian of affable address, as well as flintiness of face, were placed on duty here, where the people come almost in actual contact with the great man within, whom they learn to love or dislike, according to their treatment by his underlings. The President is affable and kind, but his immediate subordinates are snobby and unpopular.[115] A wide corridor opens on the left into the private rooms of the Secretaries, and on the right to the office of the Private Secretary, J. G. Nicolay, and to the private office of the President. The room of the Secretary is a small office, very meagerly furnished, and old-fashioned in appearance as, in fact, is all of the upper part of the mansion—the dark mahogany doors, old style mantels and paneled wainscoting being more suggestive of the days of the Madisons and Van Burens than of the present. There are usually three Private Secretaries to the President, of which one only is contemplated by law, receiving a yearly salary of $2,500, carriage and perquisites; but the extraordinary exigencies of the public service have obliged the President to employ two assistants, who are clerks detailed from the Departments and drawing their salaries therefrom.[116] These three Secretaries are all young men, and the least said of them the better, perhaps.[117]

When the President lives in town he commences his day's work long before the city is astir, and before breakfast he consumes two hours or more in writing, reading or studying up some of the host of subjects which he has on hand. It may be the Missouri question, the Maryland imbroglio, the Rosecrans removal question, or the best way to manage some great conflicting interest which engrosses his attention, but these two best hours of the fresh day are thus given to the work. Breakfast over, by nine o'clock he has directed that the gate which lets in the people shall be opened upon him, and then the multitude of cards, notes and messages which are in the hands of his usher come in upon him. Of course, there can be no precedence, except so far as the President makes it; and, as a majority of the names sent in are new to him, it is very much of a lottery as to who shall get in first. The name being given to the usher by the President, that functionary shows in the gratified applicant, who may have been cooling his heels outside for five minutes or five days, but is now ushered into a large square room, furnished with green stuff, hung around with maps and plans, with a bad portrait of Jackson over the chimney piece, a writing table piled up with documents and papers, and two large, draperied windows looking out upon the broad Potomac, and commanding the Virginia Heights opposite, on which numberless military camps are whitening

in the sun. The President sits at his table and kindly greets
whoever comes. To the stranger he addresses his expectant
"Well?" and to the familiar acquaintance he says, "And how
are you to-day, Mr. ———?" though it must be confessed that
he likes to call those whom he likes by their first names, and it
is "Andy" (Curtin), "Dick" (Yates), and so on. Seward he
always calls "Governor," and Blair or Bates is "Judge;" the rest
are plain "Mister," never "Secretary." With admirable patience
and kindness, Lincoln hears his applicant's requests, and at
once says what he will do, though he usually asks several questions, generally losing more time than most business men will
by trying to completely understand each case, however unim-
portant, which comes before him. He is not good at dispatch-
ing business, but lets every person use more time than he
might if the interview were strictly limited to the real necessi-
ties of the case. Consequently Lincoln cannot see a tithe of
the people who daily besiege his ante-chamber; and, in his
anxiety to do equal and exact justice to all, excludes or delays
those who might see him sooner if he did not try to do so
much. No man living has a kinder heart or a more honest purpose than Abraham Lincoln, and all who meet him go away
thoroughly impressed with the preponderance of those two
lovable and noble traits of his character. Is the petitioner a
poor widow who wants a writership in one of the departments—the President has read her credentials, asked a question or two in his quiet but shrewd way, and he takes a card on
which he writes a plain request to a Cabinet Minister to give
the bearer what she craves, and the grateful woman goes out,
blessing the good-natured President whose very next act may
be to receive a distinguished foreign diplomat whose Government is hovering on the doubtful verge of an American war;
or it may be a Brigadier wanting promotion, an inventor after
a contract, a curiosity hunter with an autograph book, a Major

General seeking a command, a lady with a petition for a pass
to Richmond, a Cabinet Minister after a commission for a
favorite, a deputation asking an impossibility, or a Committee
demanding an impertinence; it may be all or any of these who
come next, and the even-tempered statesman who patiently
sits there, interlarding the dull details of business with a good-
natured joke or anecdote, must wisely and quickly decide
upon questions which vary in importance from a small favor
to an humble dependent to the adjustment of one of the most
momentous National interests of the times. Is it not wonderful that so little that is open to criticism is done by him, rather
than that we have anything to find fault with? When we
recollect that every day, except Sunday, is occupied in the
manner thus described, from nine o'clock until three o'clock
in the afternoon, and that during the sessions of Congress
several hours of the evening are also thus taken up, it is a
matter of surprise that the President can find time to do so
wisely and so well the various work which comes from his
hands. Of course, during all of these interviews he is liable to
interruption from his Cabinet Ministers, who have free access
to him at all business hours; Senators and Governors of States
come next in precedence, and Representatives come last
before "citizens generally." Usually, no foreign functionary
seeks an interview with the President except through the pre-
scribed channel of the State Department, and etiquette
requires that all foreigners shall be presented to the Secretary
of State by the Minister of the country to whom the person
seeking an interview belongs, and in this roundabout way the
party follows up the clue of red tape until he arrives in the
presence chamber.

The President dines at six o'clock, and often invites an
intimate friend to take pot luck with him, but he and his
estimable wife are averse to dinner-giving or party-making,

only deviating from their own wishes in such matters for the purpose of gratifying people who expect it of them. They much prefer the same sort of social, unrestrained intercourse with the family that most sensible people do, and have a wholesome horror of state dinners, which are invariably prolific of discord, ill feeling and big expenses. Lincoln is strictly temperate and simple in his habits; to this and his faculty of throwing off the oppressive weight of care, the like of which no man ever bore before him, he owes his life, and the country owes its security in these perilous times, when a cool head, a firm hand and an honest heart are needed at the head of our vast public affairs. While the most enthusiastic admirer of Lincoln would reluct to claim for him a combination of all the endowments and acquirements of his predecessors in office, it does appear to me that it is impossible to designate any man in public life whose character and antecedents would warrant us in the belief that we have any one now living whose talents and abilities would fit him to administer this Government better than it has been conducted through the past three stormy years by the honesty, patriotism and far-sighted sagacity of Abraham Lincoln. That is merely an opinion, to be sure, but it is not an unintelligent one, and the writer hereof shares it in common with a great cloud of candid witnesses.

The wife of the President has been so frequently and cruelly misrepresented and slandered that, though hesitating to approach so delicate a subject, your correspondent cannot refrain from saying a word in strict justice to this distinguished and accomplished woman. When the present Administration came into power, the National Capital was infested as well as besieged by rebels, and every conceivable means was adopted to render the members of the new Administration unpopular. To this end slanders innumerable were circulated concerning the habits of the President and his family; and it is not many months since when candid and loyal men were to be found believing that our temperate President drank to excess, and that Mrs. Lincoln was a vulgar, ill-bred woman. Such stories are scandalous, and though time has done justice to the President, who is seen and read of all men, Mrs. Lincoln is denied the privilege of defense, and in the privacy of a household clad in mourning has not yet had justice done her by the public. The slanderous tales of those who prayed daily that "Lady Davis" might occupy the White House are still circulated and believed, and loyal people, more shame to them, without knowing the truth of what they repeat, still allow themselves to become the media for the dispersion of scandals as base as they are baseless. It is not a gracious task to refute these sayings, but the tales that are told of Mrs. Lincoln's vanity, pride, vulgarity and meanness ought to put any decent man or woman to the blush, when they remember that they do not *know* one particle of that which they repeat, and that they would resent as an insult to their wives, sisters or mothers that which they so glibly repeat concerning the first lady in the land. Shame upon these he-gossips and envious retailers of small slanders. Mrs. Lincoln, I am glad to be able to say from personal knowledge, is a true American woman, and when we have said that we have said enough in praise of the best and truest lady in our beloved land.

Republican simplicity and Republican virtues reign at the home of the American President; thousands of private citizens in our prosperous country are more luxuriously lodged, and more daintily fed; but, search the wide nation over and you will not find a more united household or a more noble and loving family than that which to-day dwells in all of the anxious cares of the White House.[118]

On the Sunday before he went to Gettysburg, Lincoln invited me to go to Gardner's photography gallery where he was to sit for his picture.[120] He took along a two-page supplement of the "Boston Journal" in which was printed Mr Everett's Gettysburg oration which Mr E. had sent him. In the carriage, on Lincoln's showing me the speech, occurred the conversation which Major Lambert quotes.[121] When he came back from Gettysburg, Lincoln told me that he made several changes in the manuscript of his own address after he got to Gettysburg, and others "as he went along" while delivering it on the field. But all of these changes did not appear in the fac-simile afterwards produced under Lincoln's own supervision. The explanation of this [is] sufficiently obvious. Lincoln, who did not appear to think very highly of his own speech, could not remember just what changes he did make while he read it on the field.

11 NOVEMBER 1863 (7 DECEMBER)

Starving National Soldiers.

All accounts from rebeldom agree that the condition of our brave fellows now in the prisons of Richmond is very unhappy and full of privations. After enduring for some time a meager and bad supply of food, the National prisoners at Richmond have been cut off from any supply whatever of meat, and they now diet on a scanty ration of rice, flour and molasses. The excuse for this is that the rebel authorities have no meat for their own soldiers, and that if their own men are deprived of what we consider one of the necessaries of life our men cannot expect any better treatment. If this is true, and it probably is, we ought to expect that starvation would force the rebels to come to some reasonable terms by which a satisfactory exchange of prisoners can be effected. But right here is the inevitable "nigger in the fence." The rebels refuse to exchange any of the officers or men of the colored regiments in their possession, and our Government insists that no discrimination shall be made as to color or position of any soldier or officer in their hands, but a uniform of the United States shall entitle its wearer to the privileges of the National Government, whatever his color may be. With their usual insane pertinacity upon this subject, the rebels strenuously object, but insist that they shall reserve these colored soldiers and their white officers "to deal with them after their own laws," whatever that may be. Uncle Sam is firm, and will not give up his protection of his soldiers. As we cannot get our soldiers home, where wholesome rations are to be had, the President has determined to feed them in Richmond, and negotiations are now going forward under his direction by which provisions will be forwarded and dealt out to our fellows there by a regular agent from the United States Commissary General's office.[122] Good for Father Abraham.

14 NOVEMBER 1863 (12 DECEMBER)

Gossipping.

. . . The whirl of dust of the bridal cortege, which went from Secretary Chase's to the railroad depot last night, has subsided—but not so the gentle flow and ebb of small talk which so grand an event as the marriage of Senator Sprague and Miss Kate Chase has created.[123] Who was there and who was not there; how the bride looked in her white velvet dress, real point lace veil and orange flowers; how the President went in solitary state and a white cravat and things; how Mrs. Lincoln did not go because she is yet in black wear and had an opportune chill betimes;[124] how the President stayed two hours and a half "to take the cuss off" the meagerness of the Presidential party. . . .[125]

When Senator Conness was in Washington last Summer the President saw and admired, in his observant way, a stout hickory cane which the Senator from California usually carried; so Conness privately sent to California for a similar stick which was given him years ago by the lamented and gifted Broderick.[126] The stick came on in due season, and after being feruled with Washoe silver was presented to the President by Senator Conness.

As the time for the assembling of Congress draws near the President is overwhelmed with visitors, most of whom engross a great deal of time each day; and, in addition to other duties, he has his message now in course of preparation, so that he is bothered beyond all account to so dispose of his time as to satisfy a tithe of the demand upon it. Day before yesterday an unusually large crowd of persons were in attendance, going through the slow process of being admitted one by one, each consuming many golden moments in small affairs of their own. The President executed a *coup d'etat* which soon dispatched business, by opening his doors and having the whole posse admitted at once to his cabinet; and, hearing each case in the presence of the waiting assembly, he soon went through with all of the calls of that day.

Sitting in the office of the Superintendent of Public Printing the other day,[127] a tidy-looking young woman came in with a card on which was written the following:

"My Dear Defrees: The bearer, a poor girl, has a brother in our lines, as prisoner of war, who wishes to take an oath of allegiance. Be good enough to look into the facts and report to me. Yrs, A. LINCOLN."[128]

It appeared that one Dennis Mack, a brother of the young woman, had been impressed by the rebels early in the war, being caught near Alexandria. Being unable to escape, he was found in the ranks of the rebels at one of the late Rappahannock fights, but persists that he is a Union man, and is ready to take the oath of allegiance. The girl had been turned away by the surly officials of the War Department, but had got access to the President, whose kind heart was at once enlisted, and he determined that justice should be done, so he sent the sister of the prisoner to the kindly Defrees, who likes to do a generous act, and we may hope that the sequel will prove that the President's kindness will be useful, as it has been in so many thousands of instances of which the world knows nothing.[129]

17 NOVEMBER 1863 (16 DECEMBER)

"The Condemned Yankees."

There was to-day a grand review in this city of the Invalid Corps, or, as the rebels call it, the "Condemned Yankees," there being over three thousand in number.[130] The day was perfect and the display very fine, and a great crowd was present, although no public notice of the review was given. The President and distinguished officers of the military service reviewed the corps. Their regimental uniform is of a sky blue color throughout, and each regiment has six battalions armed with muskets, and four battalions armed with sabers and pistols, the arms indicating the extent of injuries which the soldier has received. Being all veterans, the drill of the Invalids is well-nigh perfect.

2 DECEMBER 1863 (28 DECEMBER)

Burnside in Jeopardy.

We are still in great doubt here as to the safety of Burnside, who at last accounts was stoutly besieged in Knoxville. . . . Visitors at the White House remarked in the course of a discussion as to the fate of Burnside, that heavy firing had been heard at Knoxville during a few days past, upon which the President said; "I am glad of it. I am glad of it." Surprise being expressed at such an abrupt remark, the President said that he was in the same situation as an old lady in Sangamon county who had a great flock of children, who were almost out of her keeping, they were so numerous. When she heard one of them crying or bawling in some out-of-the-way place, she would say, "There is one of my children who is not dead yet." Burnside is one of the lost children.

The Winter Programme at the White House.

With the opening of Congress commences a series of daily levees by Mrs. Lincoln, who will receive from noon to three o'clock, afternoon, and from seven to ten o'clock in the evening. The President will also appear, whenever his time will allow, at the evening levees. No standard of dress will be established other than that people shall appear in decent and clean clothes. Mrs. Lincoln will put off her mourning dress upon the first of January, and will wear purple during the Winter season.

12 DECEMBER 1863 (18 JANUARY 1864)

What People Say of the Message.

The reputation of President Lincoln for originality is pretty general now, but nobody expected such an original Message as that communicated to the first session of the Thirty-Eighth Congress.[131] It has taken everybody completely by surprise; and, I am glad to add, the surprise is an agreeable one, for it is temperate, wise, statesmanlike and broad in its proposed treatment of the vexed questions of this hour and of the coming hour. I am not now thrusting individual opinions upon the reader, but am trying to reflect average public sentiment here.

It was expected that the President would either ignore recon-struction altogether or give an elaborate and decisive pro-gramme therefor. He has done neither; but has pleased the radicals and satisfied the conservatives by plainly projecting a plan of reconstruction, which is just alike to popular rights, to the cause of liberty and to the loyal people of all sections of the Union. Nor is this programme a finality as to its detail, for it is generally understood here that the President weaves through the whole a thread of contingency, plainly implying that while its broad, general principles are immovable and abiding, events yet to arise may change materially the plan and theory laid down. It is obvious that we are at sea in this whole matter of reconstruction, and that we must trust to Providence, whose overruling care has thus far led us, for a safe pilotage to the haven of security and rest. The President has been forced by premature discussions and ill-digested theories of others to announce what the policy of the Admin-istration will probably be in the premises, and his Message, a worthy document in itself, has found its only significance in being the reflection of his views upon this mooted question of reconstruction. As such, then, it gives, probably, more general satisfaction than any Message since the days of Washington. As no Administration since Jackson has been able to preserve in both branches of Congress a majority of its own, until now, so no President since that same period, certainly, has suc-ceeded so well in satisfying the various political antagonisms of the times as Abraham Lincoln in his last Message; and it is generally remarked that this has not been done by skillful trimming or by a noncommittal, emasculate policy; but bold, high and original ground is taken, apparently disregardful of the claims of either of the great factions which profess to own the President and the next Presidency.

Of course, everybody is not satisfied. The Copperheads

were determined not to be satisfied; the Missouri destructives
expected that one-half of the annual Message would have
been devoted to a resume of their difficulties, which they
fondly deem the center of all political questions; and Senator
Sumner is irate because his doctrine of State suicide finds no
responsive echo in the generous amnesty and magnanimous
offers of the Chief Magistrate of the United States of America.[132] During the delivery of the Message the distinguished
Senator from Massachusetts exhibited his petulance to the
admiring galleries of the Senate chamber by eccentric motions
in his chair, pitching his documents and books upon the floor
in ill-tempered disgust, as a vent to his half-concealed anger
at so effectual extinguisher upon his pet theory.[133] Nobody
expected, however, that his plan of territorializing the con-
quered rebel States would be accepted or indorsed either by
the President or by Congress. As it is, both Chase and Blair—
the two antipodes of public political sentiment—are perfectly
satisfied; and, after all, when that is said, we have said that all
who are reasonable and practicable are conciliated, pleased
and satisfied. For fear of doing injustice to our long-suffering
Missouri friends, it should be also said that they concur in the
general verdict of approval of the Message, and, despite the
non-indorsement of Missouri radicalism in theory, heartily
applaud the plan of reconstruction, and are fain to believe that
their distracted State can be harmonized, emancipated and
secured to the Union forever upon the basis laid down in the
Message. When "the Blair family" and the Missouri radicals
are alike agreed to accept so bold and original propositions as
those contained in the last annual Message of the President,
we may well conclude that the political millennium has well
nigh come, or that the author of the Message is one of the
most sagacious men of modern times.

16 DECEMBER 1863 (20 JANUARY 1864)

... Since the arrest of the Chapman pirates, lately convicted in San Francisco,[134] frequent application has been made to the President for the pardon of one of them—Alfred Rubery, an English subject—by that ardent and unwearied friend of America in England, John Bright.[135] The application of Bright was made through Senator Sumner, who consulted Senator Conness and Justice Field,[136] before the latter of whom Rubery was convicted, and those gentlemen assented to the proposition to pardon. The President has accordingly directed that the man shall be pardoned; but he takes the ground that his proclamation of amnesty, lately promulgated, does not cover the case of the Chapman pirates, as has been alleged by some of their friends in California, consequently only Rubery escapes; and furthermore, the President says that if any construction can be placed upon his late proclamation so as to include persons who have been convicted of piracy or sedition by the Courts, he will issue a supplemental proclamation disallowing such a construction. ...

19 DECEMBER 1863 (20 JANUARY 1864)

Sundry Items of News.

To-day cards are issued for the first reception at the White House this season. Only members of Congress, the diplomatic corps and Cabinet officers are invited; and the reception will be held from one o'clock to three, the President and Mrs. Lincoln both being present.

The President has recovered his health so as to go out. He was at the theater four nights this week to see Hackett as Falstaff,[137] and received the usual formal call of the Justices of the Supreme Court yesterday. While he had the varioloid he said that he at last had something that he could give all his friends—the disease. . . .[138]

. . . How do you like the [President's] message and proclamation down your way? Here it has been received with a general expression of satisfaction and relief, as indicating the most feasible method of settling reconstruction. Of course, Sumner and the few disciples of the doctrine of State suicide are disappointed, but those radical fanatics are but few. Congress has no idea of supporting their views. It is also very generally concluded that Lincoln's message settles the question of his renomination; if there was before any doubt of it, there is none now, unless unforeseen combinations and unforeseen events may arise to change the course which everything is taking. Chase, I hear, says that he is willing to leave the destinies of the country to the hands of Mr. Lincoln, being satisfied that the President is coming over to his views. Magnanimous, ain't he? Chase will never give up, however, that is positive, though he may land on the Supreme Bench. The Blairs are a great drawback to Lincoln, and so are Halleck and Stanton, the two last being excessively unpopular. The Blair Family are thrusting themselves upon Mr. Lincoln, as his natural allies, so that it is difficult for people to believe that they are not the exponents of his policy, but he knows and seems to care nothing about their political views. He tolerates Montgomery Blair in the cabinet because he is efficient in his Department, but, to my certain knowledge, he never read his Rockville speech until months after it was delivered. He appears to care nothing at all about the political opinions of his cabinet provided they are useful in the separate departments. But Blair, though a good Postmaster General, is the meanest man in the whole government. Stanton is coarse, abusive and arbitrary; decides the most important questions without thought and never reconsiders anything, and abuses people like a fish-wife when he gets *mad*, which is very frequent; nevertheless he is industrious and apparently devoted to the interests of the Government.[140] But he and Halleck have blundered all along.

People here generally feel sanguine that the war will close with another summer and that it will be terminated more by operations from the West and Southwest than from any other quarter. The Army of the Potomac is an utter failure so far as aggressive operations are concerned, and Meade is the greatest failure of all of its Generals. . . .

2 DISPATCHES & LETTERS
1864

1 JANUARY 1864 (4 FEBRUARY)

A Happy New Year.

. . . Here in Washington, New Year's day was kept after the usual fashion of visiting and being visited. The day was fearfully cold and windy, it being a *galey* day, if not a gala day, and last night was the coldest of the season, water pipes freezing up as tight as the money market, while the morning newspaper and the milkman were alike snapped up by the nipping frosts. Yesterday the President received his friends and the public generally at the White House, beginning with the Diplomatic Corps, army officers and naval and marine officers, at eleven o'clock in the day. These gentry made a brave show, as they marched up in all of their gold lace and toggery, General Halleck heading the military crowd, Seward leading his pet lambs of the diplomacy, and Admiral Davis sailed in at the head of the squadron of naval officers.[1] The foreign Ministers were especially gorgeously arrayed, being covered with stars, garters and medals of honor; the rush for a glimpse of these gay birds was very great, and Secretary Seward looked very like a molting barnyard fowl among peacocks, in such illustrious company. The rush of the great multitude was as great as in former years; and the crushing and jamming of bonnets and things was fearful. One woman became separated from her family, and a tender female shriek being heard, the paterfamilias of the lost one was sure that it was the voice of his beloved which he heard; likewise, his son, a youth of tender years, was led to believe that his mother was killed; whereat he bawled exceedingly, and there was a great deal of excitement at the entrance to the great drawing-room, where all of this took place, until every Jack got his Gill and all went well again.

The President looks better since he has had the varioloid. I don't mean to insinuate that the disease has added any new charms to his features; but his complexion is clearer, his eyes less lack-luster and he has a hue of health to which he has long been a stranger. He stood up manfully against the great crush and bore the hand-shaking like a blessed old martyr, as he is. My feminine readers will be interested to know that Mrs. Lincoln wore a purple velvet dress, decorated with white satin flutings (isn't that what you call it?) around the bottom; Valenciennes lace was on the sleeves, and an immense train flowed out behind. Mrs. Lincoln never looked better than in the dark, rich tones of her reception dress, in which she has, for the first time, left off her mourning garb. . . .

Lincoln versus Halleck.

This place is just as good as any other to recall a conversation held in this city, early last Summer, by the President and General Halleck upon Charleston matters. One evening, just after the reception of the official report of the repulse at Charleston, the President asked Halleck why it was not possible to land a strong infantry and artillery force upon Morris Island, under cover of the gunboats, to co-operate with the navy in the attack upon the works at Cummings Point; thus Sumter could be reduced, and, by gradual approaches, we could get within range of the city. Halleck would not say that it was impracticable to land troops upon the southeast end of the island, but insisted that they could do nothing after they got there, and he made a strong point upon the statement that the strip of land between Fort Wagner and the place of landing was so narrow that zigzag approaches after the usual scientific rule could not be made. Assistant Secretary Fox, of the Navy Department,[2] here came in, and the President appealed to him, and Fox coincided with him in opinion, which encouraged the President to press his views upon Halleck, who always replied: "If it were practicable; otherwise the plan would be ultimately futile, for the reason that there was not room enough for the approaches which must be made." Halleck, though he treated the suggestions of Lincoln with respect, evidently entertained a profound contempt for his generalship; yet, it will be remembered, that this plan is the only one which has thus far ever accomplished anything at Charleston and affords us any promise of eventual success. I have, before this, said that Lincoln is a better General than Halleck, but I don't think that is saying much. Lincoln was not disappointed at the Charleston fizzle.[3] Halleck was.

Odds and Ends of News.

R. J. Stevens, late Superintendent of the San Francisco Branch Mint, is still here, and is endeavoring to have his character cleared and justified by a new appointment.[4] He has failed in making the President see it in that light. . . .

9 JANUARY 1864 (5 FEBRUARY)

Odds and Ends.

The National Academy of Arts and Sciences is now in session at the Capital,[5] there being present, among others, Professor Agassiz, A. D. Bache, Admiral Davis, Commodore John Rodgers of the Weehawken-Atlanta fight; Major General A. A. Humphreys, Brigadier General Totten,[6] and others.

Yesterday the members waited upon the President and had a social interview. . . .

27 JANUARY 1864 (27 FEBRUARY)

The President's Levees.

For some reason not specially apparent, the semi-weekly levees at the White House are unusually popular this Winter, and the crowds which go there are better dressed than heretofore, when people went into the Presidential mansion in a garb which no decent man would allow in his family sitting room. The levees are held on Tuesday evenings and Saturday afternoons, the former being "dress" receptions, and the Saturday afternoon levees being less formal in character. The President has been present at all of these receptions, and he intends to meet the people always when his duties will permit.[7] Of course, there is a great variety of costume at the evening affair, but most of the visitors go in party dress—the women being rigged out in full fig, with laces, feathers, silks and satins rare, leaving their bonnets in an anteroom; and the gentlemen appear in light kids and cravats, got up in great agony by their hairdressers. Mixed in with these are the less airy people, who wear sober colors and dress in more quiet style. At the morning receptions ladies wear their walking dress, and the show is not half so fine as by gaslight, when the glittering crowd pours through the drawing rooms into the great East Room, where they circulate in a revolving march to the music of the Marine Band, stationed in an adjoining room. The gentlemen deposit their hats and outside peeling in racks, provided with checks, and then join the procession which presses into the crimson drawing room, where it is met by the train of ladies which files in from a retiring room. Uncle Abraham stands by the door which opens into the Blue Room, flanked by Marshal Lamon and his private secretary, who introduce the new arrivals, each giving his name and that of the lady who accompanies him. The President shakes hands, says "How-do," and the visitor is passed on to where Mrs. Lincoln stands, flanked by another private secretary and B. B. French, the Commissioner of Public Buildings,[8] who introduce the party; then all press on to the next room, where they admire each other's good clothes, criticise Mrs. Lincoln's new gown, gossip a little, flirt a little, yawn, go home, and say "What a bore!" Such is our Republican Court, and the most bored man in it is Old Abe, who hates white kid gloves and a crowd.

19 FEBRUARY 1864 (18 MARCH)

The Discharge of the Pirate Greathouse.
Considerable astonishment has been expressed here at the discharge of the convicted pirate Greathouse by Judge Hoffman,[9] under the operation of the amnesty proclamation, as telegraphed from California a day or two since. . . . The President never contemplated that any person who should have been convicted in the United States Courts should have any new rights or benefits under the proclamation; and it has been his intention to issue a supplemental proclamation to that effect.[10] But the mischief has been done, and the extraordinary decision of Judge Hoffman will only serve to hasten the issuance of the supplemental proclamation. . . .[11]

9 MARCH 1864 (9 APRIL)

Enter the Lieutenant General.
[Elihu B.] Washburne had the pleasure of delivering Grant's commission as Lieutenant General into the hero's own hand; but he might have saved the journey which he took for that purpose, as Grant arrived in this city last evening about dusk.

He went very quietly to Willard's, and it was not until he had half-finished his dinner that people knew that he was in town. As soon as it was discovered that he was at the table, eating his dinner, just like ordinary mortals, there was a shout of welcome from all present, an immense cheer going up from the crowd in the dining-room. After dinner the assemblage was introduced to the General by ex-Governor Morehead of Pennsylvania,[12] and a general and cordial hand-shaking took place. General Grant is rather slightly built, has stooping shoulders, mild blue eyes and light brown hair and whiskers, with a foxy tinge to his mustache. He has a frank, manly bearing, wears an ordinary-looking military suit, and doesn't put on any airs whatever. Last evening he attended the President's levee, where he met the President for the first time in his life, though many letters have passed between these two distinguished men since Grant achieved eminence as a commander. The crowd at the levee was immense, and for once the interest was temporarily transferred from the President to the newcomer. The mass of people thronged about him wherever he moved, everybody being anxious to get at least a glimpse of his face. The women were caught up and whirled into the torrent which swept through the great East room; laces were torn, crinoline mashed, and things were generally much mixed. People mounted sofas and tables to get out of harm's way or to take observations, and for a time the commotion was almost like a Parisian *emeute*; but the cause of all this disturbance soon withdrew, and the tumult subsided. . . .

17 MARCH 1864 (16 APRIL)

Consolidation.

This is now the order of the day, and Judges, Surveyors and Indian Agents are rolled up into one by Acts of Congress

without as much as "by your leave." As the bill to consolidate
the judicial districts of California into one United States
Judicial District contains some important features, I will
condense it as follows: The first section proposes that on and
after June 1, 1864, the State of California shall constitute, for
judicial purposes, one district, within and for which there shall
be but one District Court. . . .

Of course this bill will legislate out of office both of the
present Judges of the United States District Courts for California, with all of their train of clerks and other attaches; and
it becomes an interesting question to them whether any of
them will be retained. It is a delicate matter and one affording
bad precedent, to legislate upon the subject of the Courts, but
in this instance it seems unavoidable. As long as the districts
are to be consolidated for economical reasons, it would be
invidious for the authorities here to retain either of the present learned Judges of the two judicial districts of California;
hence, it is most likely that both these gentlemen will lose
their heads. This will not be so much regretted at Washington, so far as Judge Hoffman is concerned, as it would have
been had he not recently made himself notorious here by his
extraordinary decision in the Greathouse case. To say that the
President and most legal men here were astounded at the
decision of Judge Hoffman would be using a mild term. The
President said, among other strong things, that he would
naturally expect that a Judge, while placing his own construction upon the law, as given in the amnesty proclamation,
might have had at least grace enough to place some weight or
consideration upon the evident intentions of the framer of the
proclamation. He wondered how a man with a thimbleful of
brains could have so stretched that proclamation as to cover
the case of a pirate, seized upon the coast of California, where
no war or rebellion has ever existed.

The friends of Judge Hoffman in San Francisco appear to have found out that the Consolidation Bill is before Congress and that it is aimed at Hoffman; influential Californians in Washington have been the recipients of frequent telegraphic dispatches from California, remonstrating against legislating him out of office, and alleging that the public confidence in him is great and that his removal would be a public loss. As before stated, the consolidation, while it has other healthy effects, originated in a desire to practice economy, and not in any spirit of hostility to the present Judge of the California District Courts.

7 APRIL 1864 (7 MAY)

An English "Member of Parliament" in the House of Representatives.

George Thompson, the famous English Abolitionist, eight or ten years ago was mobbed in radical, anti-slavery Massachusetts. I saw him egged in the Boston Tremont Temple. Last night he spoke upon the topics of the times in the Hall of the House, being introduced to the audience by John Pierpont, another sufferer at the hands of a pro-slavery people.[13] The Vice President of the United States sat upon the platform beside him, and the President, Secretaries and other notables of our nation were among his auditors. The audience was tremendous, and the vast crowd heaved and surged with enthusiasm at the burning and stirring words of the eloquent speaker. He defined the causes of the war, as understood in England; assured us of the hearty support of the masses of the British people in our struggle for our integrity, and passed upon the President a hearty eulogium, which was received with wild applause. . . .

25 APRIL 1864 (23 MAY)

A Grand Military Display.

There was a great rush about town to see Burnside's thirty
thousand as the corps marched into the city on Fourteenth
street, across Long Bridge to Alexandria, on their way to the
front. Both branches of Congress took a recess in order to
see the show, and Senators, Representatives and Governors
mingled in the mob which lined the route of the column.
The President, attended by General Burnside and his Staff,
reviewed the troops from a balcony on the Fourteenth street
side of Willard's Hotel, as they filed past, banners flying,
music swelling on the air, horses prancing, the steady, mea-
sured tramp of marching feet, the rolling of the drum and the
harsher music of thundering artillery—all of these conspired
to make the scene a memorable one for Washington, which
seldom sees so large a force moving at one time through the
city. But a stranger sight for this Capital, so long slavery-
ridden, was the array of seven thousand American citizens of
African descent, all bravely armed and equipped, their banners
flying and their brawny limbs clad in the uniform of Uncle
Sam. These colored troops were greeted with cheers and
applause as they passed the central crowd along Fourteenth
street, and such shouts as "Remember Fort Pillow!"[14] were
flung out to them as they marched by. All of the troops
cheered lustily the President and Burnside as they caught
sight of them, and Uncle Abraham smiled benevolently down
upon them. . . .

10 MAY 1864 (6 JUNE)

Washington under the Influence of Good News.

The past few days of suspense and intense anxiety have been
succeeded by a relief of substantial good news; our most

ardent hopes have been realized by the good tidings from the front of battle, and yesterday and last night the excitement over the glorious news was unparalleled, even in Washington. On every street corner and public place hundreds of men were gathered in knots, discussing or inquiring about the military situation, and last evening the entire city was ablaze with joy upon learning that Grant had pressed the rebels past their old battle ground of the Wilderness, and was driving them before him toward Richmond.[15] About nine o'clock in the evening, the excitement of the populace having risen to a fever heat, an impromptu procession was formed in front of Willard's, and preceded by a band of music the crowd marched up to the White House, where a fine serenade was given to the President, and he appeared at the door, stepping out among the sovereigns who were crowded around the entrance. Order being restored, he proceeded to thank the assemblage for the compliment, which he thought would not have been bestowed if they were not anxious to hear from his own lips the confirmation of the good news which was in circulation on the street.[16]

13 MAY 1864 (9 JUNE)

The Schofield Quarrel.

Another drop of bitterness was added to the cup of the Missouri malcontents yesterday, by the confirmation by the Senate of Schofield as a Major General. B. Gratz Brown,[17] I happen to know from the President himself, was the man who first suggested, as a peaceful solution of the Schofield difficulty, that he be removed from the Missouri command and be made a Major General as a salve to his wounded feelings. It will be a long time before the people will be disabused of the belief that the plan, so novel and temporizing, originated with the Presi-

dent. But Brown, having procured the nomination of Schofield, secured his being hung up in the Senate until common
decency demanded that this man, who may now be lying dead
upon the battle fields of Georgia, should be relieved of the
disgraceful suspense; and yesterday he was confirmed, in the
absence of Brown, who is never in his seat, being at the head of
the Fremont harlotry at Cleveland.[18]

19 MAY 1864 (16 JUNE)

The Tide of Battle.

At this present writing our people, who have been unduly
elated at the successes of Grant, are unduly cast down at the
temporary check which has attended the National arms in the
Shenandoah Valley, where Sigel has been unable to cope with
the superior numbers of the rebel force under Breckinridge,
and has retired with considerable loss, and has probably
allowed a heavy reinforcement to join Lee's army, at present
held in check by Meade.[19] Then, too, the heavy rains of the
past week have served to lay an embargo upon active operations in Central Virginia, and to-day the public feeling is
decidedly blue, everybody forgetting, apparently, that reverses,
great and small, must form a part of every campaign; and also
forgetting, or refusing to notice, that Crooks [Crook] has
retrieved in West Virginia all that Sigel has lost,[20] and that
Sherman in Georgia has secured a more substantial victory
than we hoped of the Army of the Potomac at first. The great
public, like a spoiled child, refuses to be comforted, because
Richmond is not taken forthwith, and because we do not
meet with an unbroken success at every point. We must learn,
possibly by greater reverses, that as there can be but *one issue*
in this war, it is not of the first importance how each individual fight terminates. All of this moralizing may be read duly in

the light of the lightning dispatches which will yet outstrip it, but I am penning the soberer thoughts of our own sober President, who feels depressed only when he knows that the people are disheartened. I think he has seen the end from the beginning, but he always feels for his clients—the people.

10 JUNE 1864 (4 JULY)

Congratulations.

People generally have congratulated each other upon the harmonious action of the Convention and the fruit of its labors, as presented to the people in the shape of a ticket for President and Vice President. Abraham Lincoln himself has also been the recipient of a multitude of congratulations from all sorts of people, among them being the delegations from several of the States represented in the Convention.[21] Among others was the Ohio delegation, which serenaded the President last night in fine style, in response to which he spoke as follows:

> Gentlemen: I am very much obliged to you for this compliment. I have just been saying, and as I have just said it, I will repeat it: The hardest of all speeches which I have to answer is a serenade. I never know what to say on such occasions. I suppose that you have done me this kindness in connection with the action of the Baltimore Convention which has recently taken place, and with which, of course, I am very well satisfied. [Laughter and applause.] What we want still more than Baltimore Conventions or Presidential elections is success under General Grant. [Cries of "Good," and applause.] I propose that you constantly bear in mind that the support you owe to the brave officers and soldiers in the field is of the very first importance, and we should therefore bend all our energies to that point. Now, without detaining you any longer, I propose that you help me to close up what I am now saying with three rous-

ing cheers for General Grant and the officers and soldiers under his command.

The President's request was acceded to, and three rousing cheers were given, the President waving his hat as enthusiastically as anybody else. The National Union League also has sent a large delegation to wait upon the President with their congratulations, all of which were duly attended on yesterday at the White House.[22]

Yesterday afternoon the Committee appointed at the Convention to wait upon the President and notify him of his nomination was received in the East Room of the White House, a large number of delegates from various States being present, when ex-Governor Dennison of Ohio,[23] President of the Baltimore Convention (and a mighty poor presiding officer he was), spoke as follows:

> Mr. President: The National Union Convention, which closed its sittings at Baltimore yesterday, appointed a Committee, consisting of one from each State, with myself as its Chairman, to inform you of your unanimous nomination by that Convention for election to the office of President of the United States. That Committee, I have the honor of now informing you, is present. On its behalf I have also the honor of presenting you with a copy of the resolutions or platform which were adopted by that Convention, as expressive of its sense and of the sense of the loyal people of the country which it represented; of the principles and the policy that should characterize the administration of the Government in the present condition of the country. I need not say to you, sir, that the Convention, in thus unanimously nominating you for re-election, but gave utterance to the almost universal voice of the loyal people of the country. To doubt of your triumphant election would be little short of abandoning the hope of the final suppression of the rebellion and the restoration of the authority of the Government over the

insurgent States. Neither the Convention nor those represented by that body entertain any doubt as to the final result. Under your Administration, sustained by that loyal people and by our noble army and gallant navy, neither did the Convention nor do this Committee doubt the speedy suppression of this most wicked and unprovoked rebellion. [A copy of the resolutions were here handed to the President.] I should add, Mr. President, it would be the pleasure of the Committee to communicate to you, within a few days, through one of its most accomplished members, Curtis of New York,[24] by letter, more at length the circumstances under which you have been placed in nomination for the Presidency.

The President appeared to be deeply affected, and, with considerable emotion, spoke as follows:

Mr. Chairman and Gentlemen of the Committee: I will neither conceal my gratification nor restrain the expression of my gratitude that the Union people, through their Convention, in the continued effort to save and advance the nation, have deemed me not unworthy to remain in my present position. I know no reason to doubt that I shall accept the nomination tendered; and yet, perhaps, I should not declare definitely before reading and considering what is called the platform. I will say now, however, I approve the declaration in favor of so amending the Constitution as to prohibit slavery throughout the nation. When the people in revolt, with a hundred days of explicit notice that they could within those days resume their allegiance without the overthrow of their institutions, and that they could not resume it afterwards, elected to stand out, such amendment to the Constitution as is now proposed became a fitting and necessary conclusion to the final success of the Union cause. Such alone can meet and cover all cavils. Now, the unconditional Union men, North and South, perceive its importance and embrace it. In the joint names of liberty and Union let us labor to give it legal form and practical effect.

14 JUNE 1864 (9 JULY)

The Military Prospect.

Looking out upon the military situation from a stand point not specially affected by the movements upon the James river or in Georgia, the view is not enlivening. The struggle in Virginia has been prolonged beyond the popular expectation, and though our people are beyond all precedent patient and hopeful they are bound to be disappointed yet again in the duration of the war in Virginia. The President said the other day: "I wish when you write and speak to people you would do all you can to correct the impression that the war in Virginia will end right off victoriously. To me the most trying thing in all of this war is that the people are too sanguine; they expect too much at once. I declare to you, sir, that we are to-day further ahead than I thought one year and a half ago we should be, and yet there are a plenty of people who believe that the war is about to be substantially closed. As God is my judge I shall be satisfied if we are over with the fight in Virginia within a year. I hope we shall be 'happily disappointed,' as the saying is, but I am afraid not—I am afraid not." These words of one who is so cool and correct in judgment, and who stands at the fountain head of all knowledge of the workings of the military mechanism of the country, must have great weight with those who hear or read them, and for myself, I am free to say that they materially damped the ardor of my own expectations.[25]

BROOKS TO GEORGE WITHERLE, WASHINGTON, 15 JUNE 1864[26]

. . . How is the result of the Baltimore Convention recieved in your region? I suppose Maine people are somewhat disappointed that Hamlin was not renominated, but New England generally was not united on him, and Maine did not support

him with the earnestness which I had expected.[27] My own
choice was Dickinson,[28] but our delegation was equally divided
between Johnson and Hamlin. I have never seen any consider-
ations which would influence me to vote for Hamlin's renomination, had I a vote in the convention; he has been very much
of a nonentity here, though he may have great influence at
home. Washington gossips have it that Hamlin desires to succeed Fessenden in the Senate;[29] in my humble judgment the
exchange would be a poor one, though Fessenden is a narrow
man. By the way, Hale's defeat in the N. H. Legislature for the
Senate is to be attributed to the fact that he has an itching
palm.[30] I am sorry to say that this early friend of freedom is
notoriously corrupt and given to "taking bribes here of the
Sardians," not to say sardines. Lincoln's renomination was a
foregone conclusion, a great majority of the delegates having
been instructed beforehand in his favor, and the popular feeling was all so evidently for him that the few chagrined and
disappointed politicians hereabouts who were disposed to
oppose his nomination, were quite swallowed up in the great
wave of popular will. The Chase men and other [   ]
people who do not know who or what they want, make up in
virulence what they lack in numbers and talk of terrible things
which may happen, we cannot guess what. Much depends
upon the action of the Chicago Copperhead Convention, of
course; if they postpone until August,[31] as they appear likely to,
it will be an indication that neither McClellan or Seymour are
their choice,[32] as either of them are as available now as at any
time hereafter; but a postponement will indicate that they
propose taking up Grant or some other man whose availability
will be made apparent by the campaign now in progress. What
do you think of Fremont's operations? In my mind he does not
even rise to the height of respectability as a presidential candidate, while it is yet apparent that he seeks the nomination of

the copperheads, while he is put forth by the ultra radical sore-
heads of all ranks. If the Democrats do accept him, it will be
only that they are willing to take him up at the cost of their
organization; they may be willing to go into a political liquida-
tion under his name. . . .

20 JUNE 1864 (12 JULY)

Imposing Funeral Solemnities.

Yesterday (Sunday) witnessed a remarkable and imposing
funeral pageant in Washington, the occasion being the burial
of the victims of the late terrible calamity at the Arsenal, when
eighteen young women were instantly hurried to death by the
explosion of the cartridges upon which they were working.[33]
Several of the bodies were taken in charge by the friends of the
deceased; but fifteen were buried yesterday from the Arsenal
grounds, under the charge of the United States Government.
A pavilion, lined and covered with white, and decorated with
flags, was erected upon the grounds, and the coffins, fifteen in
number, were ranged upon an altar in the midst of the same.
The ceremonies were brief and impressive and admirably
adapted to the occasion, a vast concourse listening to them
with profound attention. The funeral cortege was headed by a
band playing mournful music, and was made up of friends of
the deceased, the associates of the victims of the disaster—all
clad in white—various benevolent societies, high officials of
the Government, the employes of the Arsenal and a very long
procession of citizens generally. Among the officials was the
President, Secretary of War, Chief of Ordnance, Commandant of the Arsenal,[34] and others. Along the route the vast
procession was joined by several other funeral trains, being the
private obsequies of other victims, until eighteen hearses were
moving to the Congressional Burying Ground, where the

remains were finally interred. It is estimated that over twenty-five thousand persons were present at this mournful spectacle, the streets being for a space impassable, on account of the great crowd. . . .

22 JUNE 1864 (18 JULY)

Military Matters.

Just now the public feeling about military matters is one of depression and anxiety. The repulse at Petersburg and the previous failure of Gilmore [Gillmore] at the same point,[35] together with the long deferred direct attack upon Richmond, serve to make our mercurial people somewhat downhearted. They have always had too much hopefulness, and now their over-sanguine expectations are dashed by the tardiness of the grand *coup* which was considered sure to come. Probably, if the facts were all known, our heads of the Government do not share in the public feeling of disappointment in the Petersburg affair. Gillmore, so long the object of much respect and confidence on the part of the public, has failed sorrowfully, not having carried out his orders, in consequence of which the golden opportunity to capture Petersburg was lost. If he had assaulted the city in front when Kautz was ready to fall upon the rear,[36] we should not now be laying a long siege to Petersburg; so the people coincide in the justice of the removal of Gillmore, who arrived in Washington almost unheralded, when he would have been the object of intense enthusiasm if he had visited this city any time during his active and brilliant operations before Charleston. The abrupt decay of the military reputation of such men as Banks, Sigel and Gillmore are among the painful features of the war, which seem to lift men up to dazzling heights only to dash them down again.

The visit of the President to General Grant excites the

apprehensions of our people,[37] always on the alert for bad omens, it being considered that the President, tired of suspense, had gone down to the front to see for himself what is the real state of the case, and what the prospects are. Last night the continual succession of good news from the front was broken by the circulation of the absurd rumor that Grant had been obliged to recross the James with a loss of thirty thousand men. This was the progeny of the secesh, who are always ready with baseless rumors whenever the popular feeling is weary or agitated.

The President and an Oregon "League."

Some time since, at the instance of Senator Nesmith,[38] the President appointed James [Joseph] W. Drew, of Oregon,[39] as an Assistant Paymaster of volunteers, which appointment an Oregon Union League denounced on the ground that the appointee was disloyal, and when the Delegates to the Baltimore Union Convention came on here a copy of their resolutions asking Drew's removal was sent on by one of them, T. H. Pearne,[40] who was advised to confer with the delegation before asking the removal. The League Minister Plenipotentiary, however, preferred standing on his own dignity, and in due time the resolutions were referred to G. R. McBride, of Oregon,[41] and upon his statement that the Paymaster complained of was as loyal as Nesmith himself, the War Department and the President decided that that was good enough, and the League diction was tabled, much to the disgust of the envoy referred to.

1 JULY 1864 (26 JULY)

The Latest Nine Days Wonder.

Yesterday morning the town was set all agog by the announcement that Secretary Chase had resigned his portfolio of the

Treasury Department, and that David Tod, late Governor of Ohio,[42] had been named as his successor. There was a general feeling of regret and apprehension among public men and citizens when the rumor of the fact became a certainty and it was positively known that Chase was no longer in the Cabinet. The Senate, which now has its session at eleven o'clock in the morning, went into executive session at half-past eleven, when the name of David Tod was submitted as the successor of the outgoing Secretary. The Chase men were nearly frantic, asserting that the movement would cost Lincoln his re-election; that Tod was an idiot, and that Chase had been driven out by the machinations of Blair. A careful sifting of the facts, however, showed that the disagreement between the President and the Secretary was twofold in character, the first being the refusal of the President to accede to the demand of Chase that Maunsell B. Field, now Assistant Secretary of the Treasury, should be Assistant Treasurer at New York, in place of Cisco,[43] resigned. The second was that the Ways and Means Committee of the House had declined to accede to Chase's request, just made, that Congress should provide, before the adjournment, for $100,000,000 additional to the estimate and appropriations already made, on account of a deficiency in the estimates of the Treasury Department. It is well known that the great moneyed interest of New York has the real control of Secretary Chase's policy, and that circumstances have rendered it possible for the Wall street magnates to tell him that unless certain things were done, Wall street would not support him to carry on this system. Chase had designated Field as the successor of Cisco, and the Register of the Treasury, L. E. Chittenden, was to succeed Field, while Risley, a special agent, was to succeed Chittenden.[44] The President insisted upon spoiling his programme, and named Hillhouse, an able financier, for Cisco's place.[45] He also declined sending a special message to Congress asking for a supplemental tax bill to raise the additional $100,000,000 asked by Chase, preferring to postpone all such requests for this session.

Chase responded, and ex-Governor Tod was nominated, but not accepted by the Senate, that body refusing to confirm. The Finance Committee waited on the President asking him to send in a more acceptable name; while the Senate demurred, Tod had the good sense to telegraph from Columbus his non-acceptance of the dazzling gift offered him.[46] The Chase men were disconsolate—they had hoped that some second rate man would succeed Chase; and if Chase, who is cold-hearted, obstinate and enormously self-conceited, had desired that a lesser man than he should be shown to be behind him, he could not have named a better man than David Tod—at least so say the Ohioans, who are supposed to know. Then there were not lacking those who said that Chase had resigned as soon as the report of the Treasury Investigating Committee had been made, for the purpose of embarrassing the Administration, and that he had named his own successor for the same purpose. That does not seem probable.

This morning, bright and early, Senator Fessenden, of Maine, Chairman of the Finance Committee, was named by the President as Secretary of the Treasury, and was immediately confirmed without the formality of sending his name to the Finance Committee. Everybody was pleased, and the only ones who had aught unpleasant to say were the Chase impracticables, who were bound not to be pleased. They said that gold was up in New York on the report—keeping out of sight that gold had gone up on the report that Hooper, of Massachusetts, the author of the Gold Bill,[47] had gone into Chase's place, and also forgetting, apparently, that gold had gone down and Government stocks up when Chase's resignation was positively known, the money interest persisting in believing that any change would be for the better, or that things could be no worse. But we all suffered a relapse by three o'clock in the afternoon, when it was announced that Fessenden had declined the place also, believing his physical ability was unequal to the task. He is one of your narrow-chested, thin men, who have not much vitality nor physical endurance, and he did a prudent thing for himself to resign; but he would make a better Secretary than Chase, beyond a doubt; and so at this present writing matters stand *in statu quo.* . . .

A Political Intriguer.

It is a matter of regret that a man of so much oratorical ability and legal sharpness as Henry Winter Davis should be so much of a political charlatan as he is; but he is, like the Blairs, insatiate in his hates, mischievous in his schemes and hollow hearted and cold blooded.[48] It is not supposed that he honestly differs in opinion with any member of the present Cabinet, except Blair, but he has seized upon every occasion to quarrel with nearly every one of them, and he stands to-day in an attitude of such intense hostility to Lincoln that he is ready to jeopardize the success of the Union party in the campaign about opening, simply that he may gratify his personal malice toward the President. Revengeful, sore-headed and proud, Davis, like others of his sort here, appears to forget that the defeat of Lincoln, the nominee of the people and the Union organization, would necessarily be the triumph of a Copperhead minority, under whose rule the status of these individuals would be worse than it now is under an Administration which has failed to satisfy their personal demands. . . .

5 JULY 1864 (27 JULY)

The Last Days of the Session.

On the Saturday before the Fourth there was a strong endeavor to get through all of the business on hand, so as to adjourn before Sunday; but in vain; there were too many important bills on hand for either branch of Congress to go home satisfied with their work. Among the bills thus impeding the adjournment were the new Conscript Bill, the Fortification Bill, Henry Winter Davis' Reconstruction Bill, sundry appropriation bills, and others of less public note. Saturday night, at eleven o'clock, witnessed in the House the usual disorderly and exciting scenes incident to a night session late in the term. Members were gathered in groups, smoking, chatting, watching the fate of pet measures with intense anxiety. The amendment to the Conscript Law got a severe handling from the Copperheads, who were likely at one time to defeat it; but it finally squeezed through in substantially the shape sent to you by telegraph, allowing fifty days notice of a draft, no commutation, substitutes granted, recruiting in rebel States allowed, and liberal bounties given. Whisky on hand also created a brisk breeze, Washburne's irrepressible crochet to tax coming up to vex the last dying moments of Congress; but whisky went out of the struggle triumphant, and Washburne was floored once more. Some men never will learn anything. The night wore on, and a few conscientious members who would not break the Sabbath in law-making left the House and Senate still hard at work, the Union men struggling with fatigue and the Copperheads until past three o'clock on Sunday morning, when a recess was taken until ten o'clock on Monday morning.

Fourth of July did not seem like the old-fashioned "Independence Day" of other years, when Congress went to work winding up affairs for the season. The Chaplain was not on hand at the early hour of ten o'clock, consequently the House came to its end without the benefit of the clergy as represented in the person of the poetical and flowery parson. Washburne of Illinois, with a laudable desire to avail himself of the last inch of time to distinguish himself with a little speech, offered a resolution of thanks to our soldiers in the field, and the ambitious member was safely delivered of his speech, most of the members considering themselves imposed upon by a speech made for bunkum when other matters of more importance were pressing. But, after divers interruptions by messages from the Senate and the President, the affair was over and the House proceeded to take up a lot of "little bills" rushed in at the last moment to catch Congressmen when the whirl of business was setting through the hall in such manner as to daze the minds of the most alert. Among these were resolutions to pay all sorts of claims, such as extra compensation for Committee Clerks, a subsidy for the publishers of the *Globe*, and such like. At ten minutes before the hour of twelve, a message from the Senate announced that that body had extended the time of adjournment ten minutes, which gave the House until ten minutes past twelve for finishing up its work. Pages darted to and fro with messages and bills; Enrolling Clerks rushed madly about with big sheets of parchment for the signatures of the Speaker and Clerk; Heads of Departments were buzzing among the members; lobbyists squeezed in upon the floor of the House, and a general scene of disorder spread over the hall, upon which the observant people looked down from the thronged galleries above. Suddenly the clock, which had marked the hour of noon, went back ten minutes without giving any reasons upon the face of it. Eldridge [Eldredge] of Wisconsin tried to be funny over the affair, but the Speaker reminded him that it had only followed the example of the Senate and had gone back ten minutes. Morrill introduced a joint resolution to establish a Commission, to be appointed by the President, for the purpose of ascertaining the public resources and the best means of levying judicious taxation on the same.[49] The Copperheads revolted at once, and showed that they would filibuster through the few remaining moments of the session if the resolution were pressed; so, after the ayes and noes had been demanded on a few dilatory motions, the proposition was withdrawn. Then Eldredge called for the reading of Washington's Farewell Address, in which he was not sustained; red-faced Secretary Forney came in with Senate bills by the score, among them being one to grant every member of this Congress a complete set of the *Globe* from the commencement of the publication until the close of this Congress—a nice little job of $100,000 only; the bill passed, and the Senate sent in word that it had agreed to extend the time of adjournment ten minutes longer. The reading of the Declaration of Independence was called for, and the stentorian voice of the Reading Clerk began to sound it forth; but "When, in the course of human events," was cut short by "A message from the President;" more bills were signed, and the reading went on until the end, with only occasional breaks of a similar character, when a Western member moved the previous question on the Declaration. The Senate had gone into Executive session, and now sent over a message again extending the time of adjournment, this time to half-past twelve—ten minutes longer. To this the Copperheads demurred decidedly and began to filibuster, amidst which the few last bills which were to be saved "as by fire" came in from the President, who was at the other end of the Capitol, signing with might and main whatever was brought before him. Members who had a few pets out in the cold yet grew uneasy at the prospect of not being able to rescue their darlings from death. To use the words of one of our own members, "all of our little California thieving bills" were passed and we were ready to go home. The filibusters called for the ayes and noes on agreeing to the extension of time, during which the time of adjournment was passed; but the roll-call could not be interrupted, and at half-past twelve o'clock the monotonous drone of the Clerk's voice ceased and the Speaker's pleasant tones fell on the waiting ears of the great throng, as, in a few well-chosen words, he pronounced a farewell to the members, wishing them prosperity and happiness in their homes and a reunion at the beginning of the next session, with brighter skies above us and the signs of returning peace more visible. A round of applause followed; the charm was broken, and in a few minutes the vast throng poured out of the doors on all sides, leaving the gilded and decorated hall to loneliness and dusky splendor. The first session of the Thirty-ninth [Thirty-eighth] Congress was over.

7 JULY 1864 (30 JULY)

Affairs at the Treasury Department.
Probably no man ever took up the administration of the affairs of our National finance with so much relief and satisfaction on the part of the public as has William Pitt Fessenden, ex-Senator from Maine. Even the bitterest Copperheads have not had a word to say against the purity, honesty and patriotic purposes of the new Secretary of the Treasury, and everybody admits his great ability, tact and experience. Probably no man in this nation, not excepting Chase, has so thorough a knowledge of the character and extent of our National sources of wealth, of the best means of getting at them, and of the character and complex interests of the people of the United States. He is a practical financier, which Chase was not when he assumed control of the finances. Chase was always topsy-turvy and behindhand, but Fessenden is cool, methodical and

immovable. Fessenden is democratical, and finds himself ill at
ease in the palatial splendors of Chase's newly built quarters at
the Treasury building. Chase was inaccessible, dignified
beyond all account, and aristocratical. Let me not be understood as attempting to depreciate the great abilities of the ex-
Secretary; his services are known to the country, and to the
country he will stand or fall by the system of finance which he
has himself inaugurated. There are divers opinions as to the
real merit of that system, but it is now too late to make a radical change in it, and it is too early to predict its success.

The faults of Chase above mentioned are minor in character, and the overweening weakness in his character was that
desire to control everything which finally brought on his
retirement from the Cabinet. The only issue of any moment
between Chase and the President was whether the President
or the Secretary should appoint the successor of Assistant
Treasurer Cisco; the former preferred Hillhouse, a man of
unblemished integrity and great financial ability, urged for the
place by Senator Morgan of New York.[50] Chase, who has
heretofore controlled every appointment, from that of the
humblest tide-waiter to a New York Collector, made a *sine
qua non* of his staying in the Cabinet of the appointment of
M. B. Field, a gentleman of ability, perhaps, but against whom
some popular prejudices have become fixed for the reason
that he parts his hair in the middle, wears a white neck-tie
and lemon-colored kids, and has not specially distinguished
himself in the Treasury Department as yet further than to
superintend the fitting up of Chase's private offices with
Axminster carpets, gilded ceilings, velvet furniture, and other
luxurious surroundings which go to hedge about a Cabinet
Minister with a dignity quite appalling to the unaccustomed
outsider. If Chase had been less strong in his pride of self-
opinion he would have been more practicable as a Cabinet

Minister and would always have harmonized with the President. . . .[51]

9 JULY 1864 (1 AUGUST)

Pacific Railroad Commissioners.

Senator Conness and Assistant Secretary Otto, of the Interior Department, waited upon the President yesterday to procure from him the appointment of the three Commissioners required by law to act on behalf of the Government in the examination of the work on the Pacific Railroad in California. Representative Cole and Senator McDougall had already filed their nominations for these officers, the same being Governor Low, T. G. Phelps and one Burke of San Jose.[52] The President, with his usual genius for splitting the difference, offered to Conness the nomination of two of the Commissioners if he would take one of those already named. The Senator took Governor Low and added to his name those of P. H. Sibley of Placer, and Josiah Johnson of Sacramento. The three gentlemen last named are accordingly the Commissioners appointed by the President.

12 JULY 1864 (10 AUGUST)

Beleaguered.

. . . The President and his family have been living out at the Soldiers' Home, about four miles only this side of the rebel line of skirmishers; but on Sunday night Secretary Stanton sent out a carriage and a guard and brought in the family, who are again domesticated at the White House. The lonely situation of the President's Summer residence would have afforded a tempting chance for a daring squad of rebel cavalry to run some risks for the chance of carrying off the President, whom we could ill afford to spare just now. . . .[53]

19 JULY 1864 (10 AUGUST)

More Men, More Money.

. . . The President has made a bold stroke, and, taking the
people at their word, calls for five hundred thousand men, right
in the face of a general election.[54] He is determined that he will
do his duty, let personal and political consequences be what
they may. Unquestionably, a call for five hundred thousand
men, though it strike terror to a few faint hearts, is more popular with the masses than a call for three hundred thousand
would have been. The people have become tired of that figure,
and in many States it will be easier to fill quotas by volunteering under this call than under a call for a less number. . . .

21 JULY 1864 (15 AUGUST)

Sherman's Successes.

Our people—who are, as usual, more intent upon what passes
around them than that at a more remote point—do not appear
to realize the great importance of the successes which Sherman
has achieved in the Southwest. Atlanta appears to be in our
grasp; the Government has private advices that the rebel
communications between Richmond and Atlanta and Montgomery and the besieged city are completely and effectually
severed, and all of the approaches to Mobile are now opening
before us; yet the people do not appear to see how all this is just
as important as the capture of Richmond. Indeed, I happen to
know that the President considers that the successes of Sherman in the Summer campaign have been greater than those of
Grant. As a strategic point, Atlanta is more valuable to its
belligerent possessor than Richmond, though the moral effect
of the surrender of the political Capital of the Confederacy
would be greater than would be the surrender of the economic
Capital, as Atlanta doubtless is. Some of the rebel newspapers

console themselves with the idea that Sherman will be content with the capture of Atlanta, and that when that city is thrown at his feet it will be a bribe to stay the progress of "the rapacious Northern invader;" but Sherman marches from conquest to conquest, and there will be no sitting down at Atlanta while Johnston's forces are allowed to reinforce Richmond,[55] but they will find other work to do in Georgia and Alabama before the Summer campaign closes in the South.

23 JULY 1864 (18 AUGUST)

A Poor Woman's Letter to Father Abraham.

The following letter, which was actually received by the President, and sent by him to the proper department of the Government, is a single illustration of how the worthy Chief Magistrate is made the recipient of all sorts of requests:

> Frederick, June 17, 1864.
>
> tu Abraham linkun President of the U. States at Washington— Deer Sur: I take mi pen in hand to aske yu about the munney cumming to me frum my husband Daniel Spielman who was a solger in the 2d Mariland Ridgment in cumpany C who was kill in a fite with the rebs last fal near Boonsborrow M.D. I haint got no pay as was cummin toe him and none of his bounty munney and now Mr President I am a pore widder wumman and have no munny and have borrered all what I lived on last winter and this summer toe—I have one littel gurl who is to smal toe help me—Now Mr President I can soe and cook and wash and du enny kind of wurk but I cant get none—see if you cant git me a plaice in one of your hospittles and I will goe rite toe wurk—but I dont want to leve mi little gurl so I want to git a plaice what I can take her toe—I no yu du what is rite and yu will se tu me a pore widder wumman whose husband fote in your army your younion army Mr President—So Mr President I sign myself your servant to command
>
> CATHERINE SPIELMAN.

A Military Failure.

The month of August does not open cheerfully. What with a
protracted drouth, popular discontent and a repulse at Petersburg, we have a forbidding picture to contemplate. This
morning the newspapers are full of glowing accounts of a
great success in the assault upon the enemy's lines at Petersburg on the 30th ultimo, but the real facts are becoming
known and it is evident that somebody has blundered.
Notwithstanding the favorable accounts of the newspapers,
the President received late on Saturday night, the 31st, dispatches from Grant, communicating the intelligence that we
had failed to make any progress whatever in the siege by the
assault, but had lost a large number of men.[56] The President,
accompanied by Captain Fox, the Assistant Secretary of the
Navy, immediately went down to the mouth of the James in a
naval transport, where Grant met them yesterday. From this
distinguished party, which returned this morning, I learn that
on the morning of the 30th a mine, which had been for some
time in progress, was exploded under the enemy's works,
blowing up an earthwork which was in fact a battery of four
guns in position, manned by South Carolinians. The entire
mass of earth was lifted in the air, making a vast fountain of
dirt, and when it came down it covered the cannon and the
men in its debris, leaving a great hole where the work had
stood. Simultaneously with the explosion, an assault was made
by the Ninth Corps upon the lines, but for lack of sufficient
support the column wavered and finally broke; the head of the
column—the Second Pennsylvania Heavy Artillery and the
Fourteenth New York Heavy Artillery, acting as infantry—
piled into the hole made by the explosion of the battery,
whence it was impossible to dislodge them, three field officers

being killed while endeavoring to cheer them forward. A terrific shelling now took place on both sides, the enemy's fire being chiefly directed into the hole where nearly twenty-five hundred men were piled on top of each other like frightened sheep; here the slaughter was great, the fire of the enemy being enfilading. For some inexplicable reason, the Second Corps on the right and the Fifth and Eighteenth Corps on the left did not press forward in support of the Ninth Corps, consequently the order was given to fall back, but it was next to impossible for the men in the ruined work to comply with the order, and a large proportion of them fell into the hands of the enemy. An open field intervenes between the rebel works and our own, and at last accounts numbers of our men, killed and wounded, were left on this debatable ground, covered by the guns of both armies, but out of the reach of any assistance. In this unfortunate affair there has been a failure on the part of subordinate Generals and of men. For the latter we ought to say that they were for the most part men who enlisted in the artillery service under the impression that they would not be obliged to serve in the field, but in fortifications; they are not reliable in material and have frequently broken before. We shall know more about the Generals by and by.

24 AUGUST 1864 (1 OCTOBER)

Wood and Vallandigham.

Fernando Wood doesn't like Vallandigham; per contra, Val doesn't like Fernando—the reason for such mutual lack of affection being, I suppose, that two of a trade can never agree.[57] Just after the return of Vallandigham from expatriation Wood sought an interview with the President, in which he said: "We Peace Democrats are the only Democrats; all others are impostors and bastards; there is no such thing as a War Democrat, for that is a contradiction of terms. We don't expect, Mr. President, to elect our candidate this Fall; the people of the North are not ready for peace yet; but peace must come sooner or later, and when it does the Democratic party will be the party which will act and assimilate with the dominant party in the South, and so we shall again have our rightful ascendancy. Now, Mr. President, you cannot find fault with that; it is not going to hurt you any." The President conceded that he was disposed to be generous, and asked if Vallandigham's reported return was any part of this pro-gramme. Wood replied that it was not, and added: "You may not believe me, but I assure you that I never knew or expected that he would return, though I acknowledge that I have had a letter from him since he got back. But I tell you frankly, Mr. President, that it will not do to make a martyr of Vallandig-ham. He has had more notoriety already than he deserves, and I warn you that the true policy is that he be severely let alone." To this the President replied: "I don't believe that Vallandig-ham has returned; I never can believe it, and I never shall believe it until he forces himself offensively upon the public attention and upon my attention; then we shall have to deal with him. So long as he behaves himself decently he is as effectually in disguise as a slovenly man who went to a mas-querade party with a clean face." . . .[58]

"Going Home to Die No More."

The one-hundred-days men from Ohio have mostly served out their time, and are now daily passing through Washington, bound home. Every one of [the] homeward bound regiments goes up to the White House and calls out the President, who makes a nice little speech; the men huzza; then the Colonel makes a nice little speech, and there are more huzzas; then the men march down the avenue feeling very good and singing the hymn whose title is the "subhead" of this paragraph. These men are doubtless brave enough, but for all the good they have done they "had better staid at home mit the girl they love so mooch," as the Dutch song hath it. People generally have come to the conclusion that this one-hundred day spirit was one of the stupidest blunders ever made by the War Department.

BROOKS TO JOHN G. NICOLAY, CHICAGO, 29 AUGUST 1864[59]

Agreeably to the expressed wish of the President, I will write you a few lines concerning matters and things here, taking it for granted, of course, that you will know all of the final results before this reaches you.

The assemblage of Democrats here is very large indeed and they appear to manifest a great deal of enthusiasm; indeed, all along the route of travel on the Pittsburg, Chicago and Ft Wayne railway the people, attracted by the music and cannon on our train, turned out in great numbers and manifested a great deal of interest and excitement, particularly on the subject of "Peace," blindly and ignorantly bawling for "Peace" without any comprehension or care, apparently, of how it is to come. Perhaps the Union people kept back, but I was disappointed at the tone and temper of the citizens whom we met in this way along the road. Here among the people who have assembled it is much the same; today in convention it was noticeable that peace men and measures and sentiments were applauded to the echo, while patriotic utterances, what few there were, recieved no response from the crowd, though that is more noticeable among the outsiders than the members of the Convention. Several resolutions of an incendiary character being offered, Cox moved that all resolutions be referred to the Committee without being read,[60] but he was ruled out,

and some hisses from the outsiders were given him, one calling out "Sit down and shut up, you war democrat." This was
pending Long's resolution to appoint a committee to ask the
President to postpone the draft until the people had decided
for peace or war at the polls.[61] I also noticed that the assemblage vigorously applaud "Dixie," whenever it is played, but
never cheer the patriotic airs.

Inconsistent as all of this may appear with the other fact, it
is nevertheless true that the popular current is all in favor of
McClellan and it *appears* to be a foregone conclusion that he
will be nominated. The Northwestern States are not generally
in his favor, but a majority of New York are, and a powerful
outside influence is at work for him. Auguste Belmont, with
plenty of money to use, heads the McClellan interest, and
Cox, Dean Richmond and others are his able colleagues. They
have music, fireworks &c, and they run the outside show of
Saturday last, when Amos Kendall presided over a convention
of "Conservatives," which nominated McClellan.[62]

On the other hand, Vallandigham, Wood and Pendleton
are equally determined,[63] but as they lack union upon any one
candidate, they are not able to present a strong front as a
peace party. Seymour, Guthrie, Pierce and Fillmore are their
candidates, being above written in the order of their prominence.[64] Wood is most bitter and determined and declares
that his faction will not submit to McClellan and a war platform: he and such as he point to McClellan's arrest of the
Maryland Legislature and kindred acts and sentiments as
evidences of a war spirit,[65] while many do not hesitate to say
that if a war man is to be nominated, Lincoln is good enough
for them. Both war and peace men appear to be agreed upon
an armistice as one of the steps to peace, and that suggestion
will undoubtedly be embodied in their platform.

These men are making the most of our own dissensions

and have published as a campaign document the Wade-Davis manifesto,[66] while today every seat in the convention was supplied with a printed copy of an article on that paper, written by Caspar Butz,[67] who appeals to the Chicago Convention to nominate Fremont. These things create a great deal of despondency among our own people, of course, and many of the weak-kneed already predict defeat and disaster, forgetting that up to this time we have had nothing to solidify and compact us; a platform and candidate from here will materially change all this. Wood and Vallandigham keep very quiet as yet, refusing to speak, and Vallandigham is seldom seen out of his private room. Seymour has not signified his position or intentions, but I am told on good authority that he is ready to sell out his dubious chances for nomination to McClellan for the assurance of Seward's place in the next cabinet.

The Vice Presidency is unsettled, but it appears certain that a border State man will be taken, if McClellan is nominated; accordingly, Guthrie, Phelps, Wickliffe and Campbell of Tennessee are chiefly named.[68] Pendleton would like it, and G. W. Cass, a nephew of Lewis Cass, works hard for it.[69]

Of course, the burden of the speeches made is a tirade against the "despotism" of the Government and the usurpations of the Administration. Geo[rge] Francis Train, who is here as a delegate from Nebraska, goes for Dix, and abuses the President in an insane speech whenever anybody will hear him.[70]

Above I have given hurriedly the aspect of things as they appear to me, and I trust they will serve to give an idea of the state of things here just now.

BROOKS TO JOHN G. NICOLAY, DIXON, ILLINOIS, 2 SEPTEMBER 1864[71]

While I am spending a few days of rest in my old Illinois home I cannot do better, perhaps, than write up a brief account of what I heard and saw at the Chicago Convention

after my last letter, written at Chicago, though the accounts in
the newspapers have given you all of the main facts of the
concluding days of the convention.

   The nomination of McClellan was a foregone conclusion,
the only possible obstacle thereto being the deep determination of the ultra "peace" men to carry all the points which they
could. And, failing in defeating his nomination, they secured
all possible concessions in the platform, which was the work of
Vallandigham and Weller of California.[72] There was a prolonged and bitter struggle, however, over the platform while it
was in the hands of the committee and the subcommittee, but
the "peace" men finally triumphed, yielding their adhesion to
McClellan for availability's sake. Though, as you are aware, a
few malcontents, like Long and Harris,[73] refused to the last to
vote for the nomination. Maryland, Kentucky and a great part
of Ohio and Indiana refused to support McClellan in convention in any way, and they kept their promise, not voting for
him. And yet not voting at all when his nomination was made
unanimous, as the phrase goes, for it is only a phrase so far as
that goes. I enclose, as a curiosity, the tally-list which I kept
during the roll-call for nomination for President, by which
you will see in the first three columns on the left the exact vote
of each State as first given, and the subsequent changes to
McClellan are noted in the next column, the order of their
change being placed in small figures in ink. This is more correct than any of the reports which were printed in the newspapers here. You will see that Kentucky did not change to
McClellan until nearly next to Ohio, who was the last, and that
Ohio still, even then, refused all her vote, throwing six for
Seymour; also that Missouri, who changed first, still held back
four votes for Seymour; Kansas went for McClellan unwill-
ingly, and so did Iowa. Maryland, Delaware and three and a
half votes of Indiana would not, and did not go for McClellan

at all. But Kentucky and Indiana are most dissatisfied with the nomination, the former especially considering that it has been sorely abused. It had been early conceded that a border state would have the vice presidency *certainly* in the event of McClellan's nomination, but, to secure the "peace" men, it was necessary to give it to Pendleton, who traded for it by bringing over his forces for McClellan. New York City made the trade throughout and Belmont and Dean Richmond, who managed for McC., gave the vote of their State to Pendleton on condition that he brought his strength over to McClellan. They had previously promised the same to Guthrie, and gave him the vote on the first ballot, as you will see by the enclosed, but when the second ballot was had they waited until Kentucky voted five and a half for Powell and the same for Guthrie,[74] then threw in their whole vote for Pendleton, with the explanation that having voted for Guthrie on the first ballot, *as promised*, &c &c. This turned the scale and Pendleton was at once nominated. Kentucky complains of bad faith on the part of New York, who retorts that the irrepressible conflict in her own delegation was the occasion of her own non-success. You know there were two delegations in the convention from Kentucky, both voting, but one-half vote being allowed to each.

Gov Seymour refused to have the seven votes cast for him be announced as his, and they were read by the secretary as having been given to T. H. Seymour,[75] much to the disgust of those who threw them. He was chagrined and disappointed at not being at least a prominent candidate, but his prospects were very good on the night of the second day, when Long and Harris made their attacks on McClellan; he artfully allowed them all possible advantage, and by permitting them to speak, though not in order, succeeded in staving off the nomination for that night at least, and the Seymour men were in excellent spirits when the convention adjourned for that day, without making any nomination. During that night the McClellan men, alarmed made several trades one of which was the vote of New York for Pendleton. It is also said that a written agreement was given to Seymour (by whom signed I know not) covenanting that he would have the portfolio of Secretary of State, in the event of McC's election. Several other promises were made in that direction, I believe, only one being for the West and that was the Chief Justice-ship for Judge Caton of Illinois,[76] in case Justice Taney would not die or resign before March 1865! This, it is said, secured the whole vote of Illinois on the first ballot; some such valuable consideration did, for the vote was reluctantly given, and Hickok [Hickox],[77] the chairman of the delegation did not hesitate to say that the nominee was the weakest man, *for a Democrat*, that God ever made.

He and others like him admit that McClellan's nomination was made for the soldiers' vote, which, they think, will be the decisive power in the next election. This was all that enabled Vallandigham to swallow the bitter pill, which he did with a very ill grace.

Our people hereabouts are confident and hopeful. The nomination has already served to unite them, and I feel more encouraged than when I left Washington.

Shall remain here for a few weeks and shall be glad to hear from you.

3 SEPTEMBER 1864 (1 OCTOBER)

The Peace Propositions.

The recent interviews at Niagara and at Richmond between unaccredited parties in relation to peace would have before this time been forgotten had not Judah P. Benjamin, the rebel Secretary of State, addressed a letter to Mason in England, giving the secession hue to the conversation which took place between a Colonel Jaquess and somebody else with Jeff. Davis, who managed to effect an entrance into Secessia for the purpose of feeling the pulse of that arch traitor.[78] Of course Benjamin seeks to make a good impression for the cause of those whom he serves in Europe; but the President of the United States is not disposed to let the matter pass in silence, and to counteract its effect authorized a denial that he advised in any case suggestions other than those which appear under his own signature, and certainly these were very far from yielding in the least degree a particle of the National honor.

19 OCTOBER 1864 (25 NOVEMBER)

A Survey of the General Situation.

. . . The victory [of the emancipationists] in Maryland is a moral one, and is a more positive indication of the change of opinion as to slavery than though it had been given to a candidate for office.[79] The President, conversing upon the subject yesterday, said, with his usual frank homeliness, "I had rather have Maryland upon that issue than have a State twice its size upon the Presidential issue; it cleans up a piece of ground." Any one who has ever had to do with "cleaning up" a piece of ground, digging out vicious roots and demolishing old stumps, can appreciate the homely simile applied to Maryland, where slavery has just been cleaned up effectually. . . .

Yesterday a deputation of Hebrews from Chicago, New York, Philadelphia and Baltimore called upon the President to present him with an address, assuring him that their people, as a body, were in favor of his re-election. These men were chiefly priests, and assured the President they had heretofore mingled in politics, and that the address presented had been read and adopted in their synagogues throughout the country. The President thanked them for their good wishes and

promises, and reminded them that he was only the exponent
of the wishes and opinions of a portion of the loyal States, and
while he was President he had no right to seek personal political favors at the hands of any, but he believed that the support
of the principles of the so-called Union party of the country,
whoever might now be its nominee, was a more effectual way
of putting down this rebellion than the contrary course. The
delegation departed, hugely pleased at their reception, and
wonderfully surprised at the frank, simple way with which the
President disposed of their address. We might be induced to
give more weight to this unusual movement, were it not for
the fact that men of Hebraic descent are (in these parts, at
least) notoriously given to Copperhead—not to say secesh—
proclivities. . . .

24 OCTOBER 1864 (23 NOVEMBER)

A Twelve-Month Volunteer Regiment.
Day before yesterday the One-Hundred-and-Eighty-ninth
Regiment, New York Volunteers, on its way to General
Grant's army, marched to the White House and saluted the
President, who came out and made them a little speech, in
which he thanked them on behalf of the country for the service which they proposed to render the nation by fighting our
battles, and he was glad to say that it would appear that the
soldiers voted about right as well as fought right, though he
supposed that many might differ with him as to their voting
right, but that was his private opinion. He added that though
it was important that there should be men at home to vote
and to look after the soldiers' base of supplies, we could get
along without them; but the soldiers we cannot get along
without.[80] The President was cheered enthusiastically. The
regiment is made up of all volunteers, not a drafted man being

among them, many being veterans re-enlisted; the ranks
exceed the maximum number, being 1,150.

A Magnificent Election Show.

. . . We had here last week . . . a splendid torchlight procession gotten up by the Lincoln and Johnson Club of this city.
Nothing so fine has ever been seen in this city, and seldom,
perhaps, has it been outdone elsewhere. Measuring by the
length of the avenue, the procession was over two miles long,
and it was resplendent from end to end with banners, torches,
fireworks, transparencies and all of the paraphernalia of such a
demonstration. Few finer sights could be shown than a view
of the length of Pennsylvania avenue, vanishing in the distance, gemmed with colored lights, flaming with torches, and
illuminated with the lurid glare from shooting fires of red,
green and blue Roman candles—the whole procession creep-
ing like a living thing and winding its slow length around
the White House, where the President looked out upon the
spectacle. . . .

Odds and Ends.

. . . When I had succeeded in showing the President the other
day how a California politician had been coerced into telling
the truth without knowing it, he said it reminded him of a
black barber in Illinois, notorious for lying, who once heard
some of his customers admiring the planet Jupiter rising in
the evening sky. "Sho! I've seen dat star afore. I seen him way
down in Georgy!" Said the President, "like your friend, he told
the truth, but he thought he was lying."

29 OCTOBER 1864 (2 DECEMBER)

Various, Divers, and Sundry.

Dr. Bellows has presented to President Lincoln the gold box
containing the golden crystals,[81] sent him by some of his

friends in California. The box is about three inches long, and has an oval piece of quartz on the lid, bearing the President's initials thereon. The President appears to be highly gratified with the beautiful gift, and expresses himself, again and again, as more than ever anxious to visit a State which produces such wonderful things and such a generous people. . . .

2 NOVEMBER 1864 (2 DECEMBER 1864)

Light on a Dark Subject.

Last night the colored people of this District held a jubilation in honor of the emancipation of Maryland, manifesting their intelligent appreciation of the advance into freedom of Maryland in their own style. One of the largest of their churches was thrown open, religious exercises were held, and enthusiastic addresses were made by their head men and preachers. After an hour spent in this way, they organized themselves into an impromptu torchlight procession, numbering some few hundreds, who bore aloft the borrowed torches and a few of the transparencies of the late Union torchlight procession, among which latter were some not specially adapted to the occasion, California figuring as "20,000 for the Union," and "Indiana gives us a gain of five Congressmen," while Massachusetts was represented by a picture of Bunker Hill monument, with an objurgatory remark as to Toombs' prediction concerning his roll-call of slaves.[82] With these emblems, and a hoarse band of music, the somewhat irregular procession got up to the White House, where loud and repeated cheers brought out the President, who began by saying: "I have to guess, my friends, the object of this call, which has taken me quite by surprise this evening." Whereupon a chief spokesman shouted, "The emancipation of Maryland, sah;" at which the President proceeded as follows:[83]

It is no secret that I have wished, and still do wish, mankind everywhere to be free.[84] [Great cheering and cries of "God bless Abraham Lincoln."] And in the State of Maryland how great an advance has been made in this direction. It is difficult to realize that in that State, where human slavery has existed for ages, ever since a period long before any here were born—by the action of her own citizens—the soil is made forever free. [Loud and long cheering.] I have no feeling of triumph over those who were opposed to this measure and who voted against it, but I do believe that it will result in good to the white race as well as to those who have been made free by this act of emancipation, and I hope that the time will soon come when all will see that the perpetuation of freedom for all in Maryland is best for the interests of all, though some may thereby be made to suffer temporary pecuniary loss.[85] And I hope that you, colored people, who have been emancipated, will use this great boon which has been given you to improve yourselves, both morally and intellectually;[86] and now, good night.[87]

Whereupon there was more cheering, and after some boggling about the order of march, the dark torchlighters gathered themselves up, and hurrahing, disappeared in the darkness.

11 NOVEMBER 1864 (10 DECEMBER)

How the President Took the News.

Election day was dull, gloomy and rainy; and, as if by common consent, the White House was deserted, only two members of the Cabinet attending the regular meeting of that body.[88] Stanton was sick abed with chills and fever; Seward, Usher and Dennison were at home, voting like honest citizens; and Fessenden was shut up with New York financiers; so Father Welles and Attorney General Bates were left to "run the machine." The President took no pains to conceal his anxious interest in the result of the election then going on all

over the country, but just before the hour for Cabinet meeting
he said: "I am just enough of a politician to know that there
was not much doubt about the result of the Baltimore Convention, but about this thing I am far from being certain; I
wish I were certain." Very few Union men here would have
been unwilling to be as certain of a great good for themselves
as they were of Lincoln's re-election.

The first gun came from Indiana, Indianapolis sending
word about half-past six in the evening that a gain of fifteen
hundred in that city had been made for Lincoln. At seven
o'clock, accompanied only by a friend, the President went over
to the War Department to hear the telegraphic dispatches, as
they brought in the returns, but it was nearly nine o'clock
before anything definite came in, and then Baltimore sent up
her splendid majority of ten thousand plus. The President
only smiled good-naturedly and said that was a fair beginning.
Next Massachusetts sent word that she was good for 75,000
majority (since much increased), and hard upon her came
glorious old Pennsylvania, Forney telegraphing that the State
was sure for Lincoln. "As goes Pennsylvania, so goes the
Union, they say," remarked Father Abraham, and he looked
solemn, as he seemed to see another term of office looming
before him. There was a long lull, and nothing heard from
New York, the chosen battle ground of the Democracy, about
which all were so anxious. New Jersey broke the calm by
announcing a gain of one Congressman for the Union, but
with a fair prospect of the State going for McClellan; then
the President had to tell a story about the successful New
Jersey Union Congressman, Dr. Newell,[89] a family friend of
the Lincolns, which was interrupted by a dispatch from New
York city, claiming the State by 10,000. "I don't believe that,"
remarked the incredulous Chief Magistrate, and when
Greeley telegraphed at midnight that we should have the state

by about four thousand, he thought that more reasonable. So
the night wore on, and by midnight we were sure of Pennsylvania, the New England States, Maryland, Ohio, Indiana,
Michigan, Wisconsin, and it then appeared that we should
have Delaware. Still no word came from Illinois, or Iowa, or
any of the trans-Mississippi States, and the President was
specially concerned to hear from his own State, which sent a
dispatch from Chicago about one o'clock in the morning,
claiming the State for Lincoln by 20,000 and Chicago by
2,500 majority. The wires worked badly on account of the
storm, which increased, and nothing more was heard from the
West until last night, the 10th, when the President received
two days' dispatches from Springfield, claiming the state by
17,000 and the Capital by 20 majority, Springfield having
been heretofore Democratic. By midnight the few gentlemen
in the office had had the pleasure of congratulating the President on his re-election. He took it very calmly—said that he
was free to confess that he felt relieved of suspense, and was
glad that the verdict of the people was so likely to be clear, full
and unmistakable, for it then appeared that his majority in the
electoral college would be immense. About two o'clock in the
morning a messenger came over from the White House with
the intelligence that a crowd of Pennsylvanians were serenad-
ing his empty chamber, whereupon he went home, and in
answer to repeated calls came forward and made one of the
happiest and noblest little speeches of his life. . . .[90]

The New Term.

. . . With the new term of office will come upon the President
a renewal of the crushing responsibilities of the past four
years, and I ought to say for the encouragement of loyal,
Christian hearts, who daily remember their care-worn Chief
Magistrate, "and all others in authority," that no man within

the length and breadth of this Christian land feels more
deeply than he the need of divine support, guidance and wisdom in these great straits than does Abraham Lincoln. On
the day following the election he said, "I should be the veriest
shallow and self-conceited blockhead upon the footstool if, in
my discharge of the duties which are put upon me in this
place, I should hope to get along without the wisdom which
comes from God and not from men."[91] In many loyal hearts
these simple words of trust will find a responsive thrill. God
give him grace!

Serenades and Speeches.

Last night an impromptu procession, gay with banners and
resplendent with lanterns and transparencies, marched up to
the White House, the vast crowd surging around the great
entrance, blocking up all of the semicircular avenue thereto as
far as the eye could reach. Bands brayed martial music on the
air, enthusiastic sovereigns cheered to the echo, and the roar of
cannon shook the sky, even to the breaking of the President's
windows, greatly to the delight of the crowd and Master
"Tad" Lincoln, who was flying about from window to window,
arranging a small illumination on his own private account.
The President had written out his speech,[92] being well aware
that the importance of the occasion would give it significance,
and he was not willing to run the risk of being betrayed by the
excitement of the occasion into saying anything which would
make him sorry when he saw it in print. His appearance at
the window was the signal for a tremendous yell, and it was
some time before the deafening cheers would permit him to
proceed. . . .

BROOKS TO LINCOLN, WASHINGTON, MONDAY MORNING
[21 NOVEMBER 1864?][93]

Not being able to see you when I have called, I hand you the enclosed table of election returns. The first page comprises the home *and* army vote, and the second page is the army vote alone, with recapitulation. As the figures are from returns sent to the Office of the House of Reps. by the Secretaries of States, I think that they are essentially correct.

25 NOVEMBER 1864 (27 DECEMBER)

Cabinet Making.

Your correspondent does not pen a paragraph on this subject because it is specially important, but for the reason that it is one of the leading amusements of the quid-nuncs here. If it were worth while, even the generous columns of the Sacramento Union would fail to contain one-half of all that has been written and printed during the past week or two concerning Cabinet changes. Now let me have my say, which shall be brief: The newspaper men and an excitable public have been deluded into the belief that Banks was here, backed up by a troop of friends, seeking to place him in the place of Stanton, to be rotated out, somehow, but how I do not yet see. The President first learned that Banks was a seeker for the war portfolio by letters of remonstrance from those who disapprove of the over conservative course of Banks at New Orleans;[94] up to night before last no man, woman or child had asked the President to appoint Banks to the War Department. But what Banks is really after is to be sent back to New Orleans with full power over Canby,[95] who is inimical to the new Constitution and the knot of office-seekers whom Banks has about him there. There can be no special change in the Cabinet until the 4th of March, and Stanton has no idea of going out even then, so far as my information, which is full, goes. It is certain that Fessenden will go into the Senate, but the President himself does not know who will take his place in the Treasury Department. Seward is likely to remain, but he is making a crusade against Father Welles, which may oust both of them eventually. Judge Bates has signified his intention to retire permanently from public life at the close of his term,[96] and the rest of the members of the Cabinet will be very likely to have the same opportunity; so we will not worry any more about it until March 4, 1865.

Presents to the President.

No President, it is said, has been the lucky recipient of so many presents as President Lincoln, the "simple people" everywhere testifying their love and admiration of our popular Chief Magistrate by gifts of varying value intrinsically, but of value always to the people's President. The gold box sent by Dr. Bellows, from citizens of San Francisco, was, the President thinks, the most beautiful gift he has ever had. More recently, some of his friends in Philadelphia have given him a gold medal about the size of a five dollar piece, indorsed in two hemispheres of rock crystal, bearing on one side a medallion likeness of Washington, and on the other a similar bust of Lincoln; inside the medal opens and shows another likeness of Lincoln and the inscription: "Abraham Lincoln, an honest man—the crisis demands his re-election." The latest present is one which has been brought from California by an old trapper, whose name I have vexatiously forgotten.[97] The gift is a chair of buckhorns, with the branching antlers interlaced to form the back, seat and arms. It is an unique affair, and much like one which the same trapper gave to Buchanan four or five years ago. The presentation comes off to-morrow.

29 NOVEMBER 1864 (28 DECEMBER)

Vandalism at the White House.

People who visit the White House usually have a free range over the East Room and one or two of the adjoining parlors; accordingly relic-hunters (let us hope they are no worse), have acquired the practice of cutting out and carrying off bits of rich carpet, damask hangings, and even large pieces of fringe, cords, tassels, gilt scroll-work and the covering of damask sofas. A few weeks ago an officer was caught, in company with two ladies, who had his penknife and were cutting out a square of red brocade from one of the East Room chairs, while he stood guard. The *ladies* were let off and the officer was sent to the Old Capitol [Prison]. Yesterday, a man in the garb of a private soldier was caught while skinning off the damask cover of a sofa. He was sent to the guard house. Well might an astonished Dutchman say, "Mine Gott, vat a peoples!"

5 DECEMBER 1864 (7 JANUARY 1865)

The Cabinet-Maker Surprised.

People generally were disappointed when Judge Holt[98] declined the place made vacant by the resignation of Attorney General Bates, the Judge Advocate [General] modestly telling the President that he believed that he could better serve the country in his present position. But they were surprised when, after sundry speculations concerning Caleb Cushing, J. T. Brady, W. M. Evarts and others,[99] the President adhered to his determination not to come back to the free States for his man and appointed James Speed, of Kentucky, to the place—a man not so widely known as some of the candidates before mentioned.[100] The new Attorney General is about forty years of age, is a distinguished lawyer, an early emancipationist, and upon the great question of human freedom he is a little more radical, if anything, than Judge Bates; at least, the President says so, and I suppose he knows, for he has been acquainted with Speed for a great many years. . . .

The President on Practical Religion.

A good illustration of the practical and common sense view which President Lincoln takes of whatever comes under his observation, was afforded the other day in his reply to the application of two Tennessee ladies for the release of their husbands, confined as prisoners of war on Johnson's Island, Ohio.[101] These ladies had been put off from day to day, and one of them continually reiterated, as an argument in favor of her husband, that he was a religious man. They were finally successful in their suit, and when the President agreed to the release, he said to the lady referred to: "You say that your husband is a religious man; tell him, when you see him, that I say that I am not much of a judge of religion, but that, in my opinion, the religion that sets men to rebel and fight against their Government because, as they think, that Government does not sufficiently help *some* men to eat their bread in the sweat of *other men's* faces, is not the sort of religion upon which people can get to heaven."[102] This is one of the shortest and best "political sermons" ever preached in Washington, I guess.

7 DECEMBER 1864 (11 JANUARY 1865)

How the President's Message Was Received.

Precisely at one o'clock yesterday the Private Secretary of the President appeared at the bar of the House of Representatives with the annual message of the President.[103] The ayes and noes were being called on some tom-fool proposition at the time, and it was not immediately read, but in a few minutes Clerk McPherson,[104] in a loud and clear voice, took up the document and began with the terse and litany-like exordium: "Again the blessings of health and abundant harvests claim our profoundest gratitude to Almighty God." Simultaneously with the utterance of the words a host of small, agile pages spread themselves all over the Hall, laying upon the desks of the members printed copies of the message, which were eagerly seized and read; a complete silence pervaded the vast hall and the breathless, crowded galleries, except when the Clerk rang out clarion-like the words, "Maryland is secure to liberty and Union for all the future. The genius of rebellion will no more claim Maryland. Like another foul spirit, being driven out, it may seek to tear her, but it will woo her no more." These triumphant and poetic words brought forth a loud burst of applause, and when the President's dry hit at the "instinctive knowledge" of the politicians on the Union question was reached, there was a ripple of laughter all over the House, and the sovereigns in the gallery showed their appreciation by a half-stifled rumble of applause, for *they* know that the politicians ought to know that "there is no diversity of opinion among the people on the question of Union or no Union." There were smiling faces and long sighs of satisfaction when the reader reached the President's re-statement of his own old position on the amnesty proposition, and when the noble sentences which conclude the message were read there was a long, loud and continued burst of applause, which the Speaker but feebly tried to still. The reading over, members dropped their copies of the message and shook hands kindly and smilingly over the acceptable token of the President's policy to come. Some few had expected that there would be an enunciation of some new principles concerning peace and reconstruction; but such were mistaken and had not known or appreciated the eminent sagacity and tact of Abraham Lincoln. The verdict of all men is that the message

is immensely strengthening for the President, and that while
it has all of the dignity and polish of a first-rate State paper, it
has the strong common sense, the practical knowledge of
details which will commend the document to the minds of
"the simple people." Thaddeus Stevens says that the message
is the wisest and best which the President ever sent to Congress,[105] and leading men generally concur in the opinion of
the critically wise Pennsylvanian. . . .

How the Message Was Written.

It may be a matter of interest to know that the whole of the
compact and able message just referred to exists, or did exist,
upon slips of paste-board or box-board. It is a favorite habit of
the President, when writing anything requiring thought, to
have a number of these stiff slips of board near at hand, and,
seated at ease in his arm chair, he lays the slip on his knee and
writes and re-writes in pencil what is afterward copied in his
own hand, with new changes and interlineations. Then being
"set up" by the printer with big "slugs" in the place of "leads,"
spaces of half an inch are left between each line in the proof,
when more corrections and interlineations are made, and from
this patchwork the document is finally set up and printed. . . .

Chief Justice Chase.

Next to the issuance of the Emancipation Proclamation, no
public act of President Lincoln has given such general satisfaction as the appointment of Salmon P. Chase to the proud
position of Chief Justice of the Supreme Court of the United
States. There were men who fancied that Lincoln could and
would waive his patriotic purposes and his genuine instincts in
the country's behalf, and would permit the remembrance of
personal differences and personal wrongs done himself to sway
him in his choice of a successor to Taney. But, true as ever to
what he considers the public good and popular demand com-

bined, he nominated his unsuccessful rival for the nomination of the Union party. The nomination gives satisfaction to nearly everybody. The Supreme Court is being reorganized in the interests of freedom, and as time and death cause breaks in the bench, the gaps are filled with men of purity, probity and love of liberty.

This morning many distinguished members of the bar of the Supreme Court assembled to hear the address and eulogy on Taney, which was presented to the bench by Thomas Ewing, Chairman of a meeting which adopted the address. Acting Chief Justice Wayne, of Georgia,[106] responded in a brief eulogy on the life and character of the deceased Chief Justice, when the Court was adjourned until to-morrow, but Chase will not be sworn in until Monday next.

Brief Items.

The President and R. E. Fenton, the Governor elect of New York,[107] were serenaded last evening. Fenton made a good speech, and the President said that he could never yet get over being embarrassed when he had nothing to say, and proposed three cheers for Sherman, which were given with a will. . . .

9 DECEMBER 1864 (11 JANUARY 1865)

Unsatisfied Malcontents.

There are some people in this world who never will have the manliness to be satisfied with any concession, however graceful, nor any object attained, however desirable. Of this class are some of the over-zealous and indiscreet friends of the new Chief Justice, who, now that Chase has been appointed,[108] gleefully claim that the President was coerced into making the appointment, and who, while compelled to admit the wisdom which characterizes the appointment, scornfully add that it was a popular choice forced upon the President by men who

control confirmations in the Senate. It seems a pity that when
the President has paid a noble and willing compliment to one
who has honorably been his competitor for Presidential honors, he cannot have the poor satisfaction of knowing that his
own purity of motive and fixity of intention are appreciated by
those who have made Chase and Chase's ambitions the excuse
for injuring and conspiring against the good name of the
President. Now, lest some of these narrow-minded slanderers
of a good man may be able to create in California the same
impression for which they are striving here, I will venture to
say that the President never desired to appoint any other man
than Chase to the Chief Justiceship; he never, I believe, had
any other intention.[109] It is a peculiar trait of his mind that
when doubts and objections arise concerning the expediency
of certain contemplated acts, he states to those with whom he
comes in contact those doubts and objections, not as his, but
with the express purpose of having them refuted, controverted
and removed, if possible. A careless or unobservant listener
goes away confounded and discouraged, but the crafty statesman has enjoyed seeing a false position demolished and his
own convictions made stronger. This is the explanation of the
extraordinary confusion in the minds of men who read the
President's reply to the Chicago ministerial delegation at the
same time that they read the Emancipation Proclamation,
which he refused to give a hope for to that same delegation.[110]
So, although the President made no sign to show that he had
fixed his mind on Chase, and even told those who plied him
with arguments in Chase's favor, that certain things were
urged against Chase, he only put forward those allegations,
though genuine, as straw objections, to be brushed aside, by
others. I hope that I may not be accused of toadyism in thus
simply stating this matter; but I want to see exact justice done
to Abraham Lincoln, and perhaps the trait of character here

drawn may serve as a key to other parts of his conduct, otherwise misunderstood.

A Good Point Well Put.

The Maryland Electoral College paid a visit to the President yesterday, and in the course of their formal interview expressed their gratification at the appointment of Chase to be Chief Justice; to which the President responded, that he trusted that the appointment was for the best. The country, he said, needed some assurances in regard to two great questions, and they were assurances that could better be given by the character and well known opinions of the appointee than by any verbal pledges. In the appointment of Chase, all holders of Government securities in America and Europe felt assured that the financial policy of the Government would be sustained by its highest judicial tribunal. In sustaining that policy, Judge Chase would only be sustaining himself, for he was the author of it. His appointment also met the public desire and expectations as regarded the emancipation policy of the Government. His views were well known upon both of these great questions, and while there were other distinguished gentlemen whose names had been suggested for this great trust, whose views he believed were sound upon these important issues, yet they did not hold the same relations to them as did Chase.[111]

BROOKS TO GEORGE WITHERLE, WASHINGTON, 10 DECEMBER 1864[112]

. . . I watched for the election returns from Maine with an interest second only to that which I felt for the news from California; not that I felt any anxiety for either state, but because I wanted to know just how they went. The general result was what I had expected, and we have every reason to be grateful and thankful to God that in the midst of an exhaustive civil war the people did and could go to work in a constitutional manner and elect a chief magistrate. I have never felt the lack of confidence in Mr. Lincoln that some of our own friends have expressed, but have believed and still do believe that he is *the man* for these times; I know him well— very well, and I do not hesitate to say that he is a far greater and better man than our own people think. The time will come when people generally will concede his true merit and worth. How do you like his last message? Here the expression is very general in enthusiastic praise thereof. Thad Stevens of Pa., a man who has never "believed" in Lincoln, says that it is the best message which has been sent to Congress in the past sixty years. It is interesting and curious to observe how the President has grown morally and intellectually since he has been at the White House; take his messages and read them through *ad seriatim* and you will see his advancement in ability, logic and rhetoric, as evident as in the letters of a youth at school. The last message is a model of compact, strong sense, practical knowledge and argument, with all needful polish. . . .

I suppose you, like the rest of our liberal people, were well-pleased with Chase's nomination for Taney's place. It was an appointment eminently fit to be made, and will, I believe, be a useful one to the country. Mr. Lincoln, I know, has never had any intention or desire of appointing any other man for that responsible and important place. . . .[113]

3 DISPATCHES & LETTERS
1865

1 JANUARY 1865 (21 FEBRUARY)

A Venerable Newspaper Rejuvenated.

The ancient *Intelligencer*, erewhile a statesman's guide and
faithful councilor, but more lately a garrulous and childish
scold, has taken a new lease of life and begins the new year
under a new management, which promises good things. As
intimated in a former letter, for a time there was a prospect
that it would pass into the hands of active Administration
men, who would try to get up an "organ" for Uncle Abraham.
The parties negotiating for the purchase were Nicolay and
Hay, two young gentlemen now acting as Private Secretaries
to the President. The plan to consolidate the *Intelligencer* and
Republican under their management fell through, as also did
an attempt to buy the *Chronicle*, $100,000 being the price
asked for the latter. The purchasers of the *Intelligencer* are
Allen, Coyle and Snow, the first of these, A. G. Allen, being
well known hereabouts as the Washington correspondent of
the Baltimore *Sun*, whose letters, signed "Agate," have been an
institution for years.[1] [John F.] Coyle is the old bookkeeper of
Gales & Seaton,[2] and has gradually "absorbed" the newspaper.
Allen is editor in chief, and is an able, vigorous and experienced writer, naturally liberal, but chronically critical and a
complete encyclopedia of life and doings in Washington,

where he has resided for the past forty years. The paper is pledged "to give to the Administration an unwavering support in its war policy as long as this shall be distinguished by such energy and sense as now appear to characterize the conduct of our military operations." Good for the ancient!

10 JANUARY 1865 (22 FEBRUARY)

"Uneasy Lies the Head," Etc.

The saying is just as true of a President as of a King, and even now, I suppose, Father Abraham lies uneasy o' nights, as he thinks of the sluice of office-hunting which may shortly be opened upon him by the cruel thoughtlessness of his friends (?), as they call themselves. The President considers that as the people have voted to keep him in another term, because the public good could best be served, he ought to make no changes in office which the public good does not demand; but politicians will not see it in that light, and will avail themselves of the excuse of a new term to have a new deal. But I commenced this paragraph to tell a queer story of a well-known actor, J. H. Hackett—Falstaff Hackett—who pleased the President by playing here his well-known character. Hackett, hearing that Lincoln was pleased, sent him a copy of his book on Shakespeare,[3] with a request that it be acknowledged in a letter, in which the President would give, also, his opinion of Hackett's Falstaff—all of which our good-natured Chief Magistrate did.[4] The letter, as the reader may remember, was first published in London, and a copy was sent to the President by Hackett, who sent word at the same time that he would have the honor, he hoped, of playing before the President when he visited Washington again, which was last Winter, when the President did go to see him, the newspapers, much to his disgust, advertising the play as being "at the request of the

President." Well, the upshot of the whole matter is that the intercourse between the flattered actor and the President is, that the actor wants an office; and what do you suppose it is? Why, nothing less than the mission to the Court of St. James! [Consulate at London?][5] That's a fact, incredible as it may seem; and it goes to show how careful a man who has office[s] to give must be in taking any notice of anybody, as he is sure to have somebody grinding an ax on his friendship before he is aware of it.[6]

13 JANUARY 1865 (20 FEBRUARY)

The President and Senator Conness.

By late California papers your correspondent learns that some persons in Washington, with whom the wish is evidently father to the thought, have industriously circulated the report that the relations existing between Senator Conness and President Lincoln are not of a cordial character. Without assuming any superior intelligence, I will take the liberty of saying that I have the emphatic affirmation of the President that the relations existing between himself and Conness are most cordial and friendly, and that he (the President) felt annoyed when he was told that a baseless fabrication like that above alluded to was in circulation in California.

21 JANUARY 1865 (20 FEBRUARY)

The Death of Edward Everett.

Last Sunday the Chaplain of the House of Representatives incidentally introduced in his sermon, preached in the hall of the House, a glowing eulogium on the life and services of Edward Everett, no man present knowing that the distinguished orator was then no more in life. The President and his family were present at the preaching, and, on his arrival at the

house, after the sermon, he was met with the sad news that
Everett was dead. That afternoon, the Secretary of State, by
order of the President, made public announcement of the
death of the distinguished man to the people of the United
States. On Monday salutes were fired and the Department
buildings, Capitol and White House were draped in mourning in respect to his memory. Everett's reputation was world-
wide, but he has left no monument of his genius or his public
worth.[7]

2 FEBRUARY 1865 (1 MARCH)

Brief Mention.

. . . A strong pressure, with a fair show of success, is being
made upon the President to place Governor Andrew of
Massachusetts in his Cabinet, as a representative of the "radical" element. Strange to say, the Blairs and Weed support the
movement, which is designed to place Andrew in the Navy
Department.[8]

12 FEBRUARY 1865 (22 MARCH)

Peace Negotiations.

Your correspondent will take up the thread of discourse where
it was left last "steamer day." Then F. P. Blair, Sr.,[9] had returned
from Richmond, bearing to the President the information that
Jeff. Davis was "ready to enter into conference with a view to
secure peace to the two countries," to use the arch-rebel's own
language. The general tenor of Blair's verbal account of what
he saw and heard in Richmond, more than anything else,
encouraged the President in the belief that peace might be
obtained by negotiation, and the Union be restored upon terms
which would be acceptable to the country. Permission having
been extended to the "informal Commissioners" appointed by

Davis to come into our lines, they came over, and after some diplomatic correspondence were on the point of returning without having seen Seward, who had been sent to meet them at Fortress Monroe, charged by the President to attend a conference upon the basis of a letter to Blair, which was as follows:

> Washington, January 18, 1865.
>
> F. P. Blair, Esq.—Sir: Your having shown me Mr. Davis' letter to you of the 12th instant, you may say to him that I have constantly been, am now, and shall continue ready to receive any agent whom he or any other influential person now resisting the national authority may informally send to me with a view of securing peace to the people of our common country.
>
> Yours, etc., A. LINCOLN

The concluding phrase, so antagonistical to Davis' term, above quoted, was understood to be Lincoln's answer thereto and basis of treaty, and while Seward was not to "assume to definitely consummate anything," he was given these three indispensable terms:

1. The restoration of the national authority throughout all the States.
2. No receding by the Executive of the United States, on the slavery question, from the position assumed thereon in the late annual message to Congress, and in preceding documents.
3. No cessation of hostilities short of an end of the war and the disbanding of all forces hostile to the Government.

It is understood that the three Commissioners, Stephens, Campbell and Hunter,[10] were disappointed at not receiving permission to go to Washington and confer with the President, as they had been led to expect they might, being willing to treat upon the basis of the letter to Blair, though with reservations as to any "personal compromise" in the premises.

Grant, who had freely conversed with these Commissioners,
at once saw that their return without any communication with
the high officers of the Government would have a bad effect
on the country, and he telegraphed his views to the War
Department, expressing his regret that they could not have an
interview with the President.[11] This decided the President,
and he forthwith made an appointment to meet them at
Fortress Monroe, whither he went on the 1st of February,
actuated by a sincere desire to obtain peace, or, failing in that,
to ascertain, categorically, the rebel terms of peace.

The country looked on with wonder to see the President of
the United States, waiving ceremony and disregarding etiquette, leaving the Capital to confer with envoys of the rebel
organization. All thought something serious was in the case if
the President should go to meet them, and most people
applauded the fearlessness of criticism with which Lincoln
went on a peace mission. At this time, when the public, with a
few factious exceptions, was resting confidently in the belief of
Lincoln's wonderful sagacity and discretion would bring the
country and himself out all right, the Washington *Chronicle*,
in a series of double-leaded, sensation leaders, ablaze with all
of the clap-trap of typographical ingenuity, showed that the
editor, J. W. Forney, in his eagerness to be considered as the
oracle of the President (rushing to the conclusion that
Lincoln was going to obtain peace by compromise), had
deliberately gone to work to prepare the public mind for the
sacrifice of something vaguely dreadful, and dreadfully vague.
These articles, counselling popular acquiescence in a repeal of
the confiscation law and other kindred measures, as a condition of peace, were telegraphed all over the country, indorsed
by Greeley, as the outgivings of the President, read by astonished and indignant thousands, scouted by the Wade-and-
Davisites, debauching public sentiment, and filling the minds

of vast multitudes, who did not know all the facts, with alarm and dejection.[12] Grave hints about an official impeachment of the President were dropped by such of the so-called "radicals," who, now that their war upon the President for slowness upon the slavery question is estopped, fly to negro suffrage and a more vigorous system of retaliation upon rebel prisoners, as affording weapons of new warfare; suspicion and distrust were apparent, and it was plain that the muscle of the North was for a brief space relaxed, while the parley for peace went on. A few, no—many, good and true men, firm in their belief in the President's superior knowledge of the facts as well as his sagacity, prophesied that he would soon show the country and the world that he was doing a wise, sensible and manly act. How thoroughly their confidence was grounded, the record, made public by the President in his late message shows.[13] The country now knows that just such terms as the purest patriot in the land would offer were extended to the rebels in that famous conference; that the rebel agents rejected all such conditions; that they wanted an independent Confederacy, before anything else, and that the only result reached was the undeniable ascertainment of the fact that the Davis Government is unalterably opposed to re-union.

The House passed a resolution, on the 8th, calling for the report of the President's visit, or so much as he might choose to give them, but it was not until the 10th that the message came in, while the trial of sundry members for absence was going on. Bits of information concerning the purport of the message had dropped out, and everywhere the malcontents were being silenced by the general expression of satisfaction at the President's course; still, all were anxious to hear his own report, and when the message was announced, by unanimous consent all other business was suspended, and the document opened and read amidst a breathless silence in the hall, every member being in his seat. A low gush of satisfaction broke out when the phrase "one common country" was read in the Blair letter, and an involuntary burst followed the annunciation of the three conditions of peace, given to Seward; there was a ripple of mirth through the House when the Clerk read Lincoln's terse instruction to Seward not to assume to consummate *anything* definitely, and I guess that some men were ashamed of themselves when they remembered that they had said that Lincoln had gone to Fortress Monroe for fear that Seward would not make his terms *liberal enough*. There was a great inspiration of satisfaction at the conclusion of the reading of the message, in the midst of which Brooks, of New York,[14] got up and made a partisan speech, in which he expressed his regret that negotiations with separate States were not opened by the President; from this he went on to the usual Copperhead harangue of "effusion of blood," "fratricidal war," "enormous debt," and so on, and so on. Thad. Stevens replied briefly and pungently, and Cox said that the President deserved the thanks of the country for his noble course in disregarding mere politicians and looking over their heads to the people for their indorsement and approval.

22 FEBRUARY 1865 (22 MARCH)

The President's Last Story.

President Lincoln likes to relate any good story concerning any of his Cabinet officers, and if their dignity has been taken down a trifle he relishes it all the better. He related with great unction, how, when Stanton was at Port Royal last month, he went up Broad river in a tug with General Foster on a reconnaissance;[15] they were hailed by a picket on the bank, who inquired who was on board; the reply was, with dignity, "The Secretary of War and Major General Foster." The picket roared back: "We've got Major Generals enough up here—why don't you bring us up some hard-tack?" Stanton's dignity collapsed and Foster conceded that his pickets did not have very large veneration, phrenologically speaking.

A Senatorial Funeral.

Thomas H. Hicks, United States Senator from Maryland,[16] died on the 13th instant, of paralysis. His health had been impaired for a long time, owing to a severe attack of erysipelas which supervened just after he met with a slight accident, bruising his leg against a carriage step. Amputation was performed, and for the past year and a half the Senator has been in and out of the Senate, assisted by a servant, such was his condition. He had concluded to resign his seat, and was to have been Collector of Baltimore, after March 4th; but disease and death intervened, and on the 15th the two houses of Congress assembled in the Senate Chamber to pay their last offices of respect, as is the custom when a Senator dies during a session of Congress. Eulogies were pronounced in either house by the colleagues of the deceased, and at one o'clock the House of Representatives, headed by the Speaker, Clerk, Sergeant-at-arms and Doorkeeper, wearing long white scarfs, entered the Senate Chamber, the Senators rising to receive them; soon after the Supreme Court, attired in judicial robes, entered in procession and took seats on the right of the President of the Senate; then the President of the United States and several members of his Cabinet quietly stole in by a side door, and sat in the center of the Chamber; the Legislature and Governor and Council of the State of Maryland then came in, and the Mayor and Common Council of Baltimore, and other officials took places within the Chamber. . . .

Superfluous Leniency.

A considerable effort is being made to procure the commutation of the sentence of death upon the Indiana treason-plotters to imprisonment for life. These men, it may be remembered, plotted to murder the Governor of Indiana and other officials, plunge the State in rebellion and bring the rebel army over the border. They have organized to run off deserters from the Union to the rebel lines; have obstructed the draft, shooting enrolling officers and waylaying Provost Marshals. Convicted and sentenced, their friends are urging upon the President, with a fair show of success, that they be saved from a death which most men would say is too good for them, and be imprisoned for life, with a hope that they be gotten out when this shall have blown over. This affair has caused some feeling here, especially among the Indiana delegation in Congress, but the President, who seems to fear the dreadful responsibility of consigning men to death, is very likely to disregard their protests and will commute the sentence as above noted.[17]

12 MARCH 1865 (10 APRIL)

Inauguration Day.

The weather was as dark and drizzly as was the National sky before the day of Sumter's fall. Crowds of people kneaded the unheeded mud in the streets of Washington and stood heroically on guard in front of the Capitol, heedless of tearful skies, long before ten o'clock in the morning of the momentous 4th. As the hour of noon arrived, flocks of women streamed around the Capitol, in most wretched, wretched plight; crinoline was smashed, skirts bedaubed, and moire antique, velvet, laces and such dry goods were streaked with mud from end to end. . . .

The hour of twelve having arrived, [Vice President Hannibal] Hamlin appeared at the main entrance, arm in arm with Andrew Johnson, the Vice President elect, who sat at the right of the Chair. . . .

[After Hamlin's brief speech], Andrew Johnson . . . then stepped in front of the retiring Vice President and began his inaugural address: and here I wish that the ungrateful task of an impartial recorder of current events might be given to another than your correspondent, for it must be said that upon that momentous and solemn occasion, where were assembled the good, the brave, the beautiful, the noble of our land, and the representatives of many foreign lands, Andrew Johnson, called to be Vice President of the United States, was in a state of manifest intoxication. I write these words in humiliation of spirit, for what honest American citizen does not feel his cheek tingle with shame at such a recital of the facts; but it cannot be denied, and thousands of outraged witnesses will ever attest the shameful truth. . . .

. . . It is hard to follow the incoherences of this maudlin speech. For twenty minutes did he run on about Tennessee, adjuring Senators to do their duty when she sent two Senators here, urging that she never was out of the Union, etc.[18] In vain did Hamlin nudge him from behind, audibly reminding him that the hour for the inauguration ceremony had passed; he kept on, though the President of the United States sat before him patiently waiting for his tirade to be over.[19] . . . When Johnson had repeated inaudibly the oath of office, his hand upon the Book, he took it in his hand and facing the audience, said loudly, "I kiss this Book in the face of my nation of the United States," which he did with a theatrical gesture. He then repeated, as well as he was able, the long oath of allegiance repeated to him by the ex-Vice President, interpolating such words as "I can say that with perfect propriety" after some of the solemn asseverations of the oath. He then spoke

about five minutes upon the nature of the oath which he had
just taken, took his seat and called the Senate to order. [Secre-
tary John W.] Forney read the proclamation of the President
calling an extra session of the Senate, read the names of the
Senators elect, and those present came forward and took the
usual oath, which was administered by Secretary Forney, the
Vice President not being in a condition to do it. . . .

The ceremony of swearing in the Senators being over, the
procession, after some haggling, was formed, and proceeded to
the temporary platform in front of the Capitol. . . . The procession from the White House was like the play of Hamlet
with Hamlet left out (excuse the threadbare illustration), the
President having gone up to the Capitol at early morning to
sign bills, work which few Presidents elect ever have to do.
But as Mrs. Lincoln's carriage headed the procession it was
just as well, and the cheering crowd thought that the President was within the vehicle. The procession was a long and
gay one despite the mud, and when it filed into the open space
before the Capitol there was no room left for the crowd,
which had been kept back until the procession came. When
the cortege of the President filed out upon the platform from
the rotunda it was followed by a host of spectators from the
Senate and passages. Instantly the bases of the columns, the
statuary groups and every "*coigne* of vantage" swarmed with
people. The crush of crinolines was terrific, but vast crowds
saw the sight to a good advantage from the great steps of the
Capitol, which rose behind the platform and from the wings
on either side. Before was a literal sea of heads, tossing and
surging, as far as the eye could reach, among the budding
foliage of the park opposite. Cheer upon cheer arose, bands
bl[e]ated upon the air and flags waved over all the scene. The
Sergeant-at-Arms of the Senate, Brown by name,[20] arose and
bowed with his shiny black hat in dumb show before the

crowd, which thereupon became still, and Abraham Lincoln, rising, tall and gaunt, over the crowd about him, stepped forward to read his Inaugural Address, printed in two broad columns upon a half-sheet of foolscap. As he rose a great burst of applause shook the air, and died far away on the outer fringes of the crowd like a sweeping wave upon the shore. Just then the sun, which had been obscured all day, burst forth in its unclouded meridian splendor and flooded the spectacle with glory and light. Every heart beat quicker at the unexpected omen, and not a few mentally prayed that so might the darkness which has obscured the past four years be now dissipated by the sun of prosperity—

> "'Till danger's troubled night depart,
> And the star of peace return."[21]

The inaugural . . . was well received and well pronounced, every word apparently being audible as the clear, light tones of the President rang out over that vast throng. There was applause at the words: "Both parties deprecated war; but one of them would *make* war rather than let the nation survive, and the other would *accept* war rather than let it perish;" and the cheer was injected long enough to make a pause before he said, "And the war came." There was applause at other points, and a long burst when the crowd, with moist eyes, had listened to these noble words, which might be printed in letters of gold:

"With malice toward none, with charity for all, with firmness in the right, as God gives us to see the right, let us strive on to finish the work we are in; to bind up the nation's wounds; to care for him who shall have borne the battle, and for his widow and his orphan—to do all which may achieve and cherish a just and lasting peace among ourselves and with all nations."

Silence restored, the President turned toward Chief Justice

Chase, who held up his right hand, with his left upon the Book, held up by the Clerk of the Supreme Court, and administered the oath of office, the President laying his right hand upon the open page; then, solemnly repeating "So help me God!" he bent forward and reverently kissed the Book, and rose inaugurated President of the United States for four years from March 4, 1865. A salvo of artillery boomed upon the air, cheer upon cheer arose below, and, after bowing to the assembled host, the President retired within, resumed his carriage, and the procession escorted him back to the White House.

Closing Scenes of the Inauguration.

Space will not allow me to tell of the last levee of the season at the Presidential mansion, where there was the greatest jam ever known in the history of that establishment; how thousands upon thousands flocked in crowds to see and speak to their beloved Chief Magistrate, and how the hard-worked old man, just from the platform of the inauguration, went through the ordeal like a kind-hearted hero, as he is. . . . [S]pace will not permit me to tell . . . all about the Inauguration Ball; how such another display of laces, jewelry, silks and feathers, gold lace and things was never seen, no, not since the world began. The President was there, also Mrs. President, and the Cabinet, and Joe Hooker, and Farragut, and such another mob of hungry people I am ashamed to say that when supper was announced and the big wigs had fed and gone, they rushed in, pushed the tables from their places, snatched off whole turkies, pyramids, loaves of cake and things, smashed crockery and glassware, spilled oyster and terrapin on each other's heads, ruined costly dresses, tore lace furbelows, made the floor all sticky with food, and behaved in the almost invariably shameful manner of a ball-going crowd at supper. The ball was held in the great unoccupied Hall of Patents, Interior Building, and three similar halls were thrown open, making a complete quadrangle of four lighted and decorated halls, a fine sight, but all spoiled by the disgusting greediness of this great American people.

The Cabinet Changes.

. . . As was previously intimated, the California, Oregon and Nevada delegations in Congress made up a memorial to the President, asking that the interests of the region which they represented might be considered in making up a new Cabinet. The President appointed a meeting, and when the delegations went up, a few days before the adjournment, they were followed by another delegation of gentlemen from California, Nevada and elsewhere, headed by Congressman Cole and J. G. McCallum [McCollum], bearer of the Electoral vote of California.[22] These persons had previously extended an invitation to the Senators and Representatives to join with them in this delegation, but it had been declined, the Senators and Representatives claiming that, as they had originated the idea of asking the President for a Cabinet appointment, and were the recognized representatives of California, Oregon and Nevada, they had a right to choose their company and their time of presenting the claim of the Pacific States. A portion of the legislative party at once withdrew, Conness setting the example. The rest soon followed, and left the field to the "outsiders," Cole remaining with them. Conness went into the parlor down stairs and saw the President, and explained to him the position of affairs; afterward the President saw the people who waited up stairs for him, heard their application civilly and said he would think of it, and so it ended for the time being. Californians at home may draw their own conclusions as to the merits of the case.

A few days after the above occurrence the President made another appointment with the legislative delegation, when he met them with great cordiality and told them that he had weighed their application with care and regretted to be obliged to say that present combinations and arrangements made it impossible for him to grant their request—in short, the slate was made up. He recognized the right of the States upon the Pacific to ask for a representation in the Cabinet of the National Administration; he was sorry he was not now able to give them what they desired, and if hereafter, among the changes which would be very likely to occur, he could give to California, the oldest of the States represented, a seat in the Cabinet, he should certainly do so.[23] This result of their application was entirely satisfactory to the delegation, and was really all that they had expected. I may as well say here that the name of A. G. Henry, Surveyor General of Washington Territory, has been secondarily presented to the President as the candidate of our Pacific delegation for a Bureau in the Interior Department—that of Indian Affairs or Land being preferred. Dr. Henry is an old-time friend of the President's and his chances of success are thought to be good.

12 MARCH 1865 (11 APRIL)

Emerson Etheridge as a Stool Pigeon.[24]

The Washington public has been interested in a novel exhibition of petty spite and meanness of character made by Emerson Etheridge, of Tennessee, once Clerk of the House of Representatives, now a renegade Copperhead of the most bitter character. On the 24th of February there appeared in the *Constitutional Union*, the Washington Copperhead organ, the following communication under the caption of "How Prisoners of War May be Discharged":

During the present week a young gentleman from Gibson county, Tennessee, came to this city for the purpose, if possible, of procuring the discharge of five prisoners of war at military prisons in the Northwest. He brought letters to L. Anderson, of Kentucky, invoking his assistance.[25] This morning Anderson started him to the President with a statement in the following words and figures:

Prisoners of War
Benjamin Bobbitt, Camp Morton.
S. D. Anderson, Camp Morton.
A. V. Alford, Camp Morton.
W. L. Eastwood, Camp Douglas.
James F. Thomas, Camp Douglas.

I am not personally acquainted with the above named persons, but they are recommended by ten true men (with whom I am personally acquainted) as proper persons to be permitted to take the oath and return home. From the recommendations and information received, I ask the President to permit them to be released on taking the oath of December, 1863.

Lu. Anderson

In the forenoon of to-day, the young gentleman referred to appeared at the President's with this paper, and asked to be permitted to present it. He was informed by C. O'Leary, who is in charge of the door of the President's office, that he could not be permitted to enter.[26] Subsequently, upon being informed of the object of the call, he was taken aside and told by O'Leary that if he would pay him fifty dollars, he (O'Leary) would take charge of the papers and procure the President's order for the release of these prisoners; that otherwise he would have to remain for many days without any probability of having an interview with the President. He saw two other persons on a similar errand pay money to O'Leary, and saw the desired papers, a few minutes afterward, given by O'Leary to such persons. The young gentleman had but little money at the hotel;

nothing like that amount with him. He left the papers, however, with O'Leary, and reported the facts above recited to me.

I went with him immediately to the President's house, intending to play a simple and rustic part. With some difficulty I succeeded in disarming him of all suspicion, and arranged with him to pay the fifty dollars so soon as the President's order for the discharge of these prisoners should be handed to the gentleman above named. O'Leary promised to meet him at his room at the National Hotel (taking the number) at precisely three o'clock to-day, when he was to bring the order of the President for the release of the prisoners and receive the amount stipulated. I remained out of sight until the order for the discharge of the prisoners was delivered and the money paid. Just as O'Leary was bowing himself out I intercepted him, forced him back into the room, denounced him as a swindler, and caused him to surrender the money (thirty dollars), that being the amount he had agreed to take finally, because of the assurance that nothing would be advanced for two of the prisoners, and the inability of the gentlemen to pay more for the others.

The order of the President for the release of the prisoners is written on the paper which was signed by Anderson, and is in the following words:

"Let these men take the oath of December 8, 1863, and be discharged.

A. LINCOLN
February 23, 1865."

Just as O'Leary was taking his leave he gave to his supposed victim his address, and urged him to inform the relatives and friends of prisoners of war that they could have them released from confinement by applying to him and paying ten dollars in each case. He gave his address, which I have in his own handwriting: "C. O'Leary, Executive Mansion, Washington (D.C.)"

I make this matter public from motives of humanity. During the last year I have made many applications for the discharge of prisoners of war upon the terms mentioned in the above order of the President, but in no instance have I been successful. I have often written to the friends and kindred of prisoners that there was no end to their captivity but peace. I rejoice, however, to be able at last to inform those who feel an interest in the matter, that a cheap and expeditious remedy is within their power. Commissioners of Exchange may disagree, Butler may higgle about his niggers, but ten dollars enclosed to "C. O'Leary, Executive Mansion, Washington (D.C.)," will restore any repentant rebel to the blessings of freedom and the society of friends.

EM. ETHERIDGE

Washington (D.C.), Feb. 23, 1865.

Everybody knows that it is the constant practice of the President to discharge prisoners of war who take the amnesty oath upon proper application being made by the Congressmen who represent the districts where their homes are located. This application was made by a Union Congressman from Kentucky, and, it now appears, was laid before the President by H. W. Harrington, of Indiana,[27] into whose hands O'Leary gave the paper. The same result would have been attained if the application had been sent to the President through the hands of his Private Secretary, but Etheridge, with his innate love of intrigue, appeared to prefer bribing a servant to accomplish what any man could do in the regular way, and then, having extorted forcibly his bribe from the tempted servant, he rushed his own disgrace and shame into print, as if he had done a very fine thing. O'Leary was, of course, instantly dismissed from service when the President ascertained what had been done; but whatever may be the public verdict in his case no sane man can regard with any degree of tolerance the part which Emerson Etheridge has played in the matter.

22 MARCH 1865 (19 APRIL)

"Lame Ducks."

The President says he don't see why, because a man has been defeated for renomination or re-election for Congress, he should be returned on his hands, like a lame duck, to be nursed into something else. But he has managed to take care of several such, one being John P. Hale, who, after eighteen years service in the Senate, packed up his things and got ready to go to Spain, where he has $12,000 per annum.[28] Everybody was sorry for Hale, not that he was defeated, but that there should be any good reason—as there was—for his defeat. It was a great pity that a man who was faithful and true to the principles of freedom when it cost something to be a disciple, should go down under a cloud. Another "lame duck" is Wilkinson, late Senator from Minnesota, whose friends are urging him for the Commissionership of Indian Affairs. Another is Freeman Clarke, of the Twenty-eighth (Rochester) District of New York, who was made Controller of the Currency, vice McCulloch, Secretary of the Treasury. Similar provision had been made for Ambrose W. Clark, of the Twentieth (Watertown) District of New York, who is appointed consul to Valparaiso.[29] The few changes which have been made in foreign appointments have chiefly been made for the benefit of the "lame ducks," though not in that category comes John Bigelow, made Minister to France, who is an able diplomatist, a gentleman and a newspaper man withal, being formerly editor of the New York *Evening Post*.[30] He is succeeded in the Consulship to Paris by J. G. Nicolay, formerly Private Secretary of the President. The new Consul does not go out until about the first of June.

Various, Divers, and Sundry.

The President's health has been worn down by the constant pressure of office-seekers and legitimate business, so that for a few days he was obliged to deny himself to all comers, and he now rigidly adheres to the rule of closing the doors at three o'clock in the forenoon, receiving only those whom he prefers during the hours of evening. He is considerably better in health now. . . .

1 APRIL 1865 (8 MAY)

What the President May Do.

The peace-mongers of the *Tribune* stamp vaguely hint at negotiations and compromises, as though the President had power to initiate or consummate either. What the basis of peace is to be is not told us by the new school of Union Copperheads, but "concessions" and "liberal advances" are darkly hinted at, just as Vallandigham and Wood hinted at compromises whose terms they dare not name. If "favorable terms" are to be offered to rebels, where is the power to grant such terms or offer them? The President can pardon offenders, but his pardons are not what rebels desire or expect, other than those largely offered in the amnesty proclamation. Then nothing remains but the Union, the Constitution and the laws of Congress. The President justly says that he has no right to offer any pledge concerning emancipation or confiscation, the two great hindrances to a re-union in the rebel mind. If the emancipation proclamation was valid and effectual, it gave freedom to their slaves, and no power under the Constitution can be found to re-enslave any man now free. Lincoln cannot recall it, and the highest tribunal known to the Constitution has yet to pass upon its validity. If the confiscation of all their property is a bar to the return of the rebels, who, by that return, would place all that they have left in our hands, they must look to Congress for a repeal of that enactment; the President has no power to annul it or even to mitigate the severity of its operation. The President, then, can offer no abrogation of the Confiscation Law, no recall of a valid proclamation, no amendment of the Constitution and no pledge of future Congressional action. Any treaty must be made by high contracting powers who are to live after the treaty shall be mutually accepted, the parties thereto continuing in existence long enough to see that each other keep the terms thereof. If Lincoln makes "a treaty" with the rebels, he will be a traitor and ought to be impeached. We have one treaty in existence—the Constitution—and when the rebels submit to that, peace will return. When any terms other than those within the purview of that instrument come, they will come from the rebels, and neither the President, or Congress, or the Courts can agree to them. But if any terms of reunion which are outside of the President's functions and are within those of the Congress, shall be presented by the rebels, then the President will convene the Congress and submit to them the propositions. And that is all the President may or can do. His own individual opinions and intentions have been so frequently and lucidly stated that any new exposition, however terse, would be simply an act of supererogation.

Why Not Negotiate?

This question is asked by the *Chronicle* and a small party behind it. The President, it may be here said, has never recognized by word or deed, written or spoken, that there is or was such a being in existence as a President of the rebel States. He holds that a recognition of such a person is a virtual recognition of such an organization as a rebel Government, a thing which he holds to be a moral impossibility. He will not, therefore, permit himself to be seduced into recognizing any persons as embassadors or emissaries sent from the so-called President Davis, and any negotiation must be had with just such persons, if had at all. The President has said that he will meet with "liberal terms" any proposition coming from "an authority which can control the armies now at war against the United States." But the control of those armies has passed out of the hands of Jefferson Davis, and we all know that when Lee comes with his propositions for a surrender the "liberal terms" will be such modifications of amnesty as Executive clemency may grant. That is all. Negotiation implies that the rebellion was not without cause and that the Government stands ready to make just concessions; it argues governmental inability to conquer a peace; and, furthermore, it would leave still open the question whether the Republic of the United States has innate strength enough to maintain itself against a great revolt within itself.

Amnesty.

It is very evident that one of the most difficult questions before us will be how broad an amnesty shall be extended to the rebels. The conditions of the so-called Amnesty Proclamation are too liberal for the revengefulness of some of our own people, and are not generous enough for the rebel leaders. Just now we need not borrow trouble, but as one of the "conditions of peace," the President has very pertinently asked: "How many more lives of our citizen soldiers are the people willing to give up to insure the death penalty to Davis and his immediate coadjutors?"

The Abolition of Slavery.

Not a few of our citizens who hate slavery and fear a reconstructed Union in which it may yet have vitality are apprehensive that a sudden end to the war and a new representation in Congress from the slave States would be effectual to save the cursed institution. It still exists, and is recognized in Delaware and Kentucky, and unless Congress admits the reconstructed States of Tennessee, Louisiana and Arkansas, the proposed amendment to the Constitution will not be carried, unless, indeed, the dogma that the States in which rebellion exists are out of the Union for all Federal purposes be adopted as final in the case. Pending the solution of this problem, the best informed men are turning their attention again to the Emancipation Proclamation of the President, which applies to the States which are supposed to be about to be reconstructed on the basis of subjugation or surrender. The validity of this edict must be eventually decided by the Supreme Court of the United States, and, without claiming to speak *ex cathedra* upon so grave and delicate a matter as an unborn decision of that bench, I think it may be received as an established fact that, whenever the question arises, the Supreme Court will decide that every man is entitled to his own life, liberty and pursuit of happiness, unless a constitutional enactment to the contrary shall be shown.

Other Matters.

Samuel C. Parks, Associate Justice for the Territory of Idaho, has resigned his seat on the Bench.[31] He was here on leave, and some business occurring between himself and the Attorney General he was told that his resignation would be acceptable, and he accordingly resigned. This has no explanation, and is more singular from the fact that his appointment was originally made by the President, who "broke the slate" of the Pacific delegations for that very purpose. . . .

BROOKS TO EDWARD MCPHERSON, WASHINGTON, 5 APRIL 1865[32]

Your note of the 1st is at hand, and I would at once see the President in regard to the matter of obtaining all of that correspondence [regarding the Niagara Falls peace talks]. He is yet, however, at the front, and when I came up from there the other day, sick, he expressed a determination to stay until the first of next week. When he comes up, if not too late, I will see what can be done, but I have not very strong hopes of his consenting to the publication of the correspondence, as there were one or two other letters which have not seen the light, and other parties than the President, might not be glad to see them printed. . . .

6 APRIL 1865 (8 MAY)

The Illumination.

. . . The illumination [celebrating the capture of Richmond] was very general, especially when one considers how many people in Washington would have gladly lighted their windows at a triumphal entry of "the other fellow," as the President sometimes playfully calls the rebel crew. . . .

The President at Richmond.

When Grant commenced the movement which has eventuated in the capture of Richmond, he induced the President to prolong his stay at City Point by a promise that in a few days he should go to Richmond unhindered. Grant has proved to be a man of his word now as before. The President has made his headquarters at City Point on a small steamer, and all of his business there has been to rest from his official labors and wait the termination of events. Some of the newspapers have circulated absurd stories about his visit being to receive new propositions of peace, but I know that no such propositions were received, offered or expected. Peace is coming fast enough, and coming in the right way.

During the rush and stir of the late victorious entry of our forces into Richmond some of the sensation writers and speakers had their say about the President making his headquarters at night where Jeff. Davis had risen in the morning. They do not know Lincoln who suppose that he will make any personal parade of himself at Richmond or elsewhere, or give the character of a personal triumph to his entry of the rebel Capital. He has quietly visited Richmond and Petersburg, and will go again as soon as he is joined by Mrs. Lincoln, who came back from City Point a day or two since. The President will return to this city in a few days, refreshed in body as well as relieved in mind, with new courage to take up his own labors in the office and in the Cabinet.

BROOKS TO EDWARD MCPHERSON, WASHINGTON, 12 APRIL 1865[33]

. . . I have not had an opportunity of asking the President for that correspondence, he has been crowded all the while since coming back, but I shall see him this week, and will ask him about it. When I saw it last summer it was printed entire and was in Greeley's hands, with full consent to print, but he said that though he was willing to publish it, others might not be, and he was not sure that all of the correspondence would be accessible to him. So much for his honesty; so, though he may now say that he is willing that it shall all be published, the President knows that he is not willing—if so, why don't he print it in the *Tribune?* The President said then that he would leave the whole matter in the hands of Mr Greeley, and he will probably say so now. . . .

12 APRIL 1865 (8 MAY)

How the Good News Came to Washington.

Most people were sleeping soundly in their beds when, at daylight on the rainy morning of April 9th, a great boom startled the misty air of Washington, shaking the earth and breaking the windows of the houses about Lafayette Square, compelling the inhabitants once more to say that they would be glad when Union victories were done with, or celebrated somewhere else. But boom, boom, boom went the guns, until five hundred of them were fired. Some few people got up and raced around in the mud to see what the news was, and some few got up a procession of flags and things, wet as it was. . . .

The streets, horribly muddy, were all alive with people, cheering and singing, carrying flags and saluting everybody, hungering and thirsting for speeches. . . .

Later in the forenoon an impromptu procession came up from the Navy Yard, dragging six boat-howitzers, which were fired through the streets as they rolled on; this crowd soon swelled to a formidable size, and filled the whole area in front of the President's house, where they patiently waited for a speech, guns firing and bands playing meanwhile. The young hopeful of the house of Lincoln—"Tad"—made his appearance at the well known window from whence the President always speaks, where he was received with a great shout of applause; encouraged by which he waved a captured rebel flag, whereat he was lugged back by the slack of his trowsers by some discreet domestic, amidst the uproarious cheers of the sovereign people below. The President soon after made his appearance, and for a moment the scene was of the wildest confusion; men fairly yelled with delight, tossed up their hats and screamed like mad. Seen from the windows, the surface of the crowd looked like an agitated sea of hats, faces and men's arms. Quiet restored, the President briefly congratulated the people on the occasion which had called out such unrestrained enthusiasm, and said that as arrangements were being made for a more formal celebration, he would defer his remarks until then; for, said he, "I shall have nothing to say then if it is all dribbled out of me now," whereat the crowd good humoredly laughed. He alluded to the presence of the band, and said that our adversary had always claimed one old good tune—Dixie— but that he held that on the 8th of April we fairly captured it—

in fact, he said, he had submitted the question to the Attorney General, who had decided that the tune was our lawful property; and he then asked that the band play "Dixie," which they did with a will, following with "Yankee Doodle." The President then proposed three cheers for General Grant and the officers and men under him, then three for the navy, all of which were given heartily, and the crowd dispersed. . . .[34]

More Congratulations.

After the first ebullitions of joy, the city settled down into comparative quiet, and no demonstration was further made until last night, when the Departments were all again illuminated, and the public, more generally than ever before, followed the example. The night was misty, and the exhibition was a very splendid one, the reflection on the moist medium of the air of the illuminated dome of the Capitol being especially fine, showing for miles around. We have become used to great illuminations here, and there was nothing specially new, the same rush of people, crash and din of bands, and glare of rockets bursting in air, and unending gleam of lighted windows—all these were as before, "only more so."

The notable feature of the evening was the President's speech, delivered to an immense throng of people, who, with bands, banners and loud huzzas poured around the familiar avenue in front of the mansion. After repeated calls, loud and enthusiastic, the President appeared at the window, the signal for a great outburst. There was something terrible about the enthusiasm with which the beloved Chief Magistrate was received—cheers upon cheers, wave after wave of applause rolled up, the President modestly standing quiet until it was over. The speech was longer and of a different character from what most people had expected, but it was well received, and it showed that the President had shared in, and had considered, the same anxieties which the people have had, as this struggle has drawn to a close. . . .[35]

Reconstruction.

This difficult and oft-vexed question comes up at once, and meddlesome ultraists of the Henry Winter Davis sort are predicting an infinite deal of vexation to the Executive and to the nation. Some are already beginning to clamor for a called session of the new Congress, but I believe that the President considers that it is a fortunate thing for the country that Congress is not in session, especially if it were such a body as that which has just adjourned; it would have a baker's dozen of reconstruction bills under consideration forthwith. Everybody now congratulates the country on the firmness which the President manifested when he refused to sign the [Wade-] Davis Bill of the Thirty-eighth Congress;[36] even those who voted for it are now willing to admit that the President's sagacity was greater than theirs when he saw that this very state of things might arise when we might have before us a truly subjugated South, subjugated by force of arms, and a law, vigorous and sweeping in its provisions, not susceptible of any change for the differing circumstances of different States, would be our only rule of reconstruction for the whole territory so unexpectedly opened before us. As it is, the probability is that these States will come back in different ways, each State acting for itself in some sovereign capacity, and as the people of the States reorganize themselves, they will revive the paralyzed powers of the State, and before the present Summer closes there will be some order brought out of the chaotic mass, which Congress would have taken hold of arbitrarily, and compressed into State Governments forthwith. . . .

Those who are ready to fight the President on reconstruction and thereby carry out in 1868 the radical programme for the Presidency, which failed in 1864, are only waiting for the occasion to pounce upon the President's expected clemency toward the offending rebel leaders. As yet, we have none of them to experiment upon, but the extremists are thirsting for a general hanging, and if the President fails to gratify their desires in this direction, they will be glad, for it will afford them more pretexts for the formation of a party which shall be pledged to "a more vigorous policy." . . .

14 APRIL 1865 (15 MAY)

A Bone of Contention.

The views of the President concerning reconstruction, as enunciated in his speech of the 11th April, are very animatedly discussed and meet with widely different comments from different people. It is, of course, acceptable to the conservative element of the Union party, largely dominant, that the President shall have insisted upon the views which he was known to have entertained on the policy of reconstruction, especially as applied to Louisiana, as a sample or instance of the working of that policy. But the radicals, so called, are as virulent and bitter as ever, and they have gladly seized upon this occasion to attempt to reorganize the faction which fought against Lincoln's nomination, very much as Sidney Smith's Mrs. Partington fought with her broom against the rising tide.[37] These men were the bitter opponents of new Louisiana in the last Congress, and they are enraged that the President should dare to utter his sentiments as antagonistic to theirs. They thought that Louisiana was killed off, and now they nose out "Executive interference with legislative prerogatives;" they discern conservative policy afar off, and see an unconditional amnesty to all rebels in the signs of the times. Among these men are Benjamin F. Butler, who is here endeavoring to make all the mischief he can and get up a radical organization with himself and Caleb Cushing (*par nobile fratrum!*) at the head; he has an ally in R. C. Schenck of Ohio,[38] who it is supposed, will be the "medium" and organ of Henry Winter Davis in the next Congress. Still, these men and their associates form but an inconsiderable portion of the great mass of the loyal people. Butler, I hear, is very much disgusted at the slow response of the people to his incendiary appeals, and at their obvious reluctance to rally round his flag. One of his *clacquers* has been sending sensation telegrams from Washington to the *Tribune.* Anent "great satisfaction of the people;" "Lee's parole a bribe for a surrender;" "split in the party that elected Lincoln," etc., etc., all of which appears in ludicrous contrast with the pro-conservative views concerning amnesty, which Greeley affects of late. Of course, the Opposition press will seize upon this small diversion as a sign of the dissolution of the Union organization, forgetting or ignoring the fact that the only reports of this suppositious quarrel which have appeared in any journal are those of a single individual, responsible to nobody for his truthfulness, his candor, or his intelligence. Whatever aspect the question may now wear to the great mass of the people, they have an implicit and trustful faith in Lincoln, which is almost unreasonable and unreasoning; he has so often proved himself wiser than his critics and advisers that many truly wise men say that they have done with contending against his better judgment, while "the simple people" say, "Oh, well, Old Abe will come out all right—he always does, you know." Any man who looks over the political history of the four past years will be surprised to see how often adverse, though friendly, criticisms of the President's acts and opinions have been made foolishness by the development of events.

16 APRIL 1865 (17 MAY)

The Great Calamity.

No living man ever dreamed that it was possible that the
intense joy of the nation over the recent happy deliverance
from war could be or would be so soon turned to grief more
intense and bitter than ever nation before had known. Just
while the national Capital was in its brightest garb of joy, and
while the nation was all pervaded with a generous exaltation, a
heavy woe, filling every heart with horror, and stiffening once
more the relaxing grasps of justice, swept over the land, and all
the people stood aghast at the damnable deed which, in our
hour of triumph, took away the beloved and revered Chief
Magistrate, Abraham Lincoln. It is hard to realize that he is
gone, that we shall no more see his commanding form, hear
his kind voice or touch his pure and honest hand, with its
well-remembered earnestness. It is hard to take in the dreadful thought that the speaking eye is closed in death, and that
the kindly, genial soul has fled, and that the head of the nation
has perished by the hand of an assassin; but so it is, and we
have only now to reconcile ourselves, as a people, to the new
order of things, gather up the personal recollections of the
martyr, commit his mortal remains to the earth and perpetu-
ate his blessed memory to all coming time.

"The Deep Damnation of His Taking-Off."

At the risk of repeating some things which you have read
already, I will present the facts connected with the great crime,
as gathered from personal observation and from conversation
with members of the party who were present at the time the
deed was committed. On Friday, April 14th, General Grant
being in town, the President and the famous General were
invited to attend the performance of Laura Keene in the
"American Cousin," at Ford's Theater.[39] The General did not

remain in town that night, but went on to Philadelphia with his wife,[40] and the President, hearing that the party had been advertised to be at the Theater, consented to go rather than that people should be disappointed. He was unusually cheerful that evening, and never was more hopeful and buoyant concerning the condition of the country. Speaker Colfax and your correspondent were at the house just before he went out for the last time alive, and in his conversation he was full of fun and anecdotes, feeling especially jubilant at the prospect before us.[41] The last words he said as he came out of the carriage were: "Grant thinks that we can reduce the cost of the army establishment at least a half million a day, which, with the reduction of expenditures of the Navy, will soon bring down our national debt to something like decent proportions, and bring our national paper up to a par, or nearly so, with gold; at least so they think."[42] Mrs. Lincoln's carriage was at the door, seated in it being Miss Harris, daughter of Senator Harris of New York, and Major Rathburn [Rathbone], her step-brother.[43] The President and wife entered and drove off without any guard or escort.

Ford's Theater is situated on Tenth street, in the central portion of the city, having an alley in the rear which opens upon F Street at right angles with Tenth, and on Ninth street, next above Tenth, on this alley, is the stage entrance, by which the murderer afterward escaped. The performance had begun when the President and party entered, and their reception caused a suspension of the play, the enthusiasm being unusually great. They took seats in a double box on the right of the stage, as you face the performers, and the door was closed, Parker, one of the attendants, first seating the party and then going into the audience, contrary to the custom heretofore,[44] another of the attendants being in the dress-circle, where he sat. The box occupied by the President is in the dress-circle,

having smaller boxes below it, and being some fifteen feet
above the stage. On the left, as one enters the box from the
back, sat Miss Harris, nearest the stage; Mrs. Lincoln sat next
on that side, and the President next—those three in a slight
curve from the front, the President being almost in the center;
opposite, on the right, was a sofa, where Major Rathbone sat.
Miss Harris says that when they had been sitting there an
hour or more, she saw the door open and a man look in, take a
rapid glance at the position of the occupants of the box and go
away again, closing the door. This attracted her attention only
as being rude, and she thought it some curious person who
wanted a look at the President. John Wilkes Booth, a "condemned" actor, had been loitering about the building behind
the scenes, and this man was he. Having ascertained that the
coast was clear, he went out of the theater by the stage door,
which he left open, went around to the front of the theater,
ascended to the dress circle and entered the box. It was now
about ten o'clock, two women only were on the stage, and the
second scene of the third act was just begun, when the theater,
so often the scene of a mock tragedy, was made the scene of a
real one of which the world has never seen a parallel since
Caesar was murdered in the Roman Senate. Miss Harris,
hearing the door open a second time, looked up and saw
Booth enter deliberately but rapidly, walk up behind the President, whose face was turned toward the audience, and, applying a little pistol exactly under the left ear, fire. Oh, God!
where was thy providence at that dreadful instant of time? It
was but an instant, and, dropping his pistol, the murderer
flashed out a knife, slashed at Rathbone and sprung over the
edge of the box in front. The audience had heard the report of
the pistol, but did not notice it, as it was very likely to be supposed a part of the stage business; but a sudden movement
caused them to look up, and there was a marble face, a pair of

glittering black eyes and a flashing knife, as Booth paused on
the gilded cornice of the proscenium long enough to shout
"Sic semper tyrannis!" Then he dropped on the stage, falling
upon his knees, but quickly recovering himself he marched
across the stage to the left, with that stagy, stilted stride peculiar to his class of actors, shouting "Revenge for the South!" as
he went. Gaining the first stage entrance, left side, he pushed
aside Miss Keene, who was about to enter, met an attache of
the theater, whose coat he slashed open with his knife, dashed
out of the door which he had left open, mounted his horse,
which a boy had been holding for him, and clattered out into
the night, bearing with him the mark of Cain, which will
brand him to the day of his death. All of this happened in a
moment of time, and so completely paralyzed was every person that it was an easy thing for the wretch to flee almost
unpursued; one man only, a lawyer in this city,[45] had a dim
idea of what had happened, and leaping on the stage he pursued Booth into the alley, saw him knock down the boy who
held the horse, mount and ride away into the darkness of the
streets.

When the audience were roused by the piercing shrieks of
Mrs. Lincoln they rushed upon the stage with shouts of "hang
him! hang him!" and for a space all was confusion. Miss Harris first recovered herself, and, leaning over the box, asked for
water. Miss Keene went up, surgeons were on the spot and
everything was done that could be done to recall the bleeding,
dying President to life. Mrs. Lincoln on hearing the report
had turned, when, to her horror, she saw the head of her husband fall forward on his breast; he was laid on the sofa at
once, but breathed only with difficulty, rattling in his throat.
He never spoke or gave any sign of consciousness. The ball
had gone clear through the skull, glancing obliquely across the
brain and lodging under the right eye, where a great discol-

oration settled. He was removed to a private house opposite, and instantly mounted couriers were scouring the city; horsemen galloped to and fro; the patrol encircled the city, which was in a state of terror and alarm. Guards kept the people out of the street where the President lay dying, but crowds, anxious, tearful and enraged, besieged the place all through the night. . . .

"The Last of Earth."

Through the dreadful night which followed, the slow and labored breath of the dying President grew feebler and feebler. He lay upon a bed in an upper chamber, surrounded by the members of the Cabinet—Seward, only, absent. General Halleck, Quartermaster General Meigs, Chief Justice Chase, Senator Sumner, Speaker Colfax and several distinguished physicians, the Surgeon General being in attendance.[46] In an adjoining room was Mrs. Lincoln, attended by her son, Captain Robert Lincoln, Major Hay (Private Secretary), Miss Harris, Major Rathbone (who was severely cut in the arm), and one or two intimate friends of the family.[47] Several times during the night Mrs. Lincoln, who was by times calm and composed and by times delirious, visited the chamber where the President lay, but she could gain no satisfaction, as he was past recognizing anybody. The agony of those long, dark hours can never be estimated, and we drop a curtain over the piteous tragedy. From the first there was no hope, and the pulse which at midnight fluttered at forty-eight, rallied slowly until half-past one o'clock, when it stood at ninety-five; from this time, however, it declined steadily, and at twenty-two minutes past seven o'clock in the morning he was dead. The long labor of life was ended, and the loving, noble heart was forever still. Rev. Dr. Gurley, of the New York Avenue Presbyterian Church, had prayed by the bedside of the dying man, and now prayed in the death-chamber, surrounded by strong men who wept like children. The same devotions were had in the chamber with the mourning family, and in an hour or two after the corpse, covered by the flag and escorted by a guard of honor, and followed by the officers present, was carried back to the White House.

The Popular Feeling.

No pen can accurately describe the mingled feeling of sorrow, wrath, horror and indignation which seized upon the people as soon as the doleful tidings spread through the city. From lip to lip the tale of horror flew; men and women went weeping about the streets; no loud voice was anywhere heard; even children's prattle was hushed; gloom, sadness, mourning sat on every countenance. To adopt the eloquent language of one of the morning journals: "If tears had audible language, a shriek would go up from these States which would startle the world from its propriety. Strong men use the impressive language of women—tears. Women bow their heads in the dust. Children sleep troubledly. Words are weak and vain."

Flags were raised at half-mast everywhere; the bells tolled solemnly, and, with wonderful swiftness, the whole city went into deep and universal mourning. All stores, Government departments and offices were closed; the hum of driving wheels and busy engines ceased; everywhere, on proud residences and on humble hovels, waved the black badges of mourning. Nature seemed to sympathize in the general grief, and tears of rain fell from the moist, dark sky; while the wind sighed mournfully through the streets, crowded with sad-faced people, and broad folds of black flapped heavily in the wind, over the decorations of yesterday's rejoicings. Far and wide flashed the sore tidings, carrying real grief to millions of American homes; and from sea to sea a smitten nation wept

in agony over the announcement that God had taken away
from earth forever Abraham Lincoln. . . .

A Sorrowful Sunday.

This has been a gloomy day in Washington, and it has been
remarked that the churches were never as full as on this day,
when all hearts were naturally softened by this great national
grief and turned toward the Head of Nations over us all, with
His inscrutable providences. At the New York Avenue Presbyterian Church, where the President was a regular attendant,
the services were peculiarly impressive. The church was
draped in mourning, and the well-known pew of the Lincoln
family, vacant and robed in sable crape, spoke mutely to the
great congregation of him that was gone. The dirge-like
music, the earnest prayer and the solemn lesson inculcated by
the preacher, all made the service one which will be long
remembered by those who heard it. In all of the churches
some reference was made to the afflictive event, and everywhere one could see that the sadness of the people was something more than that of a passing hour.

Some Personal Reminiscences.

While your correspondent would not obtrude his private
griefs upon the public attention, I cannot help saying here
that I knew and loved Abraham Lincoln well. It was my good
fortune to make his acquaintance years ago, during the early
days of Republicanism, in Illinois, and since my sojourn in
Washington that early acquaintance has ripened into intimacy
near and confiding. This enables me to testify to his unspotted
integrity, his thoughtful kindness for everybody, his unselfish
modesty, his genial heartiness, his sagacity, shrewdness, and
his knowledge of human nature. Often when I would ask a
favor for some poor soldier or friendless deserving youth, he
would give his whole attention to the matter, as though that

were his most important business on hand, and would laugh-
ingly say: "It seems to me you have a knack for picking up just
such cases that nobody else thinks of." Then, with all his
geniality, which sometimes broadened into joviality, he was
pervaded with a solemn sense of his obligations as a Christian
Magistrate, which never forsook him. He was a praying man,
and daily sought from God that aid which he had long since
learned man could not give him. With great natural shrewdness and sagacity, he had a transparent simplicity which
endeared him to all who met him; and it is notable that those
who knew him best loved him best, and those who had at a
distance been hostile to him were disarmed when they came
to know the man. I could fill columns in reciting the peculiar-
ities and the virtues of this most extraordinary man, raised by
God for this special work, which being accomplished, he has
gone to his everlasting reward. It seems cruel that so good and
so kind a man should fall in such a dreadful way, but some
wise purpose was over all, and it is some comfort at least to
know that he passed away without a pang of mental or bodily
anguish. He left behind him a smitten household, a knot of
weeping friends, and a bowed and mourning nation, but he

> "—passed through glory's morning gate,
> And walked in Paradise."

A martyr to the national cause, his monument will be a
nation saved, a race delivered, and his memory shall be cherished wherever Liberty hath a home,

> "To the latest syllable of recorded time."

27 APRIL 1865 (26 MAY)

A Radical President.

. . . Lincoln used to say that the responsibilities of office had
the effect to make men conservative. . . .

5 MAY 1865 (31 MAY)

Miscellaneous.

. . . Our lamented President took a great interest in California, and said that he thought he would like to live there after his term of office was out, but he had compromised the matter with his wife, who preferred Boston for a place of residence, by agreeing to make a long visit to California and the adjoining States, with an indefinite purpose as to a permanent settlement. . . .

BROOKS TO ISAAC P. LANGWORTHY, WASHINGTON, 10 MAY 1865[48]

. . . It was long after Mr. Lincoln's death before I could trust myself to write a letter, or find any heart to speak of that which so weighed upon my mind. I suppose that we all felt a personal interest in our beloved President, from the peculiar qualities of his mind, which seemed to familiarize him with the people; but no man outside of my own family circle was ever so much to me as he was, and I cannot yet, perhaps I never may, contemplate his cruel and tragic taking-off with calmness. He was so kind, loving and gentle that no man could even partially know him and be his enemy. The plain, homely face, every *quirk* of which I knew, was sometimes suffused with a light which was almost a transfiguration, and, though he had firmness enough when it was needed, he was more devoid of anger, clamor, evil-speaking and uncharity than any human being I ever knew or heard of.

But he is gone, and even his virtues avail nothing to recall him from the world of spirits, and we have only to gather us the mementoes which we have [of] him, to finish the work which he left and to try and imitate that immortal part of him which still survives. I am glad now that I never hesitated, when proper occasion offered, to talk with him upon religious matters, for I think that the best evidences of his belief in Christ are those which I derived in free and easy conversations with him.[49] You know I had an intimate acquaintance with him, which was not hampered or embarrassed by any official or business relations, nor did he have the same undefined reluctance which a man in his position would have had in talking upon religious matters, if I had been a clergyman. . . . Mr. Frost will recollect that I repeated to him last winter part of a conversation which I held with the President soon after his re-election, when he told me that the prayers of the people had greatly sustained him, and that he had always sought from God, the source of knowledge and wisdom, that strength which he needed. This he often repeated to others, substantially. . . .

As you may be partly aware, the death of our beloved Lincoln changes all my plans. At first, when it appeared doubtful if Nicolay could be induced to go abroad, I accepted from Mr. Lincoln the promise of a lucrative place in San Francisco [Naval Officer and Surveyor of the Port], and had well-nigh concluded to go there when Nicolay concluded to go abroad. The President was then anxious for me to take the place near him [as personal secretary], but demurred at my sacrificing so much for the sake of serving him, and offered me the privilege of continuing my correspondence, which pay[s] as much as the salary of secretary.[50] This I declined, telling him that the sacrifice, such as it was, was mine, and I had a right to make it, a view of the case in which he finally acquiesced, with the understanding that he would make all of the perquisites of the place, living, &c. liberal as possible. I would have made myself poor for the sake of serving a man so dear to me, and for the sake of serving the Country by saving him for better and higher duties, as well as my influencing him unconsciously in some ways which would be useful to the cause of truth and religion. . . .

Mrs. Lincoln still remains at the White House, more dead than alive, shattered and broken by the horrors of that dreadful night, as well as worn down by bodily sickness. She will remove to Illinois next week, however, she now thinks. . . .

17 MAY 1865 (14 JUNE)

The Lincoln Family

yet remain in Washington, but will leave for the West early next week. Mrs. Lincoln's health has been comparatively restored, and nearly all of the preparations for departure have been made. No President ever received so many tokens of good will from the people as did our late lamented Lincoln; and these gifts, packed for transportation, comprise more than two car loads of bulky boxes—a single set of dining ware being large enough to require three hogsheads in packing. This was a gift from a gentleman in Philadelphia, who had the ware made to order, the Lincoln initials being beautifully emblazoned thereon in a monogram. Beside this were gifts of paintings, photographs, statuary and other works of art and virtue—some of them very beautiful, and so numerous that Mrs. Lincoln intends to have a sort of museum attached to her future residence, so that all persons may see these gifts, under proper restrictions and regulations. . . .

The private papers of the late President have been sealed up by Robert Lincoln, the oldest son of the President, and he intends to publish them after a considerable lapse of time shall have passed—not before three or four years. Then he will merely spread before the world the letters of his father, arranged in some order, with brief annotations, leaving the material to future historians or biographers to arrange at their own convenience.[51] The correspondence which the President kept in his own hands was not large, comparatively speaking, the whole accumulation of four years being in a set of pigeon-holes, locked up in a case in his room, about three by five feet in dimensions. These pigeon-holes were lettered in his own hand, alphabetically, different compartments being allotted to a few such prominent men as McClellan, Grant, "Father Blair," Horace Greeley and Halleck. One pigeon-hole was lettered "Weed and Wood," being for Thurlow and Fernando of that name. Lincoln's name will never suffer from the publication of these letters, which are copied with his own hand, and the letters and answers filed away together; but the friends of a few men who now fill a large space in public esteem will have occasion to blush when they know some things concerning their favorites. . . .

The surviving children of Abraham Lincoln are Robert and Thomas, the first of which is about twenty-three years old, a graduate of Harvard College, and is a young man of modest and agreeable manners, quiet, and with a very good share of his father's sagacity and kindness. The youngest son is a little more than eleven years old, and was nicknamed "Tad" by his father when a small boy, which nickname was an abbreviation of "tadpole," the youngster reminding his father of that creature in his short, dumpy shape. The President was passionately attached to his boys, and seldom went anywhere without "Tad," of whom he told me an amusing anecdote on the last election day. About a year before a live turkey had been brought home for the Christmas dinner, but "Tad" interceded in behalf of its life, and carried the case up to the Executive Chamber, securing a stay of proceedings until his father could be heard from. The argument was that the turkey had as good a right to live as any body else, and his plea was admitted and the turkey's life spared. The soldiers on duty about the house made a pet of the bird, and on last election day the boy came tearing up into his father's room to call his attention to the fact that the soldiers were

voting. Noticing the turkey among them, the President asked
"Tad" if the turkey was voting, too; to which the boy promptly
responded—"Oh, no; he isn't of age yet!" The indulgent father
thought that reply was a great deal better than many of the so-
called Lincoln stories.

PERSONAL RECOLLECTIONS OF ABRAHAM LINCOLN

It is natural that friends should tenderly and frequently talk of the loved and lost, descanting upon their virtues, narrating the little incidents of a life ended, and dwelling with minute particularity upon traits of character which, under other circumstances, might have remained unnoted and be forgotten, but are invested now with a mournful interest which fixes them in the memory. This, and the general desire to know more of the man Abraham Lincoln, is the only excuse offered for the following simple sketch of some parts of the character of our beloved Chief Magistrate, now passed from earth.

All persons agree that the most marked characteristic of Mr. Lincoln's manners was his simplicity and artlessness; this immediately impressed itself upon the observation of those who met him for the first time, and each successive interview deepened the impression. People seemed delighted to find in the ruler of the nation freedom from pomposity and affectation, mingled with a certain simple dignity which never forsook him. Though oppressed with the weight of responsibility resting upon him as President of the United States, he shrank from assuming any of the honors, or even the titles, of the position. After years of intimate acquaintance with Mr. Lincoln the writer can not now recall a single instance in which he spoke of himself as President, or used that title for himself, except when acting in an official capacity. He always spoke of his position and office vaguely, as "this place," "here," or other modest phrase. Once, speaking of the room in the Capitol used by the Presidents of the United States during the close of a session of Congress, he said, "That room, you know, that they call"—dropping his voice and hesitating—"the President's room." To an intimate friend who addressed him always by his own proper title he said, "Now call me Lincoln, and I'll promise not to tell of the breach of etiquette—if you won't—and I shall have a resting-spell from 'Mister President.'"

With all his simplicity and unacquaintance with courtly manners, his native dignity never forsook him in the presence of critical or polished strangers; but mixed with his angularities and *bonhomie* was something which spoke the fine fibre of the man; and, while his sovereign disregard of courtly conventionalities was somewhat ludicrous, his native sweetness and straightforwardness of manner served to disarm criticism and impress the visitor that he was before a man pure, self-poised, collected, and strong in unconscious strength. Of him an accomplished foreigner, whose knowledge of the courts was more perfect than that of the English language, said, "He seems to me one grand *gentilhomme* in disguise."

In his eagerness to acquire knowledge of common things he sometimes surprised his distinguished visitors by inquiries about matters that they were supposed to be acquainted with, and those who came to scrutinize went away with a vague sense of having been unconsciously pumped by the man whom they expected to pump. One Sunday evening last winter, while sitting alone with the President, the cards of Professor Agassiz and a friend were sent in. The President had never met Agassiz at that time, I believe, and said, "I would like to talk with that man; he is a good man, I do believe;

don't you think so?" But one answer could be returned to the
query, and soon after the visitors were shown in, the President
first whispering, "Now sit still and see what we can pick up
that's new." To my surprise, however, no questions were asked
about the Old Silurian, the Glacial Theory, or the Great
Snow-storm, but, introductions being over, the President said:
"I never knew how to properly pronounce your name; won't
you give me a little lesson at that, please?" Then he asked if it
were of French or Swiss derivation, to which the Professor
replied that it was partly of each. That led to a discussion of
different languages, the President speaking of several words in
different languages which had the same root as similar words
in our own tongue; then he illustrated that by one or two
anecdotes, one of which he borrowed from Hood's "Up the
Rhine."[1] But he soon returned to his gentle cross-examination
of Agassiz, and found out how the Professor studied, how he
composed, and how he delivered his lectures; how he found
different tastes in his audiences in different portions of the
country. When afterward asked why he put such questions to
his learned visitor he said, "Why, what we got from him isn't
printed in the books; the other things are."

At this interview, it may be remarked in passing, the President said that many years ago, when the custom of lecture-
going was more common than since, he was induced to try his
hand at composing a literary lecture—something which he
thought entirely out of his line. The subject, he said, was not
defined, but his purpose was to analyze inventions and discoveries—"to get at the bottom of things"—and to show when,
where, how, and why such things were invented or discovered;
and, so far as possible, to find where the first mention is made
of some of our common things. The Bible, he said, he found
to be the richest store-house for such knowledge; and he then

gave one or two illustrations, which were new to his hearers. The lecture was never finished, and was left among his loose papers at Springfield when he came to Washington.[2]

The simplicity of manner which shone out in all such interviews as that here noticed was marked in his total lack of consideration of what was due his exalted station. He had an almost morbid dread of what he called "a scene"—that is, a demonstration of applause such as always greeted his appearance in public. The first sign of a cheer sobered him; he appeared sad and oppressed, suspended conversation, and looked out into vacancy; and when it was over resumed the conversation just where it was interrupted, with an obvious feeling of relief. Of the relations of a senator to him he said, "I think that Senator ———'s manner is more cordial to me than before." The truth was that the senator had been looking for a sign of cordiality from his superior, but the President had reversed their relative positions. At another time, speaking of an early acquaintance, who was an applicant for an office which he thought him hardly qualified to fill, the President said, "Well, now, I never thought M[altby] had any more than average ability when we were young men together; really I did not"—a pause.—"But, then, I suppose he thought just the same about me; he had reason to, and—here I am!"

The simple habits of Mr. Lincoln were so well known that it is a subject for surprise that watchful and malignant treason did not sooner take that precious life which he seemed to hold so lightly. He had an almost morbid dislike for an escort, or guard, and daily exposed himself to the deadly aim of an assassin. One summer morning, passing by the White House at an early hour, I saw the President standing at the gateway, looking anxiously down the street; and, in reply to a salutation, he said, "Good-morning, good-morning! I am looking for a news-boy; when you get to that corner I wish you would start one up this way." There are American citizens who consider such things beneath the dignity of an official in high place.

In reply to the remonstrances of friends, who were afraid of his constant exposure to danger, he had but one answer: "If they kill me, the next man will be just as bad for them; and in a country like this, where our habits are simple, and must be, assassination is always possible, and will come if they are determined upon it." A cavalry guard was once placed at the gates of the White House for a while, and he said, privately, that he "worried until he got rid of it." While the President's family were at their summer-house, near Washington, he rode into town of a morning, or out at night, attended by a mounted escort; but if he returned to town for a while after dark, he rode in unguarded, and often alone, in his open carriage. On more than one occasion the writer has gone through the streets of Washington at a late hour of the night with the President, without escort, or even the company of a servant, walking all of the way, going and returning.

Considering the many open and secret threats to take his life, it is not surprising that Mr. Lincoln had many thoughts about his coming to a sudden and violent end. He once said that he felt the force of the expression, "To take one's life in his hand;" but that he would not like to face death suddenly. He said that he thought himself a great coward physically, and was sure that he should make a poor soldier, for, unless there was something in the excitement of a battle, he was sure that he would drop his gun and run at the first symptom of danger.[3] That was said sportively, and he added, "Moral cowardice is something which I think I never had." Shortly after the presidential election, in 1864, he related an incident which I will try to put upon paper here, as nearly as possible in his own words:

"It was just after my election in 1860, when the news had been coming in thick and fast all day, and there had been a great 'Hurrah, boys!' so that I was well tired out, and went home to rest, throwing myself down on a lounge in my chamber. Opposite where I lay was a bureau, with a swinging-glass upon it"—(and here he got up and placed furniture to illustrate the position)—"and, looking in that glass, I saw myself reflected, nearly at full length; but my face, I noticed, had *two* separate and distinct images, the tip of the nose of one being about three inches from the tip of the other. I was a little bothered, perhaps startled, and got up and looked in the glass, but the illusion vanished. On lying down again I saw it a second time—plainer, if possible, than before; and then I noticed that one of the faces was a little paler, say five shades, than the other. I got up and the thing melted away, and I went off and, in the excitement of the hour, forgot all about it— nearly, but not quite, for the thing would once in a while come up, and give me a little pang, as though something uncomfortable had happened. When I went home I told my wife about it, and a few days after I tried the experiment again, when [with a laugh], sure enough, the thing came again; but I never succeeded in bringing the ghost back after that, though I once tried very industriously to show it to my wife, who was worried about it somewhat. She thought it was 'a sign' that I was to be elected to a second term of office, and that the paleness of one of the faces was an omen that I should not see life through the last term."

The President, with his usual good sense, saw nothing in all this but an optical illusion; though the flavor of superstition which hangs about every man's composition made him wish that he had never seen it. But there are people who will now believe that this odd coincidence was "a warning."

If Mr. Lincoln's critics may be trusted, he had too much goodness of heart to make a good magistrate. Certain it is that his continually-widening charity for all, and softness of

heart, pardoned offenders and mitigated punishments when
the strict requirements of justice would have dealt more
severely with the criminal. It was a standing order of his office
that persons on matters involving the issue of life and death
should have immediate precedence. Nor was his kindness
confined to affairs of state; his servants, and all persons in his
personal service, were the objects of his peculiar care and
solicitude. They bore no burdens or hardships which he could
relieve them of; and if he carried this virtue to an extreme, and
carried labors which others should have borne, it was because
he thought he could not help it.

He was often waylaid by soldiers importunate to get their
back-pay, or a furlough, or a discharge; and if the case was not
too complicated, would attend to it then and there. Going out
of the main-door of the White House one morning, he met
an old lady who was pulling vigorously at the door-bell, and
asked her what she wanted. She said that she wanted to see
"Abraham the Second." The President, amused, asked who
Abraham the First might be, if there was a second? The old
lady replied, "Why, Lor' bless you! we read about the first
Abraham in the Bible, and Abraham the Second is our President." She was told that the President was not in his office
then, and when she asked where he was, she was told, "Here
he is!" Nearly petrified with surprise, the old lady managed to
tell her errand, and was told to come next morning at nine
o'clock, when she was received and kindly cared for by the
President. At another time, hearing of a young man who had
determined to enter the navy as a landsman, after three years
of service in the army, he said to the writer, "Now do you go
over to the Navy Department and mouse out what he is fit
for, and he shall have it, if it's to be had, for that's the kind of
men I like to hear of." The place was duly "moused out," with
the assistance of the kind-hearted Assistant-Secretary of the

Navy [Gustavus V. Fox]; and the young officer, who may read these lines on his solitary post off the mouth of the Yazoo River, was appointed upon the recommendation of the President of the United States. Of an application for office by an old friend, not fit for the place he sought, he said, "I had rather resign my place and go away from here than refuse him, if I consulted only my personal feelings; but refuse him I must." And he did.

This same gentleness, mixed with firmness, characterized all of Mr. Lincoln's dealings with public men. Often bitterly assailed and abused, he never appeared to recognize the fact that he had political enemies; and if his attention was called to unkind speeches or remarks, he would turn the conversation of his indignant friends by a judicious story, or the remark, "I guess we won't talk about that now." He has himself put it on record that he never read attacks upon himself,[4] and if they were brought persistently before him he had some ready excuse for their authors. Of a virulent personal attack upon his official conduct he mildly said that it was ill-timed; and of one of his most bitter political enemies [Henry Winter Davis] he said: "I've been told that insanity is hereditary in his family, and I think we will admit the plea in his case." It was noticeable that Mr. Lincoln's keenest critics and bitter opponents studiously avoided his presence; it seemed as though no man could be familiar with his homely, heart-lighted features, his single-hearted directness and manly kindliness, and remain long an enemy, or be any thing but his friend. It was this warm frankness of Mr. Lincoln's manner that made a hard-headed old "hunker" once leave the hustings where Lincoln was speaking,[5] in 1856, saying, "I won't hear him, for I don't like a man that makes me believe in him in spite of myself."

"Honest Old Abe" has passed into the language of our time and country as a synonym for all that is just and honest in man. Yet thousands of instances, unknown to the world, might be added to those already told of Mr. Lincoln's great and crowning virtue. He disliked innuendoes, concealments, and subterfuges; and no sort of approach at official "jobbing" ever had any encouragement from him. With him the question was not, "Is it convenient? Is it expedient?" but, "Is it right?" He steadily discountenanced all practices of government officers using any part of the public funds for temporary purposes; and he loved to tell of his own experience when he was saved from embarrassment by his rigid adherence to a good rule. He had been postmaster at [New] Salem, Illinois, during Jackson's administration, William T. Barry being then Postmaster-General,[6] and resigning his office, removed to Springfield, having sent a statement of account to the Department at Washington. No notice was taken of his account, which showed a balance due the Government of over one hundred and fifty dollars, until three or four years after, when, Amos Kendall being Postmaster-General,[7] he was presented with a draft for the amount due. Some of Mr. Lincoln's friends, who knew that he was in straitened circumstances then, as he had always been, heard of the draft and offered to help him out with a loan; but he told them not to worry, and producing from his trunk an old pocket, tied up and marked, counted out, in six-pences, shillings, and quarters, the exact sum required of him, in the identical coin received by him while in office years before.[8]

The honesty of Mr. Lincoln appeared to spring from religious convictions; and it was his habit, when conversing of things which most intimately concerned himself, to say that, however he might be misapprehended by men who did not appear to know him, he was glad to know that no thought or intent of his escaped the observation of that Judge by whose final decree he expected to stand or fall in this world and the next. It seemed as though this was his surest refuge at times when he was most misunderstood or misrepresented. There was something touching in his childlike and simple reliance upon Divine aid, especially when in such extremities as he sometimes fell into; then, though prayer and reading of the Scriptures was his constant habit, he more earnestly than ever sought that strength which is promised when mortal help faileth. His address upon the occasion of his re-inauguration has been said to be as truly a religious document as a state-paper; and his acknowledgment of God and His providence and rule are interwoven through all of his later speeches, letters, and messages. Once he said: "I have been driven many times upon my knees by the overwhelming conviction that I had nowhere else to go. My own wisdom and that of all about me seemed insufficient for that day."

Just after the last presidential election he said: "Being only mortal, after all, I should have been a little mortified if I had been beaten in this canvass before the people; but that sting would have been more than compensated by the thought that the people had notified me that all my official responsibilities were soon to be lifted off my back." In reply to the remark that he might remember that in all these cares he was daily remembered by those who prayed, not to be heard of men, as no man had ever before been remembered, he caught at the homely phrase and said: "Yes, I like that phrase, 'not to be heard of men,' and guess it's generally true, as you say; at least I have been told so, and I have been a good deal helped by just that thought." Then he solemnly and slowly added: "I should be the most presumptuous block-head upon this footstool if I for one day thought that I could discharge the duties which have come upon me since I came into this place without the aid and enlightenment of One who is wiser and stronger than all others."

At another time he said, cheerfully, "I am very sure that if I do not go away from here a wiser man, I shall go away a better man, for having learned here what a very poor sort of a man I am." Afterward, referring to what he called a change of heart, he said that he did not remember any precise time when he passed through any special change of purpose or of heart; but he would say that his own election to office, and the crisis immediately following, influentially determined him in what he called "a process of crystallization," then going on in his mind. Reticent as he was, and shy of discoursing much on his own mental exercises, these few utterances now have a value with those who knew him which his dying words would scarcely have possessed.

No man but Mr. Lincoln ever knew how great was the load of care which he bore, nor the amount of mental labor which he daily accomplished. With the usual perplexities of the office—greatly increased by the unusual multiplication of places in his gift—he carried the burdens of the civil war, which he always called "This great trouble." Though the intellectual man had greatly grown meantime, few persons would recognize the hearty, blithesome, genial, and wiry Abraham Lincoln of earlier days in the sixteenth President of the United States, with his stooping figure, dull eyes, care-worn face, and languid frame. The old, clear laugh never came back; the even temper was sometimes disturbed; and his natural charity for all was often turned into an unwonted suspicion of the motives of men, whose selfishness cost him so much wear of mind.[9] Once he said, "Sitting here, where all the avenues to public patronage seem to come together in a knot, it does seem to me that our people are fast approaching the point where it can be said that seven-eighths of them were trying to find how to live at the expense of the other eighth."

It was this incessant demand upon his time, by men who

sought place or endeavored to shape his policy, that broke down his courage and his temper, as well as exhausted his strength. Speaking of the "great flood-gates" which his doors daily opened upon him, he said, "I suppose I ought not to blame the aggregate, for each abstract man or woman thinks his or her case a peculiar one, and must be attended to, though all others be left out; but I can see this thing growing every day." And at another time, speaking of the exhaustive demands upon him, which left him in no condition for more important duties, he said, "I sometimes fancy that every one of the numerous grist ground through here daily, from a Senator seeking a war with France down to a poor woman after a place in the Treasury Department, darted at me with thumb and finger, picked out their especial piece of my vitality, and carried it off. When I get through with such a day's work there is only one word which can express my condition, and that is—*flabbiness.*" There are some public men who can now remember, with self-reproaches, having increased with long evening debates that reducing "flabbiness" of the much-enduring President.

Mr. Lincoln visited the Army of the Potomac in the spring of 1863, and, free from the annoyances of office, was considerably refreshed and rested; but even there the mental anxieties which never forsook him seemed to cast him down, at times, with a great weight. We left Washington late in the afternoon, and a snowstorm soon after coming on, the steamer was anchored for the night off Indian Head, on the Maryland shore of the Potomac. The President left the little knot in the cabin, and sitting alone in a corner, seemed absorbed in the saddest reflections for a time; then, beckoning a companion to him, said, "What will you wager that half our iron-clads are at the bottom of Charleston Harbor?" This being the first intimation which the other had had of Dupont's attack,[10] which was then begun, hesitated to reply, when the President added,

"The people will expect big things when they hear of this; but it is too late—*too late!*"

During that little voyage the captain of the steamer, a frank, modest old sailor, was so much affected by the care-worn appearance of the President, that he came to the writer and confessed that he had received the same impression of the Chief Magistrate that many had; hearing of his "little stories" and his humor, he had supposed him to have no cares or sadness; but a sight of that anxious and sad face had undeceived him, and he wanted to tell the President how much he had unintentionally wronged him, feeling that he had committed upon him a personal wrong. The captain was duly introduced to the President, who talked with him privately for a space, being touched as well as amused at what he called "Captain M——'s freeing his mind."

The following week, spent in riding about and seeing the army, appeared to revive Mr. Lincoln's spirits and to rest his body. A friend present observed as much to him, and he replied, "Well, yes, I do feel some better, I think; but, some-how, it don't appear to touch the tired spot, which can't be got at." And that, by-the-way, reminded him of a little story of his having once used that word, spot, a great many times in the course of a speech in Congress, years ago, so that some of his fellow-members called him "spot Lincoln," but he believed that the nickname did not stick.[11] Another reminiscence of his early life, which he recalled during the trip, was one con-cerning his experience in rail-splitting. We were driving through an open clearing, where the Virginia forest had been felled by the soldiers, when Mr. Lincoln observed, looking at the stumps, "That's a good job of felling; they have got some good axemen in this army, I see." The conversation turning upon his knowledge of rail-splitting, he said, "Now let me tell you about that. I am not a bit anxious about my reputation in that line of business; but if there is any thing in this world that I am a judge of, it is of good felling of timber, but I don't remember having worked by myself at splitting rails for one whole day in my life." Upon surprise being expressed that his national reputation as a rail-splitter should have so slight a foundation, he said, "I recollect that, some time during the canvass for the office I now hold, there was a great mass meeting, where I was present, and with a great flourish several rails were brought into the meeting, and being informed where they came from, I was asked to identify them, which I did, with some qualms of conscience, having helped my father to split rails, as at other odd jobs. I said if there were any rails which I had split, I shouldn't wonder if those were the rails."[12] Those who may be disappointed to learn of Mr. Lincoln's limited experience in splitting rails, may be relieved to know that he was evidently proud of his knowledge of the art of cutting timber, and explained minutely how a good job differed from a poor one, giving illustrations from the ugly stumps on either side.

An amusing yet touching instance of the President's preoccupation of mind occurred at one of his levees, when he was shaking hands with a host of visitors, passing him in a continuous stream. An intimate acquaintance received the usual conventional hand-shake and salutation; but, perceiving that he was not recognized, kept his ground, instead of moving on, and spoke again; when the President, roused by a dim consciousness that something unusual had happened, perceived who stood before him, and seizing his friend's hand, shook it again heartily, saying, "How do you do? How do you do? Excuse me for not noticing you at first; the fact is, I was thinking of a man down South." He afterward privately acknowledged that the "man down South" was Sherman, then on his march to the sea.

Mr. Lincoln had not a hopeful temperament, and, though

he looked at the bright side of things, was always prepared for disaster and defeat.[13] With his wonderful faculty for discerning results he often saw success where others saw disaster, but oftener perceived a failure when others were elated with victory, or were temporarily deceived by appearances. Of a great cavalry raid, which filled the newspapers with glowing exultation, but failed to cut the communications which it had been designed to destroy, he briefly said: "That was good circus-riding; it will do to fill a column in the newspapers; but I don't see that it has brought any thing else to pass." He often said that the worst feature about newspapers was that they were so sure to be "ahead of the hounds," outrunning events, and exciting expectations which were sure to be disappointed. One of the worst effects of a victory, he said, was to lead people to expect that the war was about over in consequence of it; but he was never weary of commending the patience of the American people, which he thought something matchless and touching. I have seen him shed tears when speaking of the cheerful sacrifice of the light and strength of so many happy homes throughout the land. His own patience was marvelous; and never crushed at defeat or unduly excited by success, his demeanor under both was an example for all men. Once he said the keenest blow of all war was at an early stage, when the disaster of Ball's Bluff and the death of his beloved Baker smote upon him like a whirlwind from a desert.[14]

It is generally agreed that Mr. Lincoln's slowness was a prominent trait of his character; but it is too early, perhaps, to say how much of our safety and success we owe to his slowness. It may be said, however, that he is to-day admired and beloved as much for what he did not do as for what he did. He was well aware of the popular opinion concerning his slowness, but was only sorry that such a quality of mind should sometimes be coupled with weakness and vacillation. Such an accusation he thought to be unjust. Acknowledging that he was slow in arriving at conclusions, he said that he could not help that; but he believed that when he did arrive at conclusions they were clear and "stuck by." He was a profound believer in his own fixity of purpose, and took pride in saying that his long deliberations made it possible for him to stand by his own acts when they were once resolved upon. It would have been a relief to the country at one time in our history if this trait of the President's character had been better understood. There was no time, probably, during the last administration, when any of the so-called radical measures were in any danger of being qualified or recalled. The simple explanation of the doubt which often hung over his purposes may be found in the fact that it was a habit of his mind to put forward all of the objections of other people and of his own to any given proposition, to see what arguments or counter-statements could be brought against them. While his own mind might be perfectly clear upon the subject, it gave him real pleasure to state objections for others to combat or attempt to set aside.

His practice of being controlled by events is well known. He often said that it was wise to wait for the developments of Providence; and the Scriptural phrase that "the stars in their courses fought against Sisera" to him had a depth of meaning. Then, too, he liked to feel that he was the attorney of the people, not their ruler; and I believe that this idea was generally uppermost in his mind. Speaking of the probability of his second nomination, about two years ago, he said: "If the people think that I have managed their case for them well enough to trust me to carry up to the next term, I am sure that I shall be glad to take it."

He liked to provide for his friends, who were often remembered gratefully for services given him in his early struggles in life. Sometimes he would "break the slate," as he called it, of those who were making up a list of appointments, that he might insert the name of some old acquaintance who had befriended him in days when friends were few. He was not deceived by outside appearances, but took the measure of those he met, and few men were worth any more or any less than the value which Abraham Lincoln set upon them.

Upon being told that a gentleman upon whom he was about to confer a valuable appointment had been bitterly opposed to his renomination, he said: "I suppose that Judge ———, having been disappointed before, did behave pretty ugly; but that wouldn't make him any less fit for this place, and I have a Scriptural authority for appointing him. You recollect that while the Lord on Mount Sinai was getting out a commission for Aaron, that same Aaron was at the foot of the mountain making a false god, a golden calf, for the people to worship; yet Aaron got his commission, you know." At another time, when remonstrated with upon the appointment to place of one of his former opponents, he said: "Nobody will deny that he is a first-rate man for the place, and I am bound to see that his opposition to me personally shall not interfere with my giving the people a good officer."

The world will never hear the last of the "little stories" with which the President garnished or illustrated his conversation and his early stump speeches. He said, however, that as near as he could reckon, about one-sixth of those which were credited to him were old acquaintances; all of the rest were the productions of other and better story-tellers than himself. Said he: "I do generally remember a good story when I hear it, but I never did invent any thing original; I am only a retail dealer." His anecdotes were seldom told for the sake of the telling, but because they fitted in just where they came, and shed a light on the argument that nothing else could. He was not witty, but brimful of humor; and though he was quick to appreciate a good pun, I never knew of his making but one, which was on the Christian name of a friend, to whom he said: "You have yet to be elected to the place I hold; but Noah's *reign* was before Abraham." He thought that the chief characteristic of American humor was its grotesqueness and extravagance; and the story of the man who was so tall that he was "laid out" in a rope-walk, the soprano voice so high that it had to be climbed over by a ladder, and the Dutchman's expression of "somebody tying his dog loose," all made a permanent lodgment in his mind.

His accuracy and memory were wonderful, and one illustration of the former quality may be given in the remarkable correspondence between the figures of the result of the last presidential election and the actual sum total. The President's figures, collected hastily, and partially based upon his own estimates, made up only four weeks after the election, have been found to be only one hundred and twenty-nine less in their grand total than that made up by Mr. McPherson, the Clerk of the House of Representatives, who has compiled a table from the returns furnished him from the official records of all the State capitals in the loyal States.

Latterly Mr. Lincoln's reading was with the humorous writers. He liked to repeat from memory whole chapters from these books; and on such occasions he always preserved his own gravity though his auditors might be convulsed with laughter. He said that he had a dread of people who could not appreciate the fun of such things; and he once instanced a member of his own Cabinet [probably Salmon P. Chase], of whom he quoted the saying of Sydney Smith, "that it required a surgical operation to get a joke into his head." The light trifles spoken of diverted his mind, or, as he said of his theatre-going, gave him refuge from himself and his weariness. But he also was a lover of many philosophical books, and particularly liked Butler's Analogy of Religion, Stuart Mill on Liberty, and he always hoped to get at President Edwards on the Will.[15] These ponderous writers found a queer companionship in the chronicler of the Mackerel Brigade, Parson Nasby, and Private Miles O'Reilly.[16] The Bible was a very familiar study with the President, whole chapters of Isaiah, the New Testament, and the Psalms being fixed in his memory, and he would sometimes correct a misquotation of Scripture, giving generally the chapter and verse where it could be found. He liked the Old Testament best, and dwelt on the simple beauty of the historical books. Once, speaking of his own age and strength, he quoted with admiration that passage, "His eye was not dim, nor his natural force abated." I do not know that he thought then how, like that Moses of old, he was to stand on Pisgah and see a peaceful land which he was not to enter.

Of the poets the President appeared to prefer Hood and Holmes,[17] the mixture and pathos in their writings being attractive to him beyond any thing else which he read. Of the former author he liked best the last part of "Miss Kilmansegg and her Golden [Precious] Leg," "Faithless Sally Brown," and one or two others not generally so popular as those which are called Hood's best poems. Holmes's "September Gale," "Last Leaf," "Chambered Nautilus," and "Ballad of an Oysterman" were among his very few favorite poems. Longfellow's "Psalm of Life" and "Birds of Killingworth" were the only productions of that author he ever mentioned with praise, the latter of which he picked up somewhere in a newspaper, cut out, and carried in his vest pocket until it was committed to memory. James Russell Lowell he only knew as "Hosea Bigelow," every one of whose effusions he knew. He sometimes repeated, word for word, the whole of "John P. Robinson, he," giving the unceasing refrain with great unction and enjoyment. He once said that originality and daring impudence were sublimed in this stanza of Lowell's:

> "Ef you take a sword and dror it,
>   An' stick a feller creetur thru,
> Gov'ment hain't to answer for it,
>   God'll send the bill to you."

Mr. Lincoln's love of music was something passionate, but his tastes were simple and uncultivated, his choice being old airs, songs, and ballads, among which the plaintive Scotch songs were best liked. "Annie Laurie," "Mary of Argyle," and especially "Auld Robin Gray," never lost their charm for him; and all songs which had for their theme the rapid flight of time, decay, the recollections of early days, were sure to make a deep impression. The song which he liked best, above all others, was one called "Twenty Years Ago"—a simple air, the words to which are supposed to be uttered by a man who revisits the play-ground of his youth.[18] He greatly desired to find music for his favorite poem, "Oh, why should the spirit of mortal be proud?" and said once, when told that the newspapers had credited him with the authorship of the piece, "I should not care much for the reputation of having written that, but would be glad if I could compose music as fit to convey the sentiment as the words now do."[19]

He wrote slowly, and with the greatest deliberation, and liked to take his time; yet some of his dispatches, written without any corrections, are models of compactness and finish. His private correspondence was extensive, and he preferred writing his letters with his own hand, making copies himself frequently, and filing every thing away in a set of pigeon-holes in his office. When asked why he did not have a letter-book and copying-press, he said, "A letter-book might be easily carried off, but that stock of filed letters would be a back-load." He conscientiously attended to his enormous correspondence, and read every thing that appeared to demand his own attention. He said that he read with great regularity the letters of an old friend who lived on the Pacific coast until he received a letter of *seventy pages* of letter paper, when he broke down, and never read another.[20]

People were sometimes disappointed because he appeared before them with a written speech. The best explanation of that habit of his was his remark to a friend who noticed a roll of manuscript in the hand of the President as he came into the parlor while waiting for the serenade which was given him on the night following his re-election.[21] Said he: "I know what you are thinking about; but there's no clap-trap about me, and I am free to say that in the excitement of the moment I am sure to say something which I am sorry for when I see it in print; so I have it here in black and white, and there are no mistakes made. People attach too much importance to what I say now." Upon another occasion, hearing that I was in the parlor, he sent for me to come up into the library, where I found him writing on a piece of common stiff box-board with a pencil. Said he, after he had finished, "Here is one speech of mine which has never been printed, and I think it worth printing. Just see what you think." He then read the following, which is copied *verbatim* from the familiar handwriting before me:

"On Thursday of last week two ladies from Tennessee came before the President, asking the release of their husbands, held as prisoners of war at Johnson's Island. They were put off until Friday, when they came again, and were again put off until Saturday. At each of the interviews one of the ladies urged that her husband was a religious man. On Saturday, when the President ordered the release of the prisoners, he said to this lady: 'You say your husband is a religious man; tell him when you meet him that I say I am not much of a judge of religion, but that, in my opinion, the religion that sets men to rebel and fight against their Government because, as they think, that Government does not sufficiently help *some* men to eat their bread in the sweat of *other* men's faces, is not the sort of religion upon which people can get to heaven."

To this the President signed his name at my request, by way of joke, and added for a caption, "The President's Last, Shortest, and Best Speech," under which title it was duly published in one of the Washington newspapers.[22] His Message to the last session of Congress was first written upon the same sort of white pasteboard above referred to, its stiffness enabling him to lay it on his knee as he sat easily in his armchair, writing and erasing as he thought and wrought out his idea.

The already extended limits of this article will not permit any thing more than a mention of many of the traits of Mr. Lincoln's peculiar character, many of which are already widely known by his published writings and speeches, and by the numerous anecdotes which have been narrated by others who have been ready to meet the general desire to know more of the man whose life was so dear to the people. His thoughtfulness for those who bore the brunt of the battles, his harmonious family relations, his absorbing love for his children, his anxiety for the well-being and conduct of the emancipated colored people, his unwavering faith in the hastening doom of human slavery, his affectionate regard for "the simple people," his patience, his endurance, his mental sufferings, and what he did for the Nation and for Humanity and Liberty—these all must be left to the systematic and enduring labors of the historian. Though he is dead, his immortal virtues are the rich possession of the nation; his fame shall grow with our young Republic; and as years roll on brighter lustre will adorn the name of Abraham Lincoln.

NOTES

INTRODUCTION

1. By far the best source on Brooks is Wayne C. Temple's 1956 doc-
   toral dissertation, "Lincoln's 'Castine': Noah Brooks," which was
   published in several installments of the *Lincoln Herald* between
   1970 and 1972. For this introduction, I have relied heavily on Dr.
   Temple's work, which characteristically rests on meticulous
   research. A biographer of Mary Todd Lincoln believed that "Lincoln really loved Noah Brooks." Ruth Painter Randall, quoted by
   Herbert Mitgang in the introduction to Mitgang's edition of
   Brooks's volume, *Washington, D.C., in Lincoln's Time* (Chicago:
   Quadrangle Books, 1971), 10. Lincoln was a surrogate father to
   many young men. Michael Burlingame, *The Inner World of Abraham Lincoln* (Urbana: University of Illinois Press, 1994), 73–91.
2. Washington correspondence, 16 April 1865 (17 May).
3. Brooks, *Abraham Lincoln and the Downfall of American Slavery*
   (New York: G. P. Putnam's Sons, 1894), vi. Judging from his personal letters reproduced in this volume, the claim is exaggerated.
4. Washington correspondence, 16 April 1865 (17 May).
5. Mary Todd Lincoln to Noah Brooks, Chicago, 18 December 1865,
   in Justin G. Turner and Linda Levitt Turner, eds., *Mary Todd Lincoln: Her Life and Letters* (New York: Knopf, 1972), 311.
6. Mary Todd Lincoln to Noah Brooks, Chicago, 11 May 1866, ibid.,
   363.
7. James Armstrong Reed, "The Later Life and Religious Sentiments
   of Abraham Lincoln," *Scribner's Monthly Magazine*, July 1873,

339–40. Reed was the pastor of the First Presbyterian Church in Springfield, Illinois.

8. John Conness to Charles Hamlin, n.p., 21 February 1896, in Charles Eugene Hamlin, *The Life and Times of Hannibal Hamlin* (1899; Port Washington, N.Y.: Kennikat Press, 1971), 485.

9. Robert J. Cole, quoting his father, Cornelius Cole, in Noah Brooks, *Abraham Lincoln by Friend and Foe*, ed. Robert J. Cole (New York: Gold Medal Library, 1922), 8–9. Cornelius Cole saw much of Lincoln between 1863 and 1865. See Cole, "Lincoln's Gettysburg Address," *Wesleyan Alumnus* 6, no. 6 (July 1922): 9. Cole had not always admired Brooks; in 1866 he maneuvered to have the journalist fired from his post in the San Francisco custom house. Temple, "Lincoln's 'Castine,'" *Lincoln Herald* 73, no. 4 (winter 1971), 212.

10. San Francisco correspondence, 31 July 1865 (2 August).

11. Anson G. Henry to his wife, Washington, 13 March 1865, in Harry E. Pratt, ed., *Concerning Mr. Lincoln: In Which Abraham Lincoln Is Pictured as He Appeared to Letter Writers of His Time* (Springfield, Ill.: Abraham Lincoln Association, 1944), 117.

12. Charles H. Philbrick to Ozias M. Hatch, Washington, 4 April 1865, Hatch Papers, Illinois State Historical Library, Springfield.

13. Washington correspondence, 7 November 1863 (4 December). Cf. Brooks, *Lincoln and the Downfall of American Slavery*, 421–22.

14. Brooks to Edward McPherson, San Francisco, 20 February 1866, McPherson Papers, Library of Congress.

15. Cf. Brooks's account written in May 1865: "As you may be partly aware, the death of our beloved Lincoln changes all my plans. At first, when it appeared doubtful if Nicolay could be induced to go abroad, I accepted from Mr. Lincoln the promise of a lucrative place in San Francisco." Brooks to Isaac P. Langworthy, Washington, 10 May 1865, in Hugh McLellan, ed., *The Character and Religion of President Lincoln: A Letter of Noah Brooks* (Champlain, N.Y.: Privately printed, 1919), 9.

16. Don E. Fehrenbacher and Virginia Fehrenbacher, eds., *Recollected Words of Abraham Lincoln* (Stanford: Stanford University Press, 1996), 41, 517–18. Actually, Brooks does not appear at all in the Civil War diaries and letters of John Hay. The Fehrenbachers were mis-

led by Tyler Dennett's edition of Hay's diary and letters, *Lincoln and the Civil War in the Diaries and Letters of John Hay* (New York: Dodd, Mead, 1939), whose index indicates that Noah Brooks was mentioned in Hay's diary on 21 and 23 June 1864. In fact, the Brooks mentioned by Hay was Thomas B. Brooks, aide-de-camp to General Quincy A. Gillmore.

17. Howard K. Beale, ed., *The Diary of Edward Bates, 1859–1866* (Washington, D.C.: U.S. Government Printing Office, 1933), 287 (entry for 4 April 1863).

18. Ben: Perley Poore, "Reminiscences of the Great Northern Uprising," *The Youth's Companion*, 26 July 1883, 301.

19. *Philadelphia Sunday Dispatch*, 25 March 1865.

20. Washington correspondence, 14 October 1863 (7 November).

21. Quoted in Temple, "Lincoln's 'Castine,'" *Lincoln Herald* 72, no. 4 (winter 1970): 178–81.

22. Undated interview with Brooks, New York, Ida M. Tarbell Papers, Allegheny College.

23. Brooks, "Personal Reminiscences of Lincoln," *Scribner's Monthly Magazine* 15 (March 1878): 673.

24. Interview with Brooks, 13 December 1896, *Los Angeles Times*, 14 December 1896.

25. Washington correspondence, 21 January 1865 (20 February).

26. Brooks, "Personal Reminiscences of Lincoln," *Scribner's Monthly Magazine* 15 (March 1878): 678.

27. *St. Nicholas: An Illustrated Magazine for Young Folks* 10, no. 1 (November 1882): 57–65; *Abraham Lincoln: A Biography for Young People* (New York: G. P. Putnam's Sons, 1888) was reissued in 1894 under a new title, *Abraham Lincoln and the Downfall of American Slavery*.

28. Brooks to George Witherle, Washington, 10 December 1864, Hatch Collection, microfilm copy courtesy of Dr. Wayne C. Temple.

29. *Washington in Lincoln's Time* (New York: Century, 1895). I have used Herbert Mitgang's edition, which Mitgang retitled *Washington, D.C., in Lincoln's Time* (Chicago: Quadrangle Books, 1971). Occasionally in his book, Brooks copied passages virtually verbatim from his dispatches.

30. Philip J. Staudenraus, ed., *Mr. Lincoln's Washington: Selections from*

the Writings of Noah Brooks, Civil War Correspondent (New York: Thomas Yoseloff, 1967).

31. "Few books concerning Lincoln in Washington fail to quote this man [Brooks]. Only his 'Castine' articles to the *Union* . . . are little known." Milton H. Shutes, *Lincoln and California* (Stanford: Stanford University Press, 1943), 211. Carl Sandburg was an exception to this rule; he read all of Brooks's dispatches.

32. Hay to Nicolay, Colorado Springs, 14 July 1888, Hay Papers, Brown University.

33. Brooks to Isaac P. Langworthy, Washington, 10 May 1865, in McLellan, ed., *Character and Religion of President Lincoln*, 8.

34. Wayne C. Temple, *Abraham Lincoln: From Skeptic to Prophet* (Mahomet, Ill.: Mayhaven Publishing, 1995), 313.

CHAPTER ONE: DISPATCHES AND LETTERS, 1862–1863

1. Phineas D. Gurley (1816–68), minister at the New York Avenue Presbyterian Church. See David Rankin Barbee, "President Lincoln and Doctor Gurley," *Abraham Lincoln Quarterly* 5, no. 1 (March 1948): 3–24.

2. William Wallace Lincoln died on 20 February 1862.

3. Cf. Brooks's 1895 recollection: "Naturally, my first thought, on arriving in Washington in [December] 1862, was to see how far the President resembled the Lincoln of Illinois before the war. The change in his personal appearance was marked and sorrowful. On the Sunday after my arrival in Washington I took a long look at him from the gallery of the New York Avenue Presbyterian Church. His eyes were almost deathly in their gloomy depths, and on his visage was an air of profound sadness. His face was colorless and drawn, and newly grown whiskers added to the agedness of his appearance. When I had seen him last in Illinois, his face, although always sallow, wore a tinge of rosiness in the cheeks, but now it was pale and colorless.

"Hearing from a friend that I was in the city, he immediately sent word that he would like to see me, 'for old times' sake'; and nothing could have been more gratifying than the cordiality and bonhomie of his greeting when I called at the White House. 'Do you suppose I ever forget an old acquaintance? I reckon not,' he

said, when we met." Brooks, *Washington, D.C., in Lincoln's Time*, ed.
Herbert Mitgang (Chicago: Quadrangle Books, 1971), 15.

4. In November Democrats had won substantial victories in New
   York, New Jersey, Illinois, and Wisconsin. Lincoln's analysis of the
   election can be found in his letter to Carl Schurz, Washington, 24
   November 1862, in Roy P. Basler et al., eds., *Collected Works of Abra-
   ham Lincoln*, 8 vols. plus index (New Brunswick, N.J.: Rutgers
   University Press, 1953–55), 5:509–10.

5. William Henry Seward (1801–72) of New York was Lincoln's secretary of state; Salmon P. Chase (1808–73) of Ohio was Lincoln's
   secretary of the treasury.

6. Gideon Welles (1802–78) of Connecticut was Lincoln's secretary of
   the navy; Montgomery Blair (1813–83) of Maryland was Lincoln's
   postmaster general. Welles's three-year-old son Hubert had died of
   diphtheria on 18 November, and Montgomery Blair's daughter
   Maria (b. 1854) had died in September.

7. Caleb Blood Smith (1808–64) of Indiana officially resigned his post
   as secretary of the interior on 8 January 1863.

8. William Kellogg (1814–72) represented an Illinois district in the
   U.S. House of Representatives (1857–63).

9. General George B. McClellan (1826–85) had commanded the
   Army of the Potomac (1861–62). On the Virginia Peninsula Gen-
   eral McClellan had waged an unsuccessful campaign against
   Richmond (March–July 1862).

10. Ward Hill Lamon (1828–93), a good friend of Lincoln's from Illi-
    nois, was marshal of the District of Columbia.

11. Cf. the unidentified reminiscence in the *Rochester Daily Democrat*,
    19 April 1865, p. 1, col. 1: "The writer of this once had an opportu-
    nity of seeing this [Lincoln's] amiability tested. It was New Year's
    Day, in 1862; and we arrived at the reception late. Thousands on
    thousands of eager men and women, high and low, rich and poor,
    had crowded in and jammed through the narrow 'blue room,' and
    shaken the hand of the President. He had been subjected to the
    ordeal something like three hours, and still he stood there, waiting
    patiently for the thousand more. There seemed to be a break in the
    thronging multitude when we approached, and seeing that he
    appeared to be quite exhausted, we asked him, after some prelimi-

nary words, 'Mr. President; you seem very tired; do you find it a relief or a burden, to leave your other duties and come here to shake hands with everybody?' 'Oh—it's hard work,' answered he, 'but it is a relief, every way; *for here nobody asks me for what I cannot give.*' And he gave his hand to the next comer."

12. In 1895 Brooks described the New Year's receptions thus: "I made the rounds of the official residences in company with a California representative in Congress, and we were struck with the artificiality of the show. One or two of the members of the President's Cabinet did not receive calls on New Year's, but there was much elegance and profuseness of hospitality at the house of the Secretary of War, and Mr. Stanton's face wore no sign of the worry that must have distressed him on that anxious, unfestive day.

"Not so with the President. He received the diplomatic corps at eleven o'clock in the forenoon, and when these shining officials had duly congratulated him and had been bowed out, the officers of the Army and Navy who happened to be in town were received in the order of their rank. At twelve, noon, the gates of the White House grounds were flung wide open, and the sovereign people were admitted to the mansion in installments. I had gone to the house earlier, and now enjoyed the privilege of contrasting the decorous quiet of the receptions at the residences of lesser functionaries with the wild, tumultuous rush into the White House. Sometimes the pressure and the disorder were almost appalling; and it required no little engineering to steer the throng, after it had met and engaged the President, out of the great window from which a temporary bridge had been constructed for an exit.

"In the midst of this turmoil the good President stood serene and even smiling. But as I watched his face, I could see that he often looked over the heads of the multitudinous strangers who shook his hand with fervor and affection. 'His eyes were with his thoughts, and they were far away' on the bloody and snowy field of Fredericksburg, or with the defeated and worn Burnside, with whom he had that very day had a long and most depressing interview. In the intervals of his ceremonial duties he had written a letter to General Halleck which that officer construed as an intimation that his resignation of the office of general-in-chief would be acceptable to the President. It was not an occasion for cheer." *Washington, D.C., in Lincoln's Time*, 48–49.

13. The Radical Republican Eli Thayer (1819–99) proposed to lead twenty thousand black short-term troops to Florida, defeat the rebel forces there, then have the discharged troops take over the confiscated territory.

14. The text of the Germans' memorial appears in cols. 3–4.

15. Dryer, originally from Indiana, had moved to Oregon, where he edited the *Oregonian*, became active in the Republican party, and befriended Senator Edward D. Baker. When he abandoned his editorial duties to stump for the Republicans in 1860, his replacement at the *Oregonian* was Lincoln's old friend Simeon Francis, former editor of the *Illinois State Journal*. Lincoln appointed Dryer commissioner on 20 March 1861, even though critics had condemned him as a drunkard. James W. Simonton declared that "the appointment of Mr. Dryer was a disgraceful one to all concerned. It was made against the earnest remonstrances of nearly every Californian in Washington at the time, and sustained only by the little clique who undertook to control the patronage of the Pacific coast, under the command of A. J. Butler & Co." Washington correspondence, 14 December 1862, *San Francisco Bulletin*, 8 January 1863, p. 2, col. 3. Cf. Washington correspondence, 24 March 1861, *New York Herald*, 25 March 1861, p. 1, col. 1; Wayne C. Temple, *Abraham Lincoln: From Skeptic to Prophet* (Mahomet, Ill.: Mayhaven Publishing, 1995), 27; John Denton Carter, "Abraham Lincoln and the California Patronage," *American Historical Review* 48, no. 3 (April 1943), 505.

16. Cf. Lincoln to Seward, Washington, 7 March 1862, Basler, *Collected Works of Lincoln*, 5:147.

17. J. W. Foard was an entry clerk at the San Francisco Customs House; Frank Soule was a recording clerk at the San Francisco Customs House. James McBride (1802–75), a prominent public figure in Oregon, replaced Dryer on 26 January 1863 and served in that post until 1866.

18. Charles Sumner (1811–74) represented Massachusetts in the U.S. Senate (1851–74), where he chaired the Foreign Relations Committee.

19. James W. Simonton reported that "Massachusetts influence is hard

at work to secure the selection of the new Commissioner to the Sandwich Islands from Boston. The California delegation, however, are equally earnest in behalf of J. W. Fo[a]rd, at present engaged in the San Francisco Custom-house. Messrs. [Frederick F.] Low and [Aaron A.] Sargent had recommended Mr. Fo[a]rd to the President for the position before the arrival here of Mr. [Timothy G.] Phelps, who of course acquiesces in, or at all events does not oppose, the wishes of his colleagues." Washington correspondence, 14 December 1862, *San Francisco Bulletin*, 8 January 1863, p. 2, col. 3.

20. A friend of assistant attorney general Titian J. Coffey observed Lincoln discuss the appointment of a commissioner to the Sandwich Islands with a group favoring a certain gentleman: "They presented their case as earnestly as possible, and, besides his fitness for the place, they urged that he was in bad health, and a residence in that balmy climate would be of great benefit to him. The President closed the interview with this discouraging remark: 'Gentlemen, I am sorry to say that there are eight other applicants for that place, and they are all sicker than your man.'" Coffey, quoted in Allen Thorndike Rice, ed., *Reminiscences of Abraham Lincoln by Distinguished Men of His Time* (New York: North American Publishing Company, 1886), 239–40.

21. In the fall of 1862, Samuel Long had urged Dryer's removal upon the president, who twice promised to comply with the request. In November, Long reported to Senator Lyman Trumbull of Illinois, "Mr. Lincoln told me himself the last time I saw him (about 1st Oct.) that Dryer should be *immediately* removed." Long to Trumbull, Collinsville, Ill., 26 November 1862, Trumbull Papers, Library of Congress.

22. Message dated 17 January 1863, Basler, *Collected Works of Lincoln*, 6:60–61.

23. Henry Wilson (1812–75) represented Massachusetts in the U.S. Senate (1855–73).

24. General Ambrose E. Burnside (1824–81) had been in command of the Army of the Potomac since November 1862.

25. John Cochrane (1813–98) commanded the First Brigade of the Third Division of the VI Corps.

26. Joseph Hooker (1814–79), one of Burnside's fiercest critics, took over command of the Army of the Potomac on 26 January 1863.

27. General William B. Franklin (1823–1903) commanded the Left Grand Division of the Army of the Potomac; General Edwin V. Sumner (1797–1863) commanded the Right Grand Division of the Army of the Potomac.

28. Clement L. Vallandigham (1820–71), a national leader of the Peace Democrats, represented an Ohio district in the U.S. House (1858–63).

29. John G. Nicolay (1832–1901) was Lincoln's principal private secretary; John Hay (1838–1905) was Lincoln's assistant private secretary.

30. Elihu B. Washburne (1816–87) of Galena, Ill., served in the U.S. House (1853–69); Henry L. Dawes (1816–1903) represented a Massachusetts district in the U.S. House (1857–75); Charles H. Van Wyck (1824–95) represented a New York district in the U.S. House (1859–63).

31. "Government Contracts," *House Report* no. 2, 37th Cong., 2d sess., vol. 1 (serial no. 1142).

32. Joseph Vial ("Victor") Smith (1826?–65) was the publisher of a Democratic weekly, the *Cincinnati Globe*. In the words of his friend Murat Halstead, Smith was "a queer man, [as] cranky as possible, imprudently partisan and zealous, always ready for a controversy" and "one of the fiercest of the devoted admirers of Chase." Halstead to Ida M. Tarbell, Cincinnati, 2 July 1900, Tarbell Papers, Allegheny College. Chase's private secretary, Jacob Schuckers, called Smith "a man not very likely to become popular on the Pacific coast—or anywhere else. He believed in spirit rappings and was an avowed abolitionist; he whined a great deal about 'progress'; was somewhat arrogant in manner and intolerant in speech, and speedily made himself thoroughly unpopular in his office." Quoted in John G. Nicolay and John Hay, *Abraham Lincoln: A History*, 10 vols. (New York: Century, 1890), 9:89. Cf. Anson G. Henry to his wife, Washington, 12 April 1863, fragment, photostatic copy, James G. Randall Papers, Library of Congress; H. D. Smiley, "Washington Territory," in Ralph Y. McGinnis and Calvin M. Smith, eds., *Abraham Lincoln and the Western Territories* (Chicago: Nelson-Hall, 1994), 131–34; Brooks, *Washington, D.C., in Lincoln's Time*, 114–17;

Harry Carman and Reinhard Luthin, *Lincoln and the Patronage* (New York: Columbia University Press, 1943), 230; Maunsell B. Field, *Memories of Many Men and Some Women* (New York: Harper & Brothers, 1874), 301–3; Lincoln to Chase, Washington, 8 May 1863, Basler, *Collected Works of Lincoln*, 6:202.

33. These charges, brought by one J. H. Merryman, were investigated by a special treasury department agent, Thomas Brown. Washington correspondence by James W. Simonton, 27 January 1863, *San Francisco Daily Evening Bulletin*, 24 February 1863, p. 2, col. 3. Also filing complaints against Smith was Lincoln's old friend Anson G. Henry. Henry to Lincoln, Washington, 13 April 1863, Lincoln Papers, Library of Congress.

34. In 1895 Brooks recalled: "Victor Smith, formerly a resident of Ohio, and a personal friend of Secretary Chase, was one of the disturbing elements that made the great Secretary's last days in the Treasury Department turbulent and unhappy. Victor Smith had been appointed by the Secretary to the place of collector of customs at Port Townsend, Washington Territory. Smith was a restless visionary, and in these later days would have been called a crank. While he was collector at Port Townsend, Smith succeeded in inducing the Government to move the custom-house from that point to another on Puget Sound. It was a foolish and harebrained scheme, and created a bitter feeling among business men. His new place was named Port Angelos. There the collector maintained himself for a time in a semi-barbaric proprietorship. It is related of him that he once invited the officers of the revenue cutter *Shubrick* to dine at his house; and the officers, considering that the collector of the port was a high functionary, arrayed themselves in full dress, with swords, gold lace, and other gorgeous insignia of their station, and went ashore in state to wait upon Collector Smith at his mansion, which was then in an unfinished condition. In due course of time the collector, assisted by his wife, brought out two carpenter's saw-horses, on which was placed a board covered with wrapping-paper. The repast, which was as simple as any ever partaken of by the hermits of olden time, was then set forth; and Smith, taking from his pockets three big apples, gave one to each of the three

officers, with a small forked stick, remarking: 'You'll have to roast your own apples.'

"This eccentric functionary once informed me that he had 'so intertwined himself in the fibers of the government that his removal from office was an impossibility.' Nevertheless, the outcry against Smith was so great that the President told Secretary Chase that the man must go. Every Federal officer, and nearly every prominent citizen in the Puget Sound collection district, had written letters or signed memorials protesting against the continuance of Smith in his office, and had demanded his removal and the return of the custom-house to the point from which it had been so needlessly carried away. The Secretary of the Treasury was obdurate; but finally, in May, 1863, the harassed President 'took the bull by the horns,' and resolved upon Smith's removal. The stream of expostulations, protests, and remonstrances that poured in upon him from the distracted region over which Victor Smith reigned had become intolerable; but, kind and considerate to the last, the President wrote to the Secretary (as we learn from the Nicolay-Hay history of Lincoln) to this effect: 'My mind is made up to remove Victor Smith as collector of the customs at the Puget Sound district. Yet in doing this I do not decide that the charges against him are true; I only decide that the degree of dissatisfaction with him there is too great for him to be retained. But I believe he is your personal acquaintance and friend, and if you desire it I will try to find some other place for him.'

"When the Secretary received this note, he made out a commission for Victor Smith's successor, wrote his own resignation as Secretary of the Treasury, and sent both to the President. This was only one of several instances in which Chase manifested his disposition to retire from the public service in case his will was thwarted in any particular; but once more the President succeeded in placating the ruffled Secretary, who still remained at the head of the Treasury Department, notwithstanding the removal of the petty officer from his distant post on Puget Sound." Brooks, *Washington, D.C., in Lincoln's Time*, 114–15.

35. Frederick F. Low (1828–94), a prosperous businessman, represented a California district in the U.S. House (1862–63). He became col-

lector of the port of San Francisco in 1863, but soon thereafter
stepped down to serve as governor (1863–67). Aaron A. Sargent
(1827–87) represented a California district in the U.S. House
(1861–63). In 1872 he became a U.S. Senator from that state. Timothy G. Phelps (1824–99) represented a California district in the
U.S. House (1861–63).

36. John Conness (1821–1909) represented California in the U.S. Senate (1863–69).

37. Ira P. Rankin, who had run unsuccessfully for Congress in 1856, was
collector of the port of San Francisco. Rankin is listed incorrectly
in the *Official Register* as John P. Rankin.

38. In 1895 Brooks wrote: "While they [the California Congressional
delegation] were in New York, I was astonished one night by
receiving from President Lincoln an urgent summons to come
immediately to the White House. Upon my arriving there, Mr.
Lincoln said that he had just learned that a number of removals
and appointments in San Francisco had been determined upon by
Secretary Chase without consulting him or the California congressmen; and that the three congressmen had departed from
Washington very angry and discomfited. With some asperity of
manner, he wanted to know if this was true. I told him that it was
true, and I recited the facts as they had come to my knowledge
from Messrs. Sargent, Low, and Phelps. The President then angrily
asked why I had not told him this before. I replied that it was not
my affair; that as long as the congressmen had seen fit to conceal
their feelings of disappointment from the President when they
bade him good-bye, it certainly was not my business to 'tell tales
out of school.' The President expressed his astonishment that he
had been kept in the dark about so grave a matter as the emptying
and filling of the most important Federal offices on the Pacific
Coast. Then he anxiously asked if there was any way by which the
California congressmen could be reached and brought back; and
when told that two of them were still in New York, he produced a
telegraph blank and insisted that I should at once write a despatch
to Messrs. Sargent and Low, and request them to return to Washington and see the President. With that careful attention to the
smallest details which always characterized Lincoln, he enjoined

upon me that I should send the despatch and collect from him the charge therefor the next time I came to the White House. The despatch was sent, the two congressmen were recalled, and the slate which Secretary Chase had so carefully prepared was eventually broken. Subsequently Mr. Lincoln informed me that Mr. Chase was 'exceedingly hurt' by the President's interference with his plans. A curious outcome of all this business was that Secretary Chase, having been disappointed in his scheme for filling the office of collector of the port of San Francisco, insisted that one of the two congressmen who had returned to Washington should be appointed in place of the person whom he (Chase) had previously selected for the post. The President suggested that all three congressmen should get together in San Francisco, agree upon the list of appointments, and send it to him for ratification and approval. This, however, seemed impracticable; and when Messrs. Sargent and Low finally sailed for California, Mr. Low carried with him his commission as collector of the port." Brooks, *Washington, D.C., in Lincoln's Time*, 112–14.

39. At Castle Thunder, a Richmond tobacco warehouse converted into a jail for spies and traitors, the guards were reputed to be especially brutal. William G. Brownlow (1805–77), a prominent Tennessee loyalist, had been captured and imprisoned by the Confederates.

40. General Ormsby M. Mitchel (1809–62) had dispatched these raiders from Nashville under the leadership of a civilian, James J. Andrews. The Confederates hanged Andrews and seven others.

41. General Danville Leadbetter (1811–66) commanded troops in Tennessee. General Edmund Kirby-Smith (1824–93) commanded the Department of East Tennessee.

42. In 1895 Brooks wrote: "Mr. Lincoln's manner toward enlisted men, with whom he occasionally met and talked, was always delightful in its bonhomie and its absolute freedom from anything like condescension. Then, at least, the 'common soldier' was the equal of the chief magistrate of the nation. One day in the latter part of March, 1863, I was at the White House with the President, and he told me to tarry for a while, as a party of Ohio soldiers who had been lately exchanged after many harassing experiences were coming to see him. It appeared that these were the survivors of what

was then known as the Marietta raid. Twenty-one men from Ohio regiments of the command of General O. M. Mitchel, then in northern Alabama, were sent on a dangerous mission to destroy the railroad communications of Chattanooga to the south and east. The expedition failed, and of the original number only six returned to Washington, after incredible hardships and suffering,—one third of the party having escaped, and another fraction having been hanged as spies, the rebel authorities deciding that the fact that these men wore citizen's clothes within an enemy's lines put them in that category.

"The men, who were introduced to the President by General E. A. Hitchcock, then on duty in Washington, were Mason, Parrott, Pittenger, Buffum, Reddick, and Bensinger. Their names were given to the President, and, without missing the identity of a single man, he shook hands all round with an unaffected cordiality and good-fellowship difficult to describe. He had heard their story in all its details, and as he talked with each, asking questions and making his shrewd comments on what they had to say, it was evident that for the moment this interesting interview was to him of supreme importance. At that time we had great difficulty in effecting exchanges of prisoners, and General Hitchcock had compiled a series of papers of startling importance bearing on the question. The stories of these long-suffering men, and the cheerful lightness with which they narrated their courageous and hazardous deeds, impressed Mr. Lincoln very deeply. Speaking of the men afterward, he said, with much feeling, that their bearing, and their apparent unconsciousness of having taken their lives in their hands, with the chances of death all against them, presented an example of the apparent disregard of the tremendous issues of life and death which was so strong a characteristic of the American soldier." Brooks, *Washington, D.C., in Lincoln's Time*, 77–78.

43. General David Hunter (1802–86) was a friend of Lincoln's who had accompanied the president-elect on his journey from Springfield to Washington in February 1861; General John G. Foster (1823–74) commanded the Department of North Carolina.

44. General William S. Rosecrans (1819–98) commanded the Army of the Cumberland.

45. Edward Bates (1793–1869) of Missouri. Lincoln's old friend from Springfield, Anson G. Henry (1804–65), had been visiting Washington in the spring. Henry told his wife that when he called on the president to say farewell, Lincoln "*ordered* [him] to take up [his] headquarters at the White House" and "insisted [he] should wait until this week & go down with him and see the Army of the Potomac." Henry to his wife, Washington, 12 April 1863, photocopy, James G. Randall Papers, Library of Congress. The third person mentioned in the party was Medorem Crawford, of Oregon.

46. In 1895 Brooks recounted the following remarks Lincoln had made on April 4: "In the course of conversation that evening, the President was communicative and in a confidential mood, and discussed the military situation with much freedom. Speaking of McClellan, he said, 'I kept McClellan in command after I had expected that he would win victories, simply because I knew that his dismissal would provoke popular indignation and shake the faith of the people in the final success of the war.'" The following month, when rumors swept Washington that McClellan would replace Hooker, who had led the Army of the Potomac to defeat at Chancellorsville, Brooks "chanced to be in the family sitting-room at the White House, where the President, Mrs. Lincoln, and several callers were assembled, when an indiscreet young lady directly attacked Lincoln with the extraordinary question: 'Mr. President, is McClellan going to be recalled to the command of the Army of the Potomac?' The President good-naturedly parried this home-thrust, but gave no satisfactory answer." Brooks then "intimated to the President that as he had not settled the matter, there probably might be some ground for the general suspicion that McClellan would be recalled." Lincoln "assumed a very severe look, and turning, said in an undertone, 'And you, too?'" Brooks, remembering the conversation of 4 April, apologized to Lincoln, who said, "I see you remember the talk we had on the *Carrie Martin*." *Washington, D.C., in Lincoln's Time*, 26–27.

47. Daniel Butterfield (1831–1901) had earlier commanded the V Corps of the Army of the Potomac.

48. George Stoneman (1822–94) commanded the cavalry of the Army of the Potomac (February–May 1863). William W. Averell (1832–

1900) won plaudits for his conduct in the cavalry battle at Kelly's Ford on March 17, 1863. In 1895 Brooks described how the general received a message from a Confederate officer who had been a classmate of his at West Point and who signed himself "A rebellious rebel." Mrs. Lincoln opined "that the officer was a rebel against the rebel government." Her husband "smiled at this feminine way of putting the case, and said that the determined gentleman . . . wanted everybody to know that he was not only a rebel, but a rebel of rebels—'a double-dyed-in-the-wool sort of rebel,' he added." *Washington, D.C., in Lincoln's Time*, 59.

49. Marshal Joachim Murat (1767–1815) of France.

50. The "Mud March" (January 19–24, 1863) came about when Burnside tried to move the thoroughly demoralized Army of the Potomac against Lee and bogged down in heavy rainstorms.

51. George Gordon Meade (1815–72) of Pennsylvania was to command the Army of the Potomac from June 1863 through the end of the war.

52. In 1895 Brooks recounted another incident of Lincoln's visiting soldiers in hospitals: "The President and Mrs. Lincoln, accompanied by Mrs. [Abner] Doubleday . . . and myself, were once visiting the Patent Office hospital, and the two ladies, being a little in advance, left us lingering by the cot of a wounded soldier. Just beyond us passed a well-dressed lady, evidently a stranger, who was distributing tracts. After she had gone, a patient picked up with languid hand the leaflet dropped upon his cot, and, glancing at the title, began to laugh. When we reached him, the President said: 'My good fellow, that lady doubtless means you well, and it is hardly fair for you to laugh at her gift.'

"'Well, Mr. President,' said the soldier, who recognized Mr. Lincoln, 'how can I help laughing a little? She has given me a tract on the "Sin of Dancing," and both of my legs are shot off.'" *Washington, D.C., in Lincoln's Time*, 19.

53. Darius N. Couch (1822–97) of Massachusetts; John Sedgwick (1813–64) was to fall in the battle of the Wilderness (May 1864); Daniel E. Sickles (1819–1914) of New York.

54. Also that night Lincoln asked Brooks, "How many of our ironclads do you suppose are at the bottom of Charleston harbor?" Brooks

recalled that "This was the first intimation I had had that the long-talked-of naval attack on Fort Sumter was to be made that day; and the President, who had been jocular and cheerful during the evening, began despondently to discuss the probabilities of defeat. It was evident that his mind was entirely prepared for the repulse, the news of which soon after reached us. During our subsequent stay at Hooker's headquarters, which lasted nearly a week, Mr. Lincoln eagerly inquired every day for the rebel newspapers that were brought in through the picket-lines, and when these were received he anxiously hunted through them for information from Charleston." *Washington, D.C., in Lincoln's Time*, 51–52. Cf. a similar account of this story in the Appendix.

55. In 1895 Brooks quoted Lincoln's words thus: "It is a great relief to get away from Washington and the politicians. But nothing touches the tired spot." Ibid., 55. Cf. a similar account in the Appendix.

56. John F. Reynolds (1820–63) of Pennsylvania would fall at the Battle of Gettysburg (1 July 1863). In 1895 Brooks described an incident of the journey to visit the I Corps: "We rode thither in an ambulance over a rough corduroy road; and, as we passed over some of the more difficult portions of the jolting way, the ambulance driver, who sat well in front, occasionally let fly a volley of suppressed oaths at his wild team of six mules. Finally Mr. Lincoln, leaning forward, touched the man on the shoulder, and said: 'Excuse me, my friend, are you an Episcopalian?'

"The man, greatly startled, looked around and replied: 'No, Mr. President; I am a Methodist.'

"'Well,' said Lincoln, 'I thought you must be an Episcopalian, because you swear just like Governor Seward, who is a church-warden.' The driver swore no more."

Brooks went on to describe the president's reaction to the wood-cutting abilities of the troops: "As we plunged and dashed through the woods, Lincoln called attention to the stumps left by the men who had cut down the trees, and with great discrimination pointed out where an experienced axman made what he called 'a good butt,' or where a tyro had left conclusive evidence of being a poor chopper." Ibid., 55.

57. Brooks in 1895 said that "Lincoln was delighted with the superb and inspiriting spectacle of the review that day." Ibid., 55–56.

58. Oliver O. Howard (1830–1909) of Maine; Henry W. Slocum (1827–94) of New York.

59. German-born Franz Sigel (1824–1902) had commanded the XI Corps (September 1862–February 1863).

60. Presumably a sobriquet for Hooker, who had led Union forces in a clash with retreating Confederates on 5 May 1862, just outside Williamsburg, Virginia.

61. German-born Carl Schurz (1829–1906) commanded the Third Division of the XI Corps.

62. In 1895 Brooks wrote that Lincoln had not been entirely satisfied with Hooker's attitude: "One of his most frequent expressions when talking with the President was, 'When I get to Richmond,' or 'After we have taken Richmond,' etc. The President, noting this, said to me confidentially, and with a sigh: 'That is the most depressing thing about Hooker. It seems to me that he is over-confident.'" *Washington, D.C., in Lincoln's Time*, 56.

63. The portrait by Edward Dalton Marchant (1806–87) hangs in the Union League Club of Philadelphia.

64. In April, Grant took his forces south of Vicksburg, crossed the Mississippi River, and began the campaign east of the river that led to the capture of Vicksburg in July.

65. During the secession winter of 1860–61, Mary Lincoln denounced Seward as an "abolition sneak" and vehemently opposed his nomination for a cabinet post: "Seward in the Cabinet! Never. If all things should go on all right—the credit would go to Seward—if they went wrong—the blame would fall upon my husband." When Lincoln tried to defend Seward, his wife replied: "Father, you are too honest for this world! You should have been born a saint. You will generally find it a safe rule to distrust a disappointed, ambitious politician. It makes me mad to see you sit still and let that hypocrite, Seward, twine you around his finger as if you were a skein of thread." Donn Piatt in Rice, ed., *Reminiscences of Lincoln*, 481; George B. Lincoln to Gideon Welles, Rivervale, N.J., 25 April 1874, in "New Light on the Seward-Welles-Lincoln Controversy?" *Lincoln Lore*, April 1981, 2–3; Elizabeth Keckley, *Behind the Scenes;*

or, *Thirty Years a Slave and Four Years in the White House* (New York: G. W. Carlton, 1868), 130–31.

66. Secretary of War Edwin M. Stanton (1814–69).

67. George Harrington (1815–92), assistant secretary of the treasury (1861–65), had been a clerk in the Treasury Department (1845–61).

68. John Palmer Usher (1816–89) of Indiana was secretary of the interior (January 1863–May 1865.) He had succeeded another Hoosier, Caleb Blood Smith.

69. In fact, several blacks worked at the White House, including the messenger William Slade, the cook Cornelia Mitchell, the butler Peter Brown, and the bodyguard William Johnson. John E. Washington, *They Knew Lincoln* (New York: E. P. Dutton, 1942), 105–34.

70. Cf. a similar incident described in the Appendix.

71. Brooks may have copied this from the *Washington Chronicle* of 2 May. Don E. Fehrenbacher and Virginia Fehrenbacher, eds., *Recollected Words of Abraham Lincoln* (Stanford: Stanford University Press, 1996), 44.

72. In 1895 Brooks recalled: "I was at the White House on Wednesday, May 6 [1863], and the President, who seemed anxious and harassed beyond any power of description, said that while still without any positive information as to the result of the fighting at Chancellorsville, he was certain in his own mind that 'Hooker had been licked.' He was only then wondering whether Hooker would be able to recover himself and renew the fight. The President asked me to go into the room then occupied by his friend Dr. Henry, who was a guest in the house, saying possibly we might get some news later on.

"In an hour or so, while the doctor and I sat talking, say about three o'clock in the afternoon, the door opened, and Lincoln came into the room. I shall never forget that picture of despair. He held a telegram in his hand, and as he closed the door and came toward us I mechanically noticed that his face, usually sallow, was ashen in hue. The paper on the wall behind him was of the tint known as 'French gray,' and even in that moment of sorrow and dread expectation I vaguely took in the thought that the complexion of the anguished President's visage was almost exactly like that of the wall. He gave me the telegram, and in a voice trembling with emotion, said, 'Read it—news from the Army.' The dispatch was from General Butterfield, Hooker's chief of staff, addressed to the War Department, and was to the effect that the Army had been withdrawn from the south side of the Rappahannock, and was then 'safely encamped' in its former position. The appearance of the President, as I read aloud these fateful words, was piteous. Never, as long as I knew him, did he seem to be so broken, so dispirited, and so ghostlike. Clasping his hands behind his back, he walked up and down the room, saying, 'My God! my God! What will the country say! What will the country say!'

"He seemed incapable of uttering any other words than these, and after a little time he hurriedly left the room." *Washington, D.C., in Lincoln's Time,* 60–61.

73. General Henry W. Halleck (1815–72), commander in chief of the Union armies (1862–64).

74. The Union casualties numbered 17,287 (1,606 killed, 9,762 wounded, and 5,919 missing).

75. General Benjamin F. Butler (1818–93) was a prominent Massachusetts Democrat who in 1860 had supported Jefferson Davis for President; Nathaniel P. Banks (1816–94) was a prominent Massachusetts politician whom Lincoln had named major general of volunteers.

76. General Irvin McDowell (1818–85) was the hapless commander of Union forces at the First Battle of Bull Run.

77. Some Republicans were upset by Seward's handling of the *Peterhof* mails controversy with Great Britain.

78. Major General William H. French (1815–81) was in charge of the Harper's Ferry district.

79. In 1895 Brooks recalled Lincoln saying that he "regarded Hooker very much as a father might regard a son who was lame, or who had some other incurable physical infirmity. His love for his son would be even intensified by the reflection that the lad could never be a strong and successful man." *Washington, D.C., in Lincoln's Time,* 63.

80. Located outside the District of Columbia on a hilltop, the Soldiers' Home, a facility for disabled troops, was far cooler than the White

House; in 1862, 1863, and 1864, the president and his family spent the summers in a stone cottage on this site.

81. "Prog" was slang term for food, usually acquired by begging. In 1847 Edwin D. Willard and Henry A. Willard took over Fuller's City Hotel, which stood two blocks from the White House, at Fourteenth Street and Pennsylvania Avenue, remodeled it, and named it the Willard Hotel. Nathaniel Hawthorne said that "it may much more justly be called the center of Washington and the Union than . . . the Capitol, the White House, or the State Department."

82. David D. Porter (1813–91) commanded the Mississippi Squadron. The Confederates surrendered Vicksburg on 4 July 1863.

83. In 1895 Brooks recalled Lincoln saying "that he never before or afterward saw Mr. Welles so thoroughly excited as he was then." *Washington, D.C., in Lincoln's Time*, 82.

84. Sickles had lost a leg in the battle of Gettysburg.

85. Alfred Pleasonton (1824–97) commanded the cavalry of the Army of the Potomac (1863–64). James S. Wadsworth (1807–64) of New York was killed at the battle of the Wilderness on 6 May.

86. In 1895 Brooks wrote: "I remember the anxiety, almost anguish, with which Lincoln had said before I left Washington [to visit the Army of the Potomac] that he was afraid that 'something would happen' to prevent that annihilation of Lee's Army, which, as he thought, was then certainly within the bounds of possibility." When Brooks reported to Lincoln all he had seen and heard at Gettysburg, Lincoln's "grief and anger were something sorrowful to behold." *Washington, D.C., in Lincoln's Time*, 91–92, 94.

87. This unit of the Second Division of the III Corps of the Army of the Potomac was made up of six New York regiments. It had been commanded earlier by General Daniel Sickles.

88. Dixon S. Miles (d. 1862) commanded Union forces at Harper's Ferry, which surrendered to Stonewall Jackson in September 1862.

89. Ulric Dahlgren (1842–64), son of Admiral John A. Dahlgren, was wounded in a cavalry engagement at Boonesboro, Maryland, and subsequently lost part of a leg. He was killed while participating in Judson Kilpatrick's raid on Richmond in March 1864.

90. Felix Octavius Carr Darley (1822–88) was a well-known artist whose

Dahlgren's Cavalry Charge at Fredericksburg was highly praised when exhibited in Paris in 1867.

91. Colonel John Cradlebaugh of the 114th Ohio.

92. William S. Rosecrans (1819–98) was thrashed at the Battle of Chickamauga, 19–20 September.

93. Admiral John Dahlgren (1809–70), USN, commanded the South Atlantic Blockading Squadron. On the night of 8–9 September, Confederates at Fort Sumter drove off a Union storming party and took many prisoners. Dahlgren recorded in his diary that "Some of the boat's crew jumped overboard at the first fire." Madeleine Vinton Dahlgren, ed., *Memoir of John A. Dahlgren* (Boston: James R. Osgood, 1882), 414.

94. These remarks may have been occasioned by the arrival of the election returns from California.

95. George M. Hanson, a Virginia native, had settled in Paradise, Coles County, Illinois, where Lincoln knew him. He later moved to California and became a prominent Republican.

96. Hanson apparently abused his office. One observer claimed that, "Notwithstanding his being a Methodist minister he skinned not only the cattle he purchased for the [Digger] Indians, but he skinned the Indians as well, sold the beef and fed the Indians on the hoofs, horns and hides." Charles H. Coleman, *Abraham Lincoln and Coles County, Illinois* (New Brunswick, N.J.: Scarecrow Press, 1955), 222.

97. Charles James succeeded Frederick Low. Secretary Chase had appointed Timothy G. Phelps to the post, but when Senator Conness demanded that James be named, Chase acquiesced. Washington correspondence by James W. Simonton, 22 January 1865, *San Francisco Daily Evening Bulletin*, 22 February 1865, p. 1, col. 1.

98. John M. Schofield (1831–1906) commanded the Department of Missouri.

99. On 25 September the XI and XII Corps were dispatched from Virginia to Alabama to relieve Rosecrans's army, which was bottled up in Chattanooga; all the troops arrived at their destination by October 2.

100. Charles Nordhoff (1830–1901) was managing editor of the *Evening Post* (1861–71).

101. Lincoln to James C. Conkling, Washington, 26 August 1863, Basler, *Collected Works of Lincoln*, 6:406–10. When the *Evening Post* prematurely ran a report of Lincoln's open letter to James C. Conkling, "Lincoln said he was 'mad enough to cry.'" Brooks, *Washington, D.C., in Lincoln's Time*, 66.

102. Lincoln confided that "he would not deny that a re-election would . . . have its gratification to his feelings" and that "it would be a very sweet satisfaction to him to know that he had secured the approval of his fellow citizens and earned the highest testimonial of confidence they could bestow." James M. Winchell, "Three Interviews with President Lincoln," *Galaxy* 16 (July 1873): 40.

103. Simon P. Hanscom had, at the beginning of the war, been a correspondent for the *New York Herald*; in 1862 he took over the *Washington National Republican*. A journalist reported in 1865 that "Every day the irrepressible Hanscom, of the *Republican*, comes after news, and brings the gossip of the day. The *Republican* is the President's favorite paper, and he gives it what news he has, but very rarely reads it or any other paper." *Philadelphia Sunday Dispatch*, 25 March 1865. Many years after the war another journalist, Ben: Perley Poore, recalled that Lincoln's "favorite among the Washington correspondents was Mr. Simon B. [*sic*] Hanscom," (see the introduction of this work). Poore quoted Lincoln, "'I see you state,' said the President to Hanscom one day, 'that my administration will be the reign of *steel*. Why not add that Buchanan's was the reign of *stealing*?'" Poore, "Reminiscences of the Great Northern Uprising," *The Youth's Companion*, 26 July 1883, 301.

104. Whitelaw Reid made a similar observation: "The Republican, now transformed into an evening paper, and edited by Mr. S. P. Hanscom, formerly Washington correspondent of the New York Herald, has been regarded as having some peculiar facilities for getting news at the White House; and it recently intimated that its views were not likely to be in conflict with those of Mr. Lincoln; but the representation that certain of its articles were 'semi-official,' has been authoritatively contradicted." Washington correspondence, 10 August 1863, *Cincinnati Gazette*, 14 August 1863, p. 1, col. 4.

105. Richard Yates (1815–73) was governor of Illinois (1861–65).

106. Rosecrans commanded Union forces at the battle of Stone's River

(Murfreesboro), Tennessee, on 31 December 1862, and 2 January 1863, and at the battle of Corinth, Mississippi (3–4 October 1862).

107. On 17 October, in keeping with the wishes of Grant, Lincoln removed Rosecrans from command of the Army of the Cumberland.

108. On 16 October 1863, Lincoln sent to Meade, through Halleck, a telegram stating, among other things, "If Gen. Meade can now attack him [Lee] on a field no worse than equal for us, and will do so with all the skill and courage, which he, his officers and men possess, the honor will be his if he succeeds, and the blame may be mine if he fails." Basler, *Collected Works of Lincoln* 6:518.

109. Maryland Congressman Henry Winter Davis (1817–65) was a leading Radical critic of Lincoln.

110. In this address, delivered on 3 October at Rockville, Maryland, Blair denounced Sumner's reconstruction plan: "The Abolition party, whilst pronouncing philippics against slavery, seek to make a caste of another color by amalgamating the black element with the free white labor of our land and so to expand far beyond the present confines of slavery the evil which makes it obnoxious to republican statesmen. And now . . . they would make the manumission of the slaves the means of infusing their blood into our whole system by blending with it 'amalgamation, equality and fraternity.'"

111. William D. "Pig Iron" Kelley (1814–90) of Philadelphia served in the U.S. House (1861–90); John Wien Forney (1817–81) was secretary of the U.S. Senate and editor of the *Washington Chronicle* and the *Philadelphia Press*. Andrew G. Curtin (1815?–94) was governor of Pennsylvania (1861–66).

112. In response to the Washington correspondent of the *New York Herald*, who denied that Forney had criticized Blair as Brooks (and also Whitelaw Reid of the *Cincinnati Gazette*) had claimed, Brooks replied: "I published almost *verbatim* the language of Colonel Forney to Blair, as given by a witness who was present at the interview." Washington correspondence, 17 November 1863 (16 December). That witness was Forney. *Washington, D.C., in Lincoln's Time*, 127.

113. Clark Mills (1810–83), of Washington, was a sculptor whose first

important commission was the equestrian statue of Andrew Jackson in Lafayette Square, across from the White House.

114. Brooks later acknowledged privately that Mary Lincoln had in fact engaged in unethical conduct in the White House. See *supra*, p. 3, Brooks to Edward McPherson, San Francisco, 20 February 1866. Abundant evidence corroborates Brooks's later belief. See Michael Burlingame, *Honest Abe, Dishonest Mary* (Racine, Wis.: Lincoln Fellowship of Wisconsin, 1994), and Burlingame, *The Inner World of Abraham Lincoln* (Urbana: University of Illinois Press, 1994), 301–7.

115. A New Yorker complained to the president early in his first term: "If the stories I hear about Nicolay . . . are true, you ought to dismiss him. If he is sick, he has a right to be cross and ungentlemanly in his deportment, but not otherwise. People say he is very disagreeable and uncivil." Robert Colby to Lincoln, New York, 18 May 1861, Lincoln Papers, Library of Congress. One of Nicolay's assistants, William O. Stoddard, described him as "the bulldog in the ante-room" with a disposition "sour and crusty." Stoddard, "White House Sketches," *New York Citizen*, 25 August 1866, and Stoddard, *Inside the White House in War Times* (New York: Webster, 1890), 104. In the latter work, Stoddard observed that "people who do not like him [Nicolay]—because they cannot use him, perhaps—say he is sour and crusty, and it is a grand good thing, then, that he is. If you will sit in that chair [Nicolay's] a month or two, you will see what has become of any easy good-nature you sat down with. . . . The President showed his good judgment of men when he put Mr. Nicolay just where he is, with a kind and amount of authority which it is not easy to describe."

116. Lincoln's assistants John Hay, N. S. Howe, Gustav Matile, and Edward D. Neill all officially worked for the Interior Department.

117. Presumably Brooks here refers to Nicolay, John Hay, and William O. Stoddard.

118. For a different view of the Lincolns' marriage, see Burlingame, *Inner World of Lincoln*, 268–326.

119. Brooks to Richard Watson Gilder, Newark, N.J., 3 February 1894, Century Collection, New York Public Library.

120. Actually it was two Sundays before his trip to Gettysburg that Lin-

coln sat for Gardner. Photographer Alexander Gardner had been an associate of Matthew Brady; in 1863 he established his own studio at Seventh and D Streets.

121. William Harrison Lambert (1842–1912) was a major collector of Lincolniana. He wrote "The Gettysburg Address: When Written, How Received, Its True Form," *Pennsylvania Magazine of History and Biography*, October 1909.

122. The War Department sent 24,000 rations to Union prisoners in Richmond's Libby prison, but reports that the Confederates had intercepted them caused Northern authorities to end the program.

123. William Sprague (1830–1915) represented Rhode Island in the U.S. Senate (1863–75). Kate Chase (1840–99), the daughter of Treasury Secretary Salmon P. Chase, was a leading Washington belle.

124. Mary Lincoln was extremely jealous of the young and beautiful Kate Chase. See Keckley, *Behind the Scenes*, 128. In January 1864, she, along with her father, Salmon P. Chase, and her husband, William Sprague, were excluded at the First Lady's insistence from the invitation list for a Cabinet dinner. When informed of this by White House secretary John G. Nicolay, the president overruled his wife, and, as Nicolay reported, "there soon arose such a rampage as the House hasn't seen for a year." Nicolay to John Hay, Washington, 18 January 1864, Nicolay Papers, Library of Congress.

125. Mary Lincoln wanted her husband to boycott the wedding, which was widely considered the social event of the season. According to one source, the First Lady scolded her husband for wanting to go "and the music of her voice penetrated the utmost end of the house." Lincoln vainly attempted to calm his infuriated wife. Inconsolable, she "made a dash at his cravat, and captured a part of his whiskers." He then left for the wedding. "Presidential Domestic Squabbles," Washington correspondence, n.d., *Rochester Union*, unidentified clipping, Judd Stewart Collection, Lincoln Scrap Books 5:44, Huntington Library, San Marino, California. For a variation on this story, see an unidentified Philadelphia artist's account, unidentified clipping, headlined "From the Philadelphia Press," ibid., 2:103.

126. David C. Broderick (1820–59) represented California in the U.S. Senate from 1857 till his death.

127. John D. Defrees of Indiana.

128. Basler, *Collected Works of Lincoln*, 7:12, quotes the letter of 12 November 1863 as given in Charles B. Boynton, *History of the Great Western Sanitary Fair* (1864), 183: "Mr. Defrees—Please see this girl who works in your office and find out about her brother, and come and tell me."

129. Defrees later said that the young man was freed on Lincoln's order. Basler, *Collected Works of Lincoln*, 7:12n.

130. This unit was established in 1862 to allow sick and wounded men to serve by performing garrison duty and other light functions. In 1864 its name was changed to the Veteran Reserve Corps. By the end of 1863 it had twenty thousand members.

131. Basler, *Collected Works of Lincoln*, 7:36–53.

132. Sumner maintained that the Confederate states had in effect committed suicide and could be treated as if they were federal territories under congressional control.

133. Sumner declared that "he is fully and perfectly satisfied" with the message and "endorses it to the fullest extent," even though some details about readmitting states into the union needed to be worked out. Washington correspondence by "Zeta" (pen name used by an unidentified correspondent), 13 December 1863, *Chicago Tribune*, 14 December 1863, p. 1, col. 5. To Orestes Brownson, Sumner said that Lincoln's stand on Reconstruction was "identical with ours." Sumner to Brownson, Washington, 27 December 1863, in Beverly Wilson Palmer, ed., *The Selected Letters of Charles Sumner*, 2 vols. (Boston: Northeastern University Press, 1990), 2:216–17.

134. On 15 March 1863, the U.S.S. *Cyane* captured the fast privateer, *J. M. Chapman*, which allegedly was on a mission to attack California coastal shipping on behalf of the Confederacy. On 12 October 1863, the defendants in *U.S. vs. Greathouse, Harpending, and Rubery* were found guilty of aiding the rebellion and sentenced to a jail term of ten years and fined $10,000. Milton H. Shutes, *Lincoln and California* (Stanford: Stanford University Press, 1943), 77–80; Robert J. Chandler, "The Release of the *Chapman* Pirates: A California Sidelight on Lincoln's Amnesty Policy," *Civil War History* 23 (1977): 129–43.

135. On 15 May 1863, Bright wrote to his friend Senator Charles Sum-

ner, urging him to assist efforts to obtain a pardon for his nephew Rubery. On 21 July, Sumner replied that "The Presdt promised to take care of yr Birmingham boy." Palmer, *Sumner's Letters* 2:184–85. Lincoln issued a pardon for Rubery effective as of 20 January 1864.

136. Stephen J. Field (1816–99) was judge of the newly created U.S. Circuit Court in California.

137. James Henry Hackett (1800–1871), a noted Shakespearean actor. David Homer Bates said that Lincoln "was very fond of Hackett personally, and of the character of *Falstaff*, and frequently repeated some of the latter's quaint sallies. I recall that in his recitation for my benefit he criticized some of Hackett's renderings." David Homer Bates, *Lincoln in the Telegraph Office: Recollections of the United States Military Telegraph Corps during the Civil War* (New York: Century, 1907), 223. In 1895 Brooks recalled Lincoln's fondness for Shakespeare thus: "President Lincoln's theater-going was usually confined to occasions when Shakespeare's plays were enacted; for, although he enjoyed a hearty laugh, he was better pleased with the stately dignity, deep philosophy, and exalted poetry of Shakespeare than with anything that was to be found in more modern dramatic writings. But I remember a delightful evening that we once spent at the old Washington Theater, where we saw Mrs. John Wood in John Brougham's travesty of 'Pocahontas.' The delicious absurdity and crackling puns of the piece gave the President food for mirth for many days thereafter. At another time we saw Edwin Forrest in 'King Lear,' and the President appeared to be more impressed by the acting of John McCullough, in the role of Edgar, than with the great tragedian's appearance as the mad king. He asked that McCullough might come to the box between the acts; and when the young actor was brought to the door, clad in his fantastic garb of rags and straw, Mr. Lincoln warmly, and yet with diffidence, praised the performance of the scene in which he had just appeared. . . . Those who are disposed to consider that Lincoln exhibited a frivolous side of his character by his play-going should reflect that the theater was almost the only place where he could escape from the clamor of office-seekers, and for a moment unfix his thoughts from the cares and anxieties that weighted upon his spirit with dreadful oppressiveness." *Washington, D.C., in Lincoln's Time*, 72–73.

138. In late November, Lincoln had contracted varioloid fever, which
lasted till December 4. To his physician he quipped, "There is one
consolation about the matter, . . . it cannot in the least disfigure
me!" Washington correspondence by "Zeta," 3 December 1863,
Chicago Tribune, 8 December 1863, p. 2, col. 4. While recuperating
from the disease, he said "that since he has been President he had
always had a crowd of people asking him to give them something,
but that *now he has something he can give them all.*" Washington correspondence, 14 December 1863, *Chicago Tribune*, 15 December 1863,
p. 1, cols. 2–3.

139. Hatch Collection, microfilm copy courtesy of Dr. Wayne C. Temple. Witherle was a childhood friend of Brooks's in Castine,
Maine.

140. In 1895 Brooks described how Lincoln tempered Stanton's wrath at
Captain Thomas T. Eckert, whom the war secretary accused of
dereliction of duty. Lincoln "expressed his amazement, and said
that he had long been in the habit of going to Captain Eckert's
office for news from the front, for encouragement and comfort
when he was anxious and depressed. He had gone there, he said, at
all hours of the day and night,—two o'clock in the day, and two
o'clock in the morning, at midday, daybreak, and sunrise,—and he
had never found the captain absent from his post of duty; and that
he should be guilty of neglect of duty was simply incredible." Stanton relented. *Washington, D.C., in Lincoln's Time*, 37–39.

CHAPTER TWO: DISPATCHES AND LETTERS, 1864

1. Charles Henry Davis (1807–77) was chief of the Bureau of Naviga-
tion.

2. Gustavus Vasa Fox (1821–83) was chief clerk of the Navy Department; he became assistant secretary of the navy on August 1, 1861.
Lincoln once asked Brooks to run an errand to the Navy Department, saying: "Here, take this card to Captain Fox; *he* is the Navy
Department." Brooks, *Washington, D.C., in Lincoln's Time*, 39.

3. Halleck was not entirely popular with Lincoln, either, as Brooks
explained in 1895: "One evening in the early summer of 1863, just
after the failure of the naval attack on Fort Sumter, the President
asked me to go with him to Halleck's headquarters for a chat with

the general. Soon after our arrival, the President and General Halleck fell into a discussion as to the possibility of landing a strong force of artillery and infantry on Morris Island, Charleston Harbor, under cover of the gunboats, to cooperate with the Navy in an attack upon the rebel fortifications on Cummings Point. The President said he thought that Fort Sumter might be reduced in this way, and that, by gradual approaches, we could get within range of the city of Charleston. He illustrated his theory of gradual approaches by means of three or four lead-pencils and pen-handles, which he arranged in parallels, shifting them from time to time to show how, according to his notion of military strategy, our lines could be advanced in the desired direction. Halleck would not say that it was impracticable to land troops on the southeast end of the island, but he insisted that they could do nothing after they got there, and he made a strong point of the statement that the strip of land between Fort Wagner and the place of landing was so narrow that the zigzag parallel lines laid out by the President, according to scientific rules, could not be made. Assistant-Secretary Fox of the Navy Department came in during the conference, and the President appealed to him for his opinion. Captain Fox agreed with Lincoln that movement could be made, but whenever the President pressed his view upon Halleck, the general invariably replied: 'If it were practicable it would have been done; but the plan would be utterly futile for the reason that there is not room enough for the approaches which must be made.' Halleck, although he treated the suggestions of Lincoln with great respect, evidently entertained profound contempt for his military knowledge. When he went away Lincoln . . . expressed himself as discouraged with what he called 'General Halleck's habitual attitude of demur.'" *Washington, D.C., in Lincoln's Time*, 42–43. When Brooks told Lincoln one day "that Halleck was disliked because many people supposed that he was too timid and hesitating in his military conduct," the president's face "at once wore a grave, almost severe expression" and he "said that he was Halleck's friend because nobody else was." Ibid., 131.

4. Robert J. Stevens was the son-in-law of Lincoln's close friend Edward D. Baker, who was killed in battle in October 1861. He was appointed superintendent of the San Francisco mint at Baker's

request. James W. Simonton reported in March 1863 "that Stevens must lose his head, there seems to be little doubt, for the President admitted that Special Agent [Thomas] Brown's report [of 30 January to Treasury Secretary Chase] against him was conclusive." But Lincoln "dislikes personally to remove Col. Baker's son-in-law." Moreover, Lincoln's old friend Anson G. Henry hastened from Oregon to Washington to lobby on behalf of Stevens. Henry to Lincoln, Washington, 9 March 1863, and Lincoln to Henry, 9 March 1863, Basler, *Collected Works of Lincoln*, 6:128–29; New York correspondence by Simonton, 17 and 27 March 1863, *San Francisco Daily Evening Bulletin*, 14 April 1863, p. 3, col. 5 and 24 April 1863, p. 1, col. 3. In late April, Stevens was replaced by Robert B. Swain. Brown's report is given ibid., 29 April 1863, p. 3, cols. 6–7. Simonton averred that "'Uncle Abe' hated terribly to be compelled to order this execution, but there was no help for it, in view of the testimony. The first witness on the Mint affairs was Mr. [Charles] Maltby. . . . His testimony was of the most damaging character to Stevens, and was at the same time of itself nearly or quite conclusive to the President, who remarked: 'I know Maltby, for I slept with him six months, and he used to be an honest man.'" Washington correspondence, 8 April 1863, ibid. (15 May). From his earliest days in New Salem, Lincoln had known Maltby, who at the time of his testimony was Internal Revenue Collector for the Fifth District of California. See Charles Maltby, *The Life and Public Services of Abraham Lincoln* (Stockton, Calif.: Daily Independent Steam Power Print, 1884).

5. On 3 March 1863, Lincoln had signed a bill establishing the National Academy of Sciences.

6. Harvard Professor Louis Agassiz (1807–73) was a renowned zoologist. The physicist Alexander Dallas Bache (1806–67) helped found the American Academy of Sciences; during the war he served as vice president of the Sanitary Commission. John Rodgers (1812–82) commanded the monitor *Weehawken*, which sank the Confederate ironclad *Atlanta* on 17 June 1863. Andrew Atkinson Humphreys (1810–83) was chief of staff to the commander of the Army of the Potomac. Joseph Gilbert Totten (1788–1864) served as chief engineer of the Union army.

7. In 1895 Brooks recalled how Lincoln was sometimes abstracted during formal receptions: "His thoughts were apt to be far away from the crowds of strangers that passed before him. On one occasion, bringing up a friend, I greeted the President as usual, and presented my friend. The President shook hands with me in a perfunctory way, his eyes fixed on space, and I passed on, knowing that he had never seen me or heard the name of my friend; but after I had reached a point seven or right persons beyond, the President suddenly seemed to see me, and, continuing the hand-shaking of strangers while he spoke, shouted out: 'Oh, Brooks! Charley Maltby is in town, and I want you to come and see me to-morrow.' . . . Lincoln's sudden outburst, naturally enough, astonished the people who heard it." *Washington, D.C., in Lincoln's Time*, 69–70.

8. Benjamin Brown French (1800–1870) said his position made him "almost a member of the President's household." French to "Brother Reynolds," Washington, 20 April 1865, unidentified clipping, French Papers, Library of Congress. In 1868 French recalled that, during the war, "No week passed that I did not see him, and I was often with him many times a week. This, of course, with a man like him, led to numerous conversations between us, and enabled me, with no particular intention of doing so, to observe the peculiar characteristics of Mr. Lincoln." French, *Address Delivered at the Dedication of the Statue of Abraham Lincoln* (Washington: McGill & Witherow, 1868), 7.

9. In October 1863, Ridgely Greathouse, a British citizen, had been convicted of participating in the attempt to use the *J. M. Chapman* as a privateer to attack U.S. coastal shipping off California on behalf of the Confederacy. Ogden Hoffman of San Francisco, U.S. District Judge, was the second son of the distinguished lawyer and politician, Josiah Ogden Hoffman (1793–1856) of New York.

10. Cf. Lincoln to Hoffman, Washington, 15 December 1863, Basler, *Collected Works of Lincoln*, 7:67–68.

11. The supplementary proclamation was issued on 26 March 1865, effectively plugging the loophole opened by Judge Hoffman in the Greathouse case.

12. James K. Moorhead (1806–84) represented a Pennsylvania district

in the U.S. House (1859–69). He never served as governor. Brooks may have been thinking of Charles S. Morehead (1802–68), who had been governor of Kentucky (1855–59).

13. In 1850 Thompson had tried to speak in Springfield, Massachusetts, where an angry mob pelted him with eggs and mud. John Pierpont was a treasury department clerk who had been a Unitarian minister.

14. On 12 April 1864, Confederates overran Union forces at Fort Pillow, Tennessee, and murdered some black troops in cold blood after they had surrendered.

15. In fact, Grant's forces suffered heavy losses in the battle of the Wilderness (5–6 May), where his advance toward Richmond was temporarily checked.

16. Basler, *Collected Works of Lincoln*, 7:334.

17. Benjamin Gratz Brown (1826–85) was a Radical Republican senator from Missouri (1863–67).

18. On 31 May, Radical Republicans, disenchanted with Lincoln, held a convention in Cleveland and nominated John C. Fremont for president and John Cochrane for vice president.

19. At the battle of New Market on 15 May, Confederate General John C. Breckinridge's forces, which included cadets from the Virginia Military Institute, defeated Franz Sigel's command.

20. General George Crook (1829–90), who commanded a corps in Sheridan's Army of the Shenandoah, participated in the battles of Winchester, Fisher's Hill, and Cedar Creek. In August 1864 he took charge of West Virginia.

21. When Brooks called to congratulate the president, he was, as he recalled, "astonished by his jokingly rallying me on my failure to send him word of his nomination. It appeared that nobody had apparently thought it worth while to telegraph him the result of the balloting for the Presidential nominee of the convention. Probably each one of the many men who would have been glad to be the sender of pleasant tidings to the President had thought that some other man would surely anticipate him by a telegram of congratulation. In the confusion that reigned in the convention nobody went to the wires that were led into the building but the

alert newspaper men, who thought only of their own business."
Washington, D.C., in Lincoln's Time, 148.

22. The Union League of America was established in 1862 to boost
Northern morale, stimulate recruiting, educate the public about the
issues of the war, and help the Republican party.

23. William Dennison (1815–82) was governor of Ohio (1860–62). In
September 1864 he became Lincoln's postmaster general.

24. George William Curtis (1824–92) was the editor of *Harper's Weekly*.

25. Brooks jotted these words down shortly after they were uttered and
had the president read them over. As he recalled in 1895, "The
solemn manner of the President, and the weightiness of his utterance, so impressed me that I drew toward me a sheet of paper and
wrote down his words then and there. Then I read to him what I
had written, in order that I might be sure that he was correctly
reported. He suggested a verbal change, and I carried the paper
away with me." *Washington, D.C., in Lincoln's Time*, 138.

26. Hatch Collection, copy courtesy of Dr. Wayne C. Temple.

27. In 1895, Brooks wrote: "The night before the meeting of the Baltimore Convention I had a long conversation with the President in
regard to the probable action of that body. He requested me to
come to him when I should return from Baltimore, and bring him
the odd bits of political gossip that I might pick up in the convention, and which, as he said, would not get into the newspapers. I
had hoped to see Mr. Hamlin renominated, and had anxiously
given Mr. Lincoln many opportunities to say whether he preferred
the renomination of the Vice-President; but he was craftily and
rigidly non-committal, knowing, as he did, what was in my mind
concerning Mr. Hamlin. He would refer to the matter only in the
vaguest phrase, as, 'Mr. Hamlin is a very good man,' or, 'You, being
a New Englander, would naturally like to see Mr. Hamlin renominated; and you are quite right,' and so on. By this time Lincoln's
renomination was an absolute certainty, and he cheerfully conceded
that point without any false modesty. But he could not be induced
to express any opinion on the subject of the selection of a candidate
for Vice-President. He did go so far as to say that he hoped that
the convention would declare in favor of the constitutional amend-

ment abolishing slavery as one of the articles of the party faith." *Washington, D.C., in Lincoln's Time*, 141–42.

28. Daniel S. Dickinson (1800–1866), a prominent Unionist from New York who had been a Democrat before the war, was a delegate to the Republican convention in Baltimore.

29. William Pitt Fessenden (1806–69) represented Maine in the U.S. Senate (1853–64). He served as Lincoln's secretary of the treasury (1864–65).

30. On 9 June 1864, John P. Hale (1806–73), who had represented New Hampshire in the U.S. Senate since 1847, was rejected by the New Hampshire state legislature. He had accepted fees from one J. H. Hunt, who was convicted of fraud. The Senate found that Hale's action did not technically violate the law, but recommended that a law be passed to outlaw such action in the future.

31. The Democrats did postpone their convention till late August.

32. Horatio Seymour (1810–86) was governor of New York.

33. The explosion occurred on 17 June.

34. General George Douglas Ramsay (1802–82) was chief of ordnance (1863–64); Major James Gilchrist Benton (1820–81) commanded the Washington Arsenal (1863–66).

35. In mid-June Federal troops vainly tried to capture Petersburg, Virginia. General Quincy A. Gillmore (1825–88) commanded the X Corps of the Army of the James, which had failed to take Petersburg.

36. General August V. Kautz (1828–95) commanded the cavalry of the Army of the James.

37. Lincoln visited Grant on 21 and 22 June.

38. Democrat James W. Nesmith (1820–85) represented Oregon in the Senate (1861–67).

39. Joseph W. Drew had been quartermaster general of Oregon in the 1850s. He also served as an Indian agent, a customs collector, and a representative to the territorial legislature of Oregon.

40. Thomas Hall Pearne was a Methodist minister active in the Republican politics of Oregon and editor of the *Pacific Christian Advocate*.

41. Probably John Rogers McBride (1832–1904), a Republican Congressman from Oregon (1863–65).

42. David Tod (1805–68) was the governor of Ohio (1862–64).

43. Maunsell B. Field (1822–75) was deputy assistant treasurer in New York and a close associate of Secretary Chase. John Jay Cisco (1806–84), a Wall Street banker, had been appointed assistant U.S. treasurer in charge of the subtreasury in New York by President Pierce in 1853. Lincoln not only retained him in that place but insisted that he serve as treasurer of the Union Pacific Railroad. *New York Times*, 24 March 1884, p. 1, col. 5.

44. Lucius E. Chittenden (1824–1902) of Vermont was register of the treasury (1861–65); Hanson A. Risley was a special Treasury Department agent for the purchase of products of insurrectionary states on behalf of the U.S. government.

45. Thomas Hillhouse (1816–97), a New York financier and politician who served as assistant adjutant general of volunteers on the staff of Governor Morgan (1861–62).

46. Tod to Lincoln, Columbus, 30 June 1864, Lincoln Papers, Library of Congress.

47. Samuel Hooper (1808–75) represented a Massachusetts district in the U.S. House from 1861 till his death. The Gold Bill, passed on 17 June 1864, outlawed speculation in gold. It was repealed on 2 July because it had driven up the gold premium dramatically.

48. According to another Washington journalist, Davis had a large "organ of combativeness," was "always spoiling for a fight," and seemed "to be ever wandering about dragging an imaginary coat upon the floor of the House and daring any one to tread upon it." Early in 1864 "his favorite object of attack" became Lincoln, who said: "Well, well, it appears to do him good, and as it does me no injury, (that is I don't feel that it does) what's the harm in letting him have his fling? If he did not pitch into me he would into some poor fellow whom he might hurt." Washington correspondence, 28 February 1864, *Chicago Tribune*, 3 March 1864, p. 2, col. 4.

49. Charles A. Eldredge (1820–96) was a Democratic Congressman from Fond du Lac, Wisconsin (1863–75); Justin S. Morrill (1810–98) was a Republican Congressman from Vermont (1855–67).

50. Edwin D. Morgan (1811–83) represented New York in the U.S. Senate (1863–69).

51. In 1895 Brooks recalled that "Lincoln was greatly exasperated by

the Victor Smith incident; and when he had finally disposed of the matter, as he thought, he was much depressed by frequent repetitions of similar complications. From him and from one of the Senators who waited upon him after Chase's resignation I learned the facts of the last trial of the patience of the long-suffering Lincoln. The crisis which made it impossible for Mr. Chase to stay any longer in the Treasury Department was brought on, as everybody knows, by his determination to have his own way in making several important appointments in the city of New York. But, as we have seen, the trouble began long before, when Secretary Chase grew more and more determined to resent interference with any of the appointments in the Treasury Department. Whether his ambition to be President of the United States had anything to do with this hardening of his will in the matter of executive patronage, it is impossible to say; but from the time that his name was brought prominently before the public by Senator Pomeroy, of Kansas, and others, until his final exit from the Treasury Department, Mr. Chase was continually in hot water. His resignation, handed in when Victor Smith's removal was determined upon by the President, was written in May 1863. "His final resignation was tendered in June, 1864. It would appear that Mr. Chase believed that his great position in the United States Government was absolutely necessary to the welfare of the republic, and that he could not be permitted to leave it without inviting disaster; and his frequent threats of resignation were intended, apparently, to coerce the President into letting him have his own way in all matters of detail.

"When the nomination of David Tod, of Ohio, went to the Senate in place of Salmon P. Chase, resigned, the Senators were struck dumb with amazement. In executive session the whole matter was at once referred to the Finance Committee, and in a few minutes Senators Fessenden, Conness, Sherman, Cowan, and Van Winkle were on their way to the White House. They had two questions to ask. One was, Why has Chase resigned, and is the act final? And the other was, Why has the name of David Tod been sent to the Senate? The President received the Senators with great affability, and there was a general and free discussion of the situation, Senator Fessenden, chairman of the Finance Committee, being the mouthpiece of the visiting statesmen. The President immediately disposed of the Tod branch of the complication by reading a telegram from Governor Tod declining the nomination. Then he gave the Senators a full history of the original formation of the Cabinet in 1861, explaining why each man had been chosen, and expressing his great confidence in Secretary Chase's abilities and integrity. Then he followed with a detailed statement of the relations that had existed between himself and the Secretary of the Treasury since the latter had taken office. He told the Senators all the incidents concerning the many times that Chase had offered his resignation, and he referred to the ill temper which the Secretary had betrayed on those occasions. Then he took from a pigeon-hole all the correspondence between himself and the Secretary, showing numerous instances of the testiness of the Secretary and the much-enduring patience of the President during a period stretching over nearly all the years of the administration down to that day.

"Lincoln said that of course Mr. Chase had a full right to indulge in his ambition to be President, and there was no question as to his claim upon the gratitude of the American people; but indiscreet friends of the Secretary had succeeded in exciting a feeling disagreeable in itself, and embarrassing to the President and to the Secretary. This had gone on, he said, until they disliked to meet each other; and to him (Lincoln) the relation had become unendurable, and he had accepted the resignation of Mr. Chase as a finality. He told the committee that he would not continue to be President with Mr. Chase in the Cabinet; that if the Senate should insist upon it, they could have his resignation, and take Mr. Hamlin for President. Of one of the appointments which Secretary Chase had insisted upon President Lincoln spoke with considerable feeling. This appointment, which Chase had adhered to tenaciously, and which Lincoln said was discreditable to the Secretary, was one which the President insisted never would be made with his consent. He told the Senators that at a party where Mr. Chase's chosen appointee was present, this person was intoxicated, and kicked his hat in the air in the presence of ladies and gentlemen. Lincoln said he had told Chase that he would take any other nomination which he (Chase) would send him, but this man he could not and would not accept. Chase, notwithstanding Lincoln's statement concerning the man's habits and character, persisted in urging the nomination upon the President. This, Lincoln said, was 'the last straw.' As we know, Tod's declination of the nomination left the President free to send another name to the Senate, and the Finance Committee of that body was then for the first time enlightened as to the unfortunate relations which had so long existed between the Secretary of the Treasury and the President.

"The way was now clear, and the next surprise to which the public was treated was the nomination and immediate confirmation of Senator William Pitt Fessenden as Secretary of the Treasury. It was a picturesque feature of this latter part of the business that Senator Fessenden was in the President's office conferring with him on the situation of affairs while his own nomination as successor to Chase was on its way to the Senate; and when Fessenden learned from the President that that nomination had actually been made, he went in hot haste to the Capitol, only to find that the appointment had been confirmed before he could enter his protest against it.

"That evening I was at the White House, and Mr. Lincoln sent for me to come into the library, where I found him lying upon his back on a sofa, with his hands clasped over his chest, and looking weary beyond description. But he was in a comfortable frame of mind; and, after going over the incidents of this exciting episode, he said cheerfully, 'When I finally struck the name of Fessenden as Governor Chase's successor, I felt as if the Lord hadn't forsaken me yet.'" *Washington, D.C., in Lincoln's Time*, 118–22.

52. William Tod Otto (1816–1905), an attorney from Indiana, had represented his state at the 1860 Republican national convention in Chicago. Cornelius Cole (1822–1924) represented a California district in the U.S. House (1863–65) and was later a U.S. Senator (1867–73).

53. In 1895 Brooks recalled: "Lincoln, very much irritated, and against his will, came back to town. He was subsequently greatly discomposed and annoyed when he found that . . . G. V. Fox had kept under orders a small Navy vessel in the Potomac for the President's

escape in case the rebel column should succeed in piercing the line of fortifications." *Washington, D.C., in Lincoln's Time*, 160. He was even more annoyed when Early was permitted to escape across the Potomac: "Speaking of their escape, afterward, he said that General Halleck's manifest desire to avoid taking any responsibility without the immediate sanction of General Grant was the main reason why the rebels . . . got off scatheless. . . . It may as well be said that throughout the long and weary months of the war which followed . . . Lincoln frequently referred to the escape of Early as one of the distressing features of his experience in the city of Washington." Ibid., 162. On 14 July John Hay recorded in his diary that Lincoln, after learning of Early's escape, was "evidently disgusted." Michael Burlingame and John R. Turner Ettlinger, eds., *Inside Lincoln's White House: The Complete Civil War Diary of John Hay* (Carbondale: Southern Illinois University Press, 1997), 223 (entry for 14 July 1864).

54. Proclamation of 18 July 1864, in Basler, *Collected Works of Lincoln*, 7:448–49.

55. General Joseph E. Johnston (1807–91) commanded the Army of the Tennessee, which was opposing Sherman's march toward Atlanta.

56. On 30 July, 4,000 Union soldiers were killed or wounded during an assault on Petersburg; the Confederates suffered only 1,500 casualties.

57. Fernando Wood (1812–81) represented a New York district in the U.S. House (1863–65). Lincoln had banished Vallandigham to the Confederacy in May 1863; the exile returned to Ohio in June 1864.

58. In 1895 Brooks recalled: "When Vallandigham, passing through the Confederacy, had, by a detour seaward, finally returned to the United States through Canada, I had occasion to mention his name to Lincoln, remarking that he had been speaking in Ohio. 'What!' exclaimed the President, looking at me quizzically, 'has Vallandigham got back?' Somewhat puzzled, I explained that everybody knew that. 'Dear me!' said Lincoln, with preternatural solemnity. 'I supposed he was in a foreign land. Anyhow, I hope I do not know that he is in the United States; and I shall not, unless he says or does something to draw attention to him.' Presently he went to his table, and, drawing out some loose sheets of paper, said

that he had there the rough notes of an interview which he had lately had with Fernando Wood. This was in August, 1864. It appeared that Wood had said to the President: 'We Peace Democrats are the only Democrats; all others are bastards and impostors; there is no such thing as a War Democrat, for that is a contradiction in terms. We don't expect to elect our candidate for President this fall: the people of the North are not yet ready for peace. But peace must come sooner or later; and when it does, the Democratic party will be the party which will act and assimilate with the dominant party in the South, and so we shall again have our rightful ascendancy. Now, Mr. President, you cannot find fault with that; it is not going to hurt you any.'

"Lincoln then said that he had told Wood that he was disposed to be generous; and he asked if Vallandigham's alleged return was any part of this program. Wood replied that it was not, and added: 'You may not believe me, but I assure you that I never knew or expected that he would return, though I acknowledge that I have had a letter from him since he got back. He has had already more notoriety than he deserves, and I warn you that the true policy is that he be severely let alone.' To this the President replied, according to his own account: 'I don't believe that Vallandigham has returned; I never can believe it until he forces himself offensively upon the public attention and upon my attention. Then we shall have to deal with him. So long as he behaves himself decently, he is as effectually in disguise as the man who went to a masquerade party with a clean face.'" *Washington, D.C., in Lincoln's Time*, 110–11.

59. Lincoln Papers, Library of Congress.
60. Samuel Sullivan "Sunset" Cox (1824–89) represented an Ohio district in the U.S. House (1857–65).
61. Democrat Alexander Long (1816–86) of Cincinnati represented an Ohio district in the U.S. House (1863–65). In April 1864 his colleagues censured him for uttering treason.
62. Auguste Belmont (1816–90) was a prosperous New York banker and leader of the national Democratic party; Dean Richmond (1804–66), a wealthy New York businessman, held power in the national Democratic party. During the Civil War, Amos Kendall (1789–1869), who had been a member of President Jackson's

"Kitchen Cabinet," championed the War Democrats against the Peace Democrats.

63. Democrat George H. Pendleton (1825–89) represented an Ohio district in the U.S. House (1857–65).

64. Democrat James Guthrie (1792–1869) of Kentucky served as secretary of the U.S. treasury (1853–57) and was to represent his state in the U.S. Senate (1865–68). Franklin Pierce (1804–69) of New Hampshire served as President of the United States (1853–57). Millard Fillmore of New York also served as President of the United States (1850–53).

65. On 12 September 1861, McClellan had, in compliance with orders from Secretary of War Cameron, instructed N. P. Banks to arrest members of the Maryland legislature as they gathered for a session scheduled to open five days later in Frederick. The administration feared that the legislators might pass an ordinance of secession.

66. The Wade-Davis manifesto, which appeared in the press on August 5, denounced Lincoln's veto intemperately. Brooks in 1895 recalled: "A day or two after the Wade-Davis manifesto appeared, Lincoln, in conversation with me, said: 'To be wounded in the house of one's friends is perhaps the most grievous affliction that can befall a man. I have tried my best to meet the wishes of this man [Davis], and to do my whole duty by the country.' Later on in the same conversation, while lamenting with sincere grief the implacable hostility which Henry Winter Davis had manifested, he said that Davis's pride of opinion led him to say and do things of which he (Lincoln) was certain in his own private judgment his (Davis's) conscience could not approve. When I said that it sometimes seemed as though Davis was mad, Lincoln replied, 'I have heard that there was insanity in his family; perhaps we might allow the plea in this case.' It was this attack upon him, apparently so needless and so unprofitable, and so well calculated to disturb the harmony of the Union party, that grieved the President more than the framing and the passage of the bill; but commenting in his own shrewd way on that bill, Lincoln said that he had somewhere read of a robber tyrant who had built an iron bedstead on which he compelled his victims to lie. If the captive was too short to fill the bedstead, he was stretched by main force until he was long enough;

and if he was too long, he was chopped off to fit the bedstead. This, Lincoln thought, was the sort of reconstruction which the Wade-Davis plan contemplated. If any State coming back into Federal relations did not fit the Wade-Davis bedstead, so much the worse for the State. Lincoln's habitual diffidence in quoting erudite or classic sayings usually induced him to refer to such stories in this vague way; and although he probably knew well who Procrustes was, he slurred over the illustration as something of which he had remotely heard." *Washington, D.C., in Lincoln's Time,* 156–57.

67. Caspar Butz (1825–85) of Chicago, editor of the *Deutsch-Amerikanische Monatsheft fuer Politik, Wissenschaft und Literatur,* had supported Lincoln in 1860 but grew disenchanted with him during the war and helped lead the pro-Fremont movement.

68. Presumably Brooks refers to John S. Phelps (1814–86) of Missouri, who was to run for governor of his state as a Democrat in 1868. Charles A. Wickliffe (1788–1869) represented a Kentucky district in the U.S. House (1861–63) as a Unionist. William Bowen Campbell (1807–67) represented a Tennessee district in the U.S. House (1837–43) and was governor of Tennessee (1851–53).

69. George Washington Cass (1810–88), president of the Pittsburgh, Fort Wayne & Chicago Railroad, had been the democratic nominee for governor of Pennsylvania in 1863. Lewis Cass (1782–1866), a prominent Democrat from Michigan, had been his party's presidential nominee in 1848.

70. George Francis Train (1829–1904) was an eccentric reformer, prolific writer, and successful financier. General John A. Dix (1798–1879), commander of the Department of the East, was a prominent Democrat from New York.

71. Lincoln Papers, Library of Congress.

72. John B. Weller (1812–75) was governor of California (1858–60) and a U.S. Senator from that state (1852–57).

73. Democrat Benjamin Gwinn Harris (1805–95) represented a Maryland district in the U.S. House (1863–67). In April 1864 his colleagues censured him for treasonable utterances.

74. Lazarus W. Powell (1812–67) represented Kentucky in the U.S. Senate (1859–65).

75. Thomas H. Seymour (1807–68) represented a Connecticut district

in the U.S. House (1843–45) and served as governor of his state (1850–53).

76. John Dean Caton (1812–95) was chief justice of the Illinois State Supreme Court (1855–64).

77. Virgil Hickox (1806–81) of Springfield, the general agent of the Chicago, Alton and St. Louis Railroad, served as chairman of the Illinois State Democratic Committee.

78. On 20 July, Lincoln's secretary John Hay met Confederate agents at Niagara Falls to investigate peace feelers that influential newspaper editor Horace Greeley mistakenly thought were serious. In that same month Col. James F. Jaquess visited Richmond and discussed possible peace terms with Jefferson Davis and Judah P. Benjamin. He was accompanied by a journalist, James R. Gilmore.

79. On 12–13 October, the voters of Maryland approved by a slight majority (375 votes out of 60,000) a new constitution, which abolished slavery. On 29 October, after court challenges had been dismissed, the governor declared the new constitution adopted, to go into effect on 1 November. On 10 October Lincoln had written a public letter urging Maryland voters to support the new constitution. Basler, *Collected Works of Lincoln*, 8:41.

80. The text can be found in Basler, *Collected Works of Lincoln*, 8:75.

81. Henry W. Bellows (1814–82), founder and president of the Sanitary Commission.

82. Before the war, Confederate General Robert Toombs (1810–85) of Georgia had declared that he would call the roll of his slaves in the shadow of Bunker Hill in Boston.

83. This brief address does not appear in Basler, *Collected Works of Lincoln*. It is printed in Fehrenbacher and Fehrenbacher, eds., *Recollected Words of Abraham Lincoln*, 51.

84. In a letter to Edward Everett Hale, San Francisco, 29 November 1865 (Hay Library, Brown University), Brooks has Lincoln use the word *men* rather than *mankind*.

85. Ibid. Brooks has Lincoln say "be made thereby to suffer" instead of "may thereby be made to suffer."

86. Ibid. Brooks has Lincoln say "intellectually and morally" rather than "morally and intellectually."

87. Ibid. Brooks says: "This speech was never in print, except in my own correspondence, published in the California press."

88. In 1895 Brooks wrote: "About noon I called on President Lincoln, and to my surprise found him entirely alone. . . . I spent nearly all the afternoon with the President, who apparently found it difficult to put his mind on any of the routine work of his office, and entreated me to stay with him." *Washington, D.C., in Lincoln's Time,* 195–96.

89. The physician William A. Newell (1817–1901) represented a New Jersey district in the U.S. House (1847–51); he was elected again to that seat in 1864.

90. Basler, *Collected Works of Lincoln,* 8:100–101.

91. Brooks later wrote that Lincoln also said on the day after the election: "Being only mortal, after all, I should have been a little mortified if I had been beaten in the canvass before the people; but the sting would have been more than compensated by the thought that the people had notified me that my official responsibilities were soon to be lifted off my back." *Washington, D.C., in Lincoln's Time,* 198.

92. Basler, *Collected Works of Lincoln,* 8:399–405.

93. Lincoln Papers, Library of Congress.

94. Some Radical Republicans believed Banks played along with the conservatives in Louisiana who wished to deny blacks the rights of citizenship.

95. General Edward Richard Sprigg Canby (1817–73) commanded the military division of West Mississippi.

96. Bates stepped down as attorney general on 1 December 1864.

97. The trapper was Seth Kinman.

98. Joseph Holt (1807–94) of Kentucky was judge advocate general of the Union army.

99. Caleb Cushing (1800–1879), a prominent Democrat before the war, supported the Union and in November 1864 endorsed Lincoln for reelection. Attorney James Topham Brady (1815–69) ran for governor of New York in 1860 as a Breckinridge Democrat. Attorney William Maxwell Evarts (1818–1901) was a New York Republican who was to serve as Andrew Johnson's attorney general (1868–69).

100. James Speed (1812–87) was the brother of Lincoln's close friend Joshua Speed.

101. Johnson's Island was a Union prisoner of war camp in the Sandusky Bay of Lake Erie.

102. Lincoln wrote this out and gave it to Brooks, asking that it be published forthwith in the *Washington Chronicle*. It appeared in that journal on 7 December beneath the headline, "The President's Last, Shortest, and Best Speech," which Lincoln wrote. Cf. Appendix.

103. Basler, *Collected Works of Lincoln*, 8:136–53.

104. Edward McPherson (1830–95) was clerk of the U.S. House of Representatives (1863–75).

105. Thaddeus Stevens (1792–1868) of Pennsylvania, the dominant Radical Republican in the U.S. House, was chairman of the powerful Ways and Means Committee.

106. Attorney Thomas Ewing (1789–1871), known as "The Logician of the West," served as secretary of the treasury (1841–45), secretary of the interior (1849–50), and U.S. Senator from Ohio (1830–36, 1850–51). James Moore Wayne (1790?–1867) of Savannah was associate justice of the U.S. supreme court (1835–67).

107. Reuben E. Fenton (1819–85) was governor of New York (1865–69).

108. On 6 December, Lincoln nominated Chase to become chief justice of the U.S. Supreme Court.

109. Lincoln nominated Chase despite his own personal feelings, for he would, to use his own language, "rather have swallowed his buckhorn chair" or "have eat[en] flat irons" than to have made that appointment. William E. Chandler, quoting Lincoln, in Beale, ed., *Welles Diary*, 2:196 (entry for 15 December 1864); Virginia Fox diary, quoted in Miers et al., eds., *Lincoln Day by Day*, 3:301 (entry for 10 December 1864).

110. "Reply to Emancipation Memorial Presented by Chicago Christians of All Denominations," 13 September 1862, in Basler, *Collected Works of Lincoln*, 5:419–25.

111. This summary of Lincoln's remarks is practically a verbatim copy of the one that appeared in the *Baltimore American Commercial Advertiser* of 9 December, as given in Fehrenbacher and Fehrenbacher, eds., *Recollected Words of Lincoln*, 15. Cf. Basler, *Collected Works of Abraham Lincoln*, 8:154.

112. Hatch Collection, microfilm copy courtesy of Dr. Wayne C. Temple.

113. Brooks later recalled a conversation with Lincoln in late 1864: "I had occasion to see the President in his private office. He was in gay humor, and asked what was the news. I said: 'Mr. President, there is no news.' 'Very well,' he said; 'what are people talking about?' 'They are guessing who will be Taney's successor,' I said, jocularly. Instantly his countenance fell, and, with a grave and serious expression, he said, pointing to a huge pile of telegrams and letters on his table: 'I have been all day and yesterday and the day before besieged by messages from my friends all over the country, as if there were a determination to put up the bars between Governor Chase and myself.' Then, after a pause, he added: 'But I shall nominate him for Chief Justice nevertheless.'" Brooks, *Statesmen* (New York: Charles Scribner's Sons, 1893), 170–71. Cf. *Washington, D.C., in Lincoln's Time*, 122, 173–77.

CHAPTER THREE: DISPATCHES AND LETTERS, 1865

1. Snow, Coyle & Co., a Washington publishing firm, bought the *National Intelligencer* on 31 December 1864. A. G. Allen (1818?–73) was a U.S. naval agent during the Pierce administration and then became a journalist for Washington papers, including the *Patriot* and the *National Intelligencer*. Allen signed his Washington dispatches "Aga." Whitelaw Reid of the *Cincinnati Gazette* used the pen name "Agate."

2. Joseph Gales (1786–1860) and William W. Seaton (1785–1866), who were brothers-in-law, ran the Washington *National Intelligencer* for many years.

3. *Notes, Criticisms, and Correspondence upon Shakespeare's Plays and Actors* (1863).

4. Lincoln to Hackett, Washington, 17 August 1863, Basler, *Collected Works of Lincoln*, 6:392–93.

5. The bracketed material appears thus in Brooks.

6. John Hay described Lincoln's relations with Hackett succinctly: "He was so delighted with Hackett in Falstaff that he wrote him a letter of warm congratulation which pleased the veteran actor so much that he gave it to the New York Herald, which printed it with abusive comments. Hackett was greatly mortified and made suitable apologies; upon which the President wrote to him again in

the kindliest manner, saying: 'Give yourself no uneasiness on the subject. . . . I certainly did not expect to see my note in print; yet I have not been much shocked by the comments upon it. They are a fair specimen of what has occurred to me through life. I have endured a great deal of ridicule, without much malice; and have received a great deal of kindness, not quite free from ridicule. I am used to it.' This incident had the usual sequel; the veteran comedian asked for an office, which the President was not able to give him and the pleasant acquaintance ceased. A hundred times this experience was repeated: a man would be introduced to the President whose disposition and talk were agreeable; he took pleasure in his conversation for two or three interviews, and then this congenial person would ask some favor impossible to grant, and go away in bitterness of spirit. It is a cross that every President must bear." "Life in the White House in the Time of Lincoln," manuscript in Hay's hand, Hay Papers, reel 22, Library of Congress. This essay was published, with slight variations, in *Century Magazine*, November 1890.

7. This opinion of Everett's legacy was Lincoln's, as Brooks later explained: "Not long after Edward Everett's death, he referred to that event as a public loss. On the evening of the day when the news of the death reached Washington, I was at the White House, and the conversation naturally fell upon that topic. Lincoln said, 'Now, you are a loyal New Englander,—loyal to New England,—what great work of Everett's do you remember?' I was forced to say that I could not recall any. The President persisted and wanted to know if I could not recollect any great speech. Not receiving satisfaction, he said, looking around the room in his half-comical fashion, as if afraid of being overheard, 'Now, do you know, I think Edward Everett was very much overrated. He hasn't left any enduring monument. But there was one speech in which, addressing a statue of John Adams and a picture of Washington, in Faneuil Hall, Boston, he apostrophized them and said, "Teach us the love of liberty protected by law!" That was very fine, it seems to me. Still, it was only a good idea, introduced by noble language.'

"Continuing his discussion of Everett, he referred to his celebrated address on Washington, which was delivered through the

South, as if in the hope that the rising storm of the rebellion might be quelled by this oratorical oil on the waters. Lincoln recalled a story told of Everett's manner. It was necessary, in his Washington oration, to relate an anecdote accompanied by the jingle of coin in the lecturer's pocket. This was done at each of the five hundred repetitions of the address, in the same manner, and with unvarying accuracy. When gold and silver disappeared from circulation, Mr. Everett procured and kept for this purpose a few coins with which, and a bunch of keys, the usual effect was produced. 'And I am told,' added Lincoln, 'that whenever Mr. Everett delivered that lecture, he took along those things. They were what, I believe, the theatrical people would call his "properties."'" "Personal Reminiscences of Lincoln," *Scribner's Monthly Magazine* 15 (March 1878), 678.

8. John A. Andrew (1818–67) was the governor of Massachusetts throughout the Civil War. Thurlow Weed (1797–1882) of New York was a leading Republican fundraiser and strategist, and he acted as the alter ego of Secretary of State Seward, who led the moderate opponents of the Radicals.

9. Francis P. Blair Sr. (1791–1876), a close advisor of President Jackson in the 1830s, offered counsel to Lincoln on many issues. He visited Richmond twice in January 1865 to promote a plan that would unite the North and the South in an attempt to drive French forces from Mexico.

10. Alexander H. Stephens (1812–83) of Georgia was vice president of the Confederacy; John A. Campbell (1811–89) of Virginia was assistant secretary of war of the Confederacy; and Robert M. T. Hunter (1809–87) of Virginia was president pro tem of the Confederate Senate.

11. Grant to E. M. Stanton, City Point, Virginia, 1 February 1865, in John Y. Simon, ed., *The Papers of Ulysses S. Grant* (Carbondale: Southern Illinois University Press, 1967–), 13:345–46.

12. Horace Greeley, longtime champion of schemes to effect a compromise peace, had inveigled F. P. Blair to undertake his peace mission. "Wade-and-Davisites" refers to the Radical Republican opponents of Lincoln.

13. Message of 10 February 1865, in Basler, *Collected Works of Lincoln*, 8:274–85.

14. James Brooks (1810–73) represented a New York district in the U.S. House of Representatives (1863–66).

15. John G. Foster (1823–74) commanded the Army of the South.

16. Thomas Holliday Hicks (1798–1865) represented Maryland in the U.S. Senate from 1862 till his death.

17. In December 1864 a military tribunal in Indianapolis condemned Lambdin P. Milligan, William A. Bowles, and Stephen Horsey to death for plotting treason. Indiana Governor Oliver P. Morton led the effort to obtain clemency. Before he could rule on Morton's appeal, the president was assassinated.

18. LeRoy P. Graf et al., eds., *The Papers of Andrew Johnson* (Knoxville: University of Tennessee Press, 1967–), 7:502–6.

19. While listening to Johnson's "incoherent harangue," the mortified president "bowed his head with a look of unutterable despondency." William Pitt Kellogg to James R. B. Van Cleave, Washington, 8 February 1909, copy, Lincoln File, Reminiscences, folder 4, Illinois State Historical Library, Springfield. Kellogg claimed that he sat near Lincoln and observed his face closely. Cf. John W. Forney, *Anecdotes of Public Men*, 2 vols. (New York: Harper and Brothers, 1874), 1:177.

20. George T. Brown (1821–80) owned and edited the *Alton Courier*, served as mayor of Alton (1846–47), led the Republican party in southern Illinois, served as secretary of the Illinois State Senate in 1855, and became sergeant-at-arms of the U.S. Senate in 1861.

21. On 5 March, Lincoln asked Brooks if he "had noticed the sunburst, and then went on to say that he was as just superstitious enough to consider it a happy omen." *Washington, D.C., in Lincoln's Time*, 74.

22. Cornelius Cole (1822–1924) represented a California district in the U.S. House (1863–65) and was later a U.S. Senator (1867–73). The bearer of the electoral vote for California was J. G. McCollum of El Dorado.

23. According to James W. Simonton, "the utter absence of unanimity in presenting a candidate from California, was the chief cause of the failure" to persuade Lincoln to name a Californian to the cabi-

net. New York correspondence, 10 March 1865, *San Francisco Daily Evening Bulletin*, 13 April 1865, p. 2, col. 2.

24. Conservative Unionist Emerson Etheridge (1819–1902) was a slaveholder from west Tennessee.

25. Lucian Anderson (1824–98) represented a Kentucky district in the U.S. House (1863–65).

26. It was alleged that Mary Lincoln had replaced doorman Edward McManus with Cornelius O'Leary and received half of the money he received as an influence peddler. *New York World*, 15 March 1865.

27. Democrat Henry William Harrington (1825–82) of Madison served in the U.S. House (1863–65).

28. Hale served as U.S. minister to Spain (1865–69).

29. Morton Smith Wilkinson (1819–94) represented Minnesota in the U.S. Senate (1859–65); he did not become Commissioner of Indian Affairs. Freeman Clarke (1809–87) represented a New York district in the U.S. House (1863–65) and served as Comptroller of the Currency (1865–67). Hugh McCulloch (1808–95) was Comptroller of the Currency from 1863 until March 1865, when he was named secretary of the treasury. Ambrose Williams Clark (1810–87) represented a New York district in the U.S. House (1861–65) and served as consul at Valparaiso (1865–69).

30. John Bigelow (1817–1911) of New York was consul-general in Paris (1861–65) and served as minister to France (1865–66).

31. Attorney Samuel C. Parks of Lincoln, Illinois, was a good friend of the president's. Parks was replaced by Milton Kelly.

32. McPherson Papers, Library of Congress.

33. Ibid.

34. Basler, *Collected Works of Lincoln*, 8:393–94.

35. Ibid., 399–405. Brooks later recalled, "I was invited to be near him at the historic window in the White House whence he was used to speak to the people. Noting my look of surprise at the roll of manuscript he had in his hand, just before we left the parlor for the upper part of the house he said: 'It is true that I don't usually read a speech, but I am going to say something to-night that may be important. I am going to talk about reconstruction, and sometimes I am betrayed into saying things that other people don't like. In a little off-hand talk I made the other day I used the phrase "Turned

tail and ran." A gentleman from Boston was very much offended by that, and I hope he won't be offended again.' On the way upstairs the President turned to me and said, with a queer smile: 'The gentleman from Boston was Senator Sumner.'" Brooks, *Statesmen*, 214. In another source, Brooks recorded that he "held a light while he [Lincoln] read, dropping the pages of his written speech one by one upon the floor as he finished them. Little Tad, who found the crowd no longer responsive to his antics, had now sought the chief point of attraction, and scrambled around on the floor, importuning his father to give him 'another,' as he collected the sheets of paper fluttering from the President's hand." *Washington, D.C., in Lincoln's Time*, 227.

36. Passed on 2 July 1864, the Wade-Davis bill, drafted by Congressman Henry Winter Davis and Senator Benjamin F. Wade, established stricter criteria for reconstruction than Lincoln had spelled out seven months earlier. The President pocket-vetoed it.

37. Sydney Smith (1771–1845), a celebrated British wit, once declared, "As for the possibility of the House of Lords preventing ere long a reform of Parliament, I hold it to be the most absurd notion that ever entered into human imagination. I do not mean to be disrespectful, but the attempt of the Lords to stop the progress of Reform reminds me very forcibly of the great storm of Sidmouth and of the conduct of the excellent Mrs. Partington on that occasion. In the winter of 1824 there set in a great flood upon that town; the tide rose to an incredible height; the waves rushed in upon the houses; and everything was threatened with destruction. In the midst of this sublime and terrible storm Dame Partington, who lived upon the beach, was seen at the door of her house with mop and pattens, trundling her mop, squeezing out the sea-water, and vigorously pushing away the Atlantic Ocean. The Atlantic was roused. Mrs Partington's spirit was up. But I need not tell you that the contest was unequal. The Atlantic Ocean beat Mrs. Partington. She was excellent at a slop or a puddle, but she should not have meddled with a tempest." Gerald Bullett, *Sydney Smith: A Biography and a Selection* (London: Michael Joseph, 1951), 77–78.

38. Robert C. Schenck (1809–90) represented an Ohio district in the U.S. House (1863–71).

39. Laura Keene (1826?–73), an English-born actress and theater manager, scored her greatest success with *Our American Cousin*.

40. On 13 April Mary Lincoln had asked Grant to escort her on a tour of the capital. He accepted, and as the two entered their coach, the people gathered near the White House shouted "Grant" several times, "whereupon Mrs. L[incoln] was disturbed, and directed the driver to let her out." But when the crowd then cheered for the president, she gave orders to proceed. This "was repeated at different stages of the drive" whenever the crowd learned the identity of the coach's occupants. Mrs. Lincoln felt it inappropriate that Grant should be cheered first. The following day the general, when invited by the president to attend *Our American Cousin* at Ford's Theater, refused, fearing a repetition of the previous night's unpleasantness. Grant told this story in 1869. Hamilton Fish Diary, 12 November 1869, Fish Papers, Library of Congress. Mrs. Grant told Fish "that she objected strenuously to accompanying Mrs. Lincoln."

41. Schuyler Colfax (1823–85) of Indiana was speaker of the U.S. House (1863–69).

   In 1895 Brooks recalled: "Late in the afternoon I filled an appointment by calling on the President at the White House, and was told by him that he 'had a notion' of sending for me to go to the theater that evening with him and Mrs. Lincoln." *Washington, D.C., in Lincoln's Time*, 229.

42. These remarks may have been "a journalist's invention." Colfax's account of his meeting with Lincoln does not mention Brooks. In his 1895 reminiscences, Brooks does not repeat these purported remarks of Lincoln and states that he spoke with Lincoln in the afternoon and met Colfax later in the day. Fehrenbacher and Fehrenbacher, eds., *Recollected Words of Lincoln*, 58.

43. Clara Harris was the daughter of Ira Harris (1802–75), who represented New York in the U.S. Senate (1861–67). In 1867, she married Major Henry R. Rathbone (1837–1911), Ira Harris's stepson and her stepbrother.

44. John F. Parker, one of four plainclothesman guards at the White House, neglected his duties that night.

45. Joseph B. Stewart.

46. Montgomery C. Meigs (1816–92) was Quartermaster General of

the Army; Dr. Joseph K. Barnes (1817–83) became acting surgeon general in 1863 and surgeon general the following year.

47. Others trying to console Mary Lincoln included her friend Elizabeth Cogswell Dixon, wife of Connecticut Senator James Dixon; Mrs. Dixon's sister, Mary Kinney; and Mrs. Kinney's daughter, Constance. Later they were joined by Emma Brooks Gurley, wife of the Rev. Dr. Phineas D. Gurley, and Mary Jane Hale Welles, wife of the secretary of the navy.

48. Hugh McLellan, ed., *The Character and Religion of President Lincoln: A Letter of Noah Brooks, May 10, 1865* (Champlain, N.Y.: Privately printed, 1919). Langworthy was a Congregational minister in Chelsea, Massachusetts. As a young man, Brooks had worshipped at Longworthy's church. Cf. Brooks's similar letter to James A. Reed, New York, 31 December 1872, in Reed, "The Later Life and Religious Sentiments of Abraham Lincoln," *Scribner's Monthly Magazine*, July 1873, 340.

49. Brooks's biographer contends that "it is extremely doubtful that he [Lincoln] talked openly to anybody about Christ's atonement for man's sins." Wayne C. Temple, *Lincoln: From Skeptic to Prophet*, 313.

50. $2,500 per year.

51. Lincoln's papers, edited by his secretaries John G. Nicolay and John Hay, were not published until 1894.

APPENDIX: PERSONAL RECOLLECTIONS OF ABRAHAM LINCOLN

This piece originally appeared in *Harper's New Monthly Magazine*, July 1865, 222–30.

1. The British poet Thomas Hood (1799–1845).

2. Lincoln wrote a lecture on discoveries and inventions in the late 1850s and left the manuscript with Mrs. Elizabeth Grimsley of Springfield when he departed for Washington in February 1861. Basler, *Collected Works of Lincoln*, 2:437–42, 3:356–63.

3. On 28 April 1864, John Hay wrote in his diary, "The Prest. tells a queer story of Meigs. When McClellan lay at Harrison's Landing, Meigs came one night to the President & waked him up at Soldier's Home to urge upon him the immediate flight of the Army from that point—the men to get away on transports & the *horses to be killed* as they cd not be saved. Thus often' says the Prest. 'I who

am not a specially brave man have had to sustain the sinking courage of these professional fighters in critical times." Burlingame and Ettlinger, eds., *Hay Diary*, 191.

4. On 11 April 1865, he said: "As a general rule, I abstain from reading the reports of attacks upon myself, wishing not to be provoked by that to which I can not properly offer an answer." Basler, *Collected Works of Lincoln*, 8:401. Cf. Burlingame, *Inner World of Lincoln*, 195–96.

5. "Hunker" was a slang term for a Democrat.

6. William Taylor Barry (1785–1835) of Kentucky served as postmaster general (1829–35).

7. Amos Kendall (1789–1869) of Kentucky served as postmaster general (1835–40).

8. Cf. Isaac N. Arnold, *The Life of Abraham Lincoln* (Chicago: A. C. McClurg, 1884), 39.

9. William O. Stoddard, who worked as an assistant to Nicolay and Hay in the White House, said "Lincoln did not retain the external equanimity of his earlier days under the galling pressure of the burdens laid upon him in 1863. The goading irritations were too many, and they gave him no rest whatever." Stoddard, *Abraham Lincoln: The True Story of a Great Life* (New York: Fords, Howard, and Hulbert, 1884), 382.

10. On 7 April 1863, Admiral Samuel F. Du Pont (1803–65), commander of the South Atlantic Blockading Squadron, led the assault on Charleston. Of the nine Union ironclads that attacked Charleston, five were disabled by Confederate batteries; one sank the following day.

11. In January 1848 Lincoln, as a Congressman, introduced a resolution into the House of Representatives demanding that President Polk give Congress information identifying the exact spot where the bloody encounter took place between Mexican and American troops that precipitated war between the two countries in May 1846. This "spot resolution" prompted Democrats to bestow upon Lincoln the derisive sobriquet "spotty."

12. This remark was made at the Illinois Republican state convention at Decatur from 8 to 10 May 1860. In the years 1830–31, Lincoln had split hundreds of rails in Macon County, Illinois.

13. Lincoln told Iowa Congressman Josiah B. Grinnell that "You flaxen men with broad faces are born with cheer, and don't know a cloud from a star. I am of another temperament." Similarly, he said to an Illinois neighbor, "I am not a man of a very hopeful temperament." J. B. Grinnell, *Men and Events of Forty Years: Autobiographical Reminiscences of an Active Career from 1850–1890* (Boston: D. Lathrop, 1891), 171; Noyes W. Miner, "Personal Reminiscences of Abraham Lincoln," manuscript dated 10 July 1881, Illinois State Historical Library, Springfield.

14. Upon learning Edward D. Baker's fate, Lincoln emerged from the telegraph office "with bowed head, and tears rolling down his furrowed cheeks, his face pale and wan, his heart heaving with emotion" and "almost fell as he stepped into the street. . . . With both hands pressed upon his heart he walked down the street, not returning the salute of the sentinel pacing his beat before the door." Charles Carlton Coffin in Rice, ed., *Reminiscences of Lincoln*, 172–73. At the funeral, the president "wept like a child." J. Wainwright Ray to John G. Nicolay, Washington, 18 October 1886, Nicolay Papers, Library of Congress.

15. Joseph Butler (1692–1752) wrote *Analogy of Religion, Natural and Revealed*; John Stuart Mill (1806–73) wrote *On Liberty* (1859); and Jonathan Edwards (1703–58) wrote *A Careful and Strict Enquiry into the Modern Prevailing Notions of That Freedom of the Will, Which is Supposed to be Essential to Moral Agency, Vertue and Vice, Reward and Punishment, Praise and Blame* (1754).

16. Ohio journalist David R. Locke created the comic character Petroleum V. Nasby. On 5 March 1865, Lincoln allegedly asked Ohio Congressman James M. Ashley to tell Locke "that for the ability to write the queer, quaint and good things he does, I'd give up my office tomorrow." Ashley to Locke, Washington, 5 March 1865, quoted in a letter by an unidentified correspondent to Benjamin P. Thomas, New York, 24 January 1953, Benjamin P. Thomas Papers, Illinois State Historical Library, Springfield.

Private Miles O'Reilly was a comic character in the writings of Charles G. Halpine, an officer in the Union army.

17. Oliver Wendell Holmes (1809–94) of Cambridge, Massachusetts.

18. Lincoln's favorite song, according to Ward Hill Lamon, was

"Twenty Years Ago," which Lamon heard him sing often in Illinois and later in the White House. The verses that most affected him were these:

I've wandered to the village, Tom; I've sat beneath the tree
Upon the schoolhouse play-ground, that sheltered you and me:
But none were left to greet me, Tom, and few were left to know
Who played with us upon the green, some twenty years ago.

Near by the spring, upon the elm you know I cut your name,—
Your sweetheart's just beneath it Tom; and you did mine the same.
Some heartless wretch has peeled the bark,—t'was dying sure but
     slow,
Just as *she* died whose name you cut, some twenty years ago.

My lids have long been dry, Tom, but tears came to my eyes;
I thought of her I loved so well, those early broken ties:
I visited the old churchyard, and took some flowers to strew
Upon the graves of those we loved, some twenty years ago.

Ward Hill Lamon, *Recollections of Abraham Lincoln, 1847–1865*, ed. Dorothy Lamon Teillard, 2d ed. (Washington, D.C.: Privately published, 1911), 150–51.

19. The poem was "Mortality," by the Scots poet William Knox (1789–1825). In 1846 Lincoln expressed a much higher opinion of the poem: "I would give all I am worth, and go in debt, to be able to write so fine a piece as I think that is." Lincoln to Andrew Johnston, Tremont, Ill., 18 April 1846, Basler, *Collected Works of Lincoln*, 1:378.

20. No such document is in the Lincoln Papers at the Library of Congress.

21. The speech was given two nights after the election.

22. It first appeared in the *Washington Daily Chronicle* on 7 December 1864.

INDEX